Principles and Theory of Political Science

Volume 1

Urmila Sharma
S.K. Sharma

ATLANTIC
PUBLISHERS & DISTRIBUTORS (P) LTD

Published by
ATLANTIC
PUBLISHERS & DISTRIBUTORS (P) LTD
7/22, Ansari Road, Darya Ganj, New Delhi-110002
Phones : +91-11-40775252, 40775214, 23273880, 23275880
Fax: +91-11-23285873
Web: www.atlanticbooks.com
E-mail: orders@atlanticbooks.com

Disclaimer

- The author and the publisher have taken every effort to the maximum of their skill, expertise and knowledge to provide correct material in the book. Even then if some mistakes persist in the content of the book, the publisher does not take responsibility for the same. The publisher shall have no liability to any person or entity with respect to any loss or damage caused, or alleged to have been caused directly or indirectly, by the information contained in this book.
- The author has fully tried to follow the copyright law. However, if any work is found to be similar, it is unintentional and the same should not be used as defamatory or to file legal suit against the author.
- If the readers find any mistakes, we shall be grateful to them for pointing out those to us so that these can be corrected in the next edition.
- All disputes are subject to the jurisdiction of Delhi courts only.

Printed & bound in India by Atlantic Print Services

Preface

Man is the only political animal among living beings. This political nature of man is responsible for the most of his progress. Man's life is very much determined by the political system in which he lives. Whatever may have been said by the idealists, the Marxists and the Anarchists, political system has been and shall be the most important feature of human society and, the most important determinant of the quality of human life. Therefore, the future of human society, better or worse, depends upon the political system of the state.

This book deals with the Principles and the Theory of Political Science. Besides the introductory portion including definition, scope, value, nature and methods of political science, this book includes the discussion on all those topics which find a place in the syllabi of Political Theory or Principles of Political Science in any Indian University. These include: Political Power, Behavioural and Post-behavioural Revolutions, The State, The Rise and Growth of Nation States, The Political System, Sovereignty, Monist and Pluralist View of Sovereignty, The Theory of Rights, Concept of Liberty, Concept of Equality, Law and International Law, Concept of Property, Concept of Justice, Political Obligation, Political Revolution, Punishment etc.

As Political Sociology is today an integral part of Political Science, this book deals with the main concepts of Political Sociology including Political Development, Political Culture, Political Socialisation, Political Participation, Political Recruitment, Political Elites, Political Alienation, Political Communication, Political Legitimacy and Effectiveness and Bureaucracy.

Principles of Political Science deals with the theories of the state and the government. Thus, this book discusses forms of government, Democracy, Socialism, Marxism, Syndicalism, Guild Socialism,

Evolutionary Socialism, Fabianism, Anarchism, Fascism, Liberalism, Individualism and *Sarvodaya*. A Bibliography has been given at the end for those, who desire to go to originals and have a wide study of the subjects.

Questions for exercise, given at the end of each chapter, have been actually asked in examination papers of the various Universities. These will help the reader to prepare for examinations.

Thus, the authors have left no stones unturned to make this book informative and an ideal textbook on Principles and Theory of Political Science.

However, suggestions for improvement will be gratefully acknowledged and incorporated in the next edition.

Urmila Sharma
S.K. Sharma

Contents

Volume I

Volume II

1

Political Science: Definition, Scope and Value

Political Science is known by several names as 'politics' (Aristotle), 'political science' (William Godwin and Mary Wollstonecraft), 'science of state' (R.G. Gettell) and 'science of politics' (Sir Fredrick Pollock). However, it lacks a precise nomenclature. Jellinek remarks that there is no science which is so much in need of a good terminology as is political science. Lowell holds that the study of politics, "lacks the first essentials of a modern science, a nomenclature incomprehensible to educated men." Referring to the amount of confusion created by different nomenclatures of this subject, Garner says: "This is regrettable, because it often leads to confusion and misunderstanding, such as one does not encounter in the literature of the natural sciences, where the terminology employed is more precise and exact."[1]

Literal Meaning

The English word 'politics' originates from three Greek words like *polis* (city-state), *polity* (government) and *politeia* (constitution). Thus, in the original Greek sense, politics is a study of the city-state and its administration in practical as well as philosophical terms. The term 'politics' has been taken by the lexicons and the writers of textbooks both as a science and an art. The original Greek meaning of 'politics' became outdated ever since Hobbes identified it with 'power' and Auguste Comte popularised the trend of 'positivism'. Hence, Gilchrist maintains that the term 'politics', when used in its original Greek sense, "is unobjectionable, but since modern usage has given it a new meaning, it is useless as a scientific term."[2]

1. Jellinek, *Political Science and Government*, p. 2.
2. Gilchrist, R.N., *Principles of Political Science*, p. 2.

Theoretical and Applied Politics

Eminent writers like Jellinek, Willoughby and Pollock have made distinction between the 'theoretical' or 'academic' and 'practical' or 'applied' dimensions of politics. It shows that while some topics relating to the origin, nature, purposes and ends of the state form part of 'theoretical politics', others relating to the actual administration of the affairs of the government belong to the sphere of applied politics. Thus, while the term 'theoretical politics' refers to the fundamental characteristics of the state without reference to its activities or the means by which its ends are attained, the term 'applied politics' refers to the state in action or state considered as a dynamic institutions?[3]

WHAT IS POLITICS?

Aristotle defined Politics as the science of state. "It corresponds to that part of the affairs of the state which centres in government and that kind or part of the government which speaks to law."[4] Some important definitions of Politics are as follows:

1. According to Max Weber, Politics is the, "striving to share power or striving to influence the distribution of power, either among states or among groups within a state."[5]
2. According to Heinz Eulau, "The behavioural persuasion in Politics is concerned with what man does politically and the meaning he attaches to his behaviour."[6]
3. In the words of Harold Lasswell, "The study of Politics is the study of influence and the influential."[7] Lasswell further defined influential as those who get the most of what there is to get.
4. According to David Easton, the political system can be identified with, "The authoritative allocation of values for a society."[8] And politics should be concerned with "that system of interactions in any society to which...binding or authoritative allocations are made and implemented."[9] Easton further points out that the allocation is authoritative in the sense that, "The people to whom it is intended to apply or who are affected by it consider that they must or ought to obey it."[10] As Vernon Van Dyke has correctly said: "This...reduces

3. Garner, *op. cit.*, p. 4.
4. Charles Hyneman, *The Study of Politics*, Urbana : University of Illinois Press, 1956, p. 26.
5. Max Weber, "Politics as a Vocation" excerpted in A. Pizzorno (ed.), *Political Sociology*, Penguin Books Ltd., England, 1971, p. 28.
6. Heinz Eulau, *The Behavioural Persuasion in Politics*, New York: Random House, 1963, p. 5.
7. *The Political Writings of Harold D. Lasswell*, The Free Press, Glencoe: Illinois, 1951, p. 295.
8. David Easton, *The Political System*, New York : Alfred A. Knopf, 1960, p. 129.
9. David Easton, *A Framework for Political Analysis*, Englewood Cliffs, N.J.: Prentice- Hall, 1965, p. 50.
10. David Easton, *The Political System*, p. 132.

the difficulties that attend a focus on politics defined as struggle over issues, for the authoritative allocation of values could be tacit, unattended by current straggle. Easton's definition encompasses the politics of consent as well as the politics of struggle."[11]

5. E.C. Banfield defined politics as, "The activity (negotiation, argument, discussion, application of force, persuasion, etc.) by which an issue is agitated or settled."[12] This definition includes wider non-political element. Politics according to it is a social activity, not invariably related with power. This is a better definition than other definitions mentioned so far.
6. Taking politics as a social activity like Banfield, Bertrand de Jouvenel included in it, "Every systematic effort performed at any place in the social field to move other men in pursuit of some design cherished by the mover."[13]
7. According to Robert Dahl, a political system is a "persistent pattern of human relationships that involves, to a significant extent, power, rule or authority."[14] Here politics very much extends to non-political.
8. Extending the above mentioned viewpoint states William Bluhm, "Reduced to its universal element, then politics is a social process characterised by activity involving rivalry and co-operation in the exercise of power, and culminating in the making of decisions for a group."[15]

Non-political Politics

The above mentioned definitions show that politics includes non-political. In the words of J.D.B. Millet, "Politics is what it is because society is what it is: because men, in their social situation, find themselves divided...politics is a natural reflex of the divergences between the members of a society."[16] "It is a permanent feature of human society because social diversities are never going to stop. It is a matter of the expression advocacy, settlement and modification of disagreements."[17]

---

11. Vernon Van Dyke, "The Optimum Scope of Political Science" in *Political Science: Introductory Essays and Readings*, Bellows, Brikson and Winter (ed.), Duxbury Press : Belmont, California, 1971, p. 18.
12. M, Myerson and E.C. Banfield, *Politics, Planning and the Public Interest*, New York: Free Press, 1955, pp. 304-305.
13. Bertrand de Jouvenel, "On the Nautre of Political Science" in *The American Political Science Review*, December 1961, p. 773.
14. Robert A. Dahl, *Modern Political Analysis*, Prentice-Hall of India (Private) Ltd., New Delhi, 1965, p. 6.
15. William Bluhm, *The Theories of the Political System*, Englewood Cliffs, N.J. : Prentice-Hall, Inc., 1965, p. 5.
16. J.D.B. Miller, *The Nature of Politics*, Gerald Duckworth & Co. Ltd., London, 1965,
17. *Ibid.*, p. 284.

NEW MEANING OF POLITICS

In its new meaning politics has been made free from the shackles of normative dimensions. It has been restated in empirical terms. Thus, it is not merely a study of the state and the government, it is a study of power, its exercise, and straggle for its sake. As Michael Curtis said, '"Politics is organised dispute about power and its use, involving choice among competing values, ideas, persons, interests and demands. The study of politics is concerned with the description and analysis of the manner in which power is obtained, exercised and controlled, the purpose for which it is used, the manner in which decisions are made, the factors which influence the making of those decisions, and the context in which those decisions take place."[18]

Thus today, there has been a striking shift from the study of state to the study of power in the meaning of Political Science. This shift has broadened the area of inquiry and served to make political analysis more realistic. It has saved Politics from narrow formalism and institutionalism which is involved in the definition of the discipline as the science of the state.

According to N.P. Guild and K.T. Palmer, this shift has two main advantages. "One advantage that power has over earlier concepts is that it focusses attention on a process not on a legal abstraction as state. Political Science becomes the study of the way power is accumulated, used and controlled in modern society. Consequently, it includes not only the legal and formal but also the extra-legal and informal processes involved in government. Another advantage of using power as the central concept is that political science pays greater heed to man, especially the political man, as a basic unit of analysis."[19]

DEFINITION OF POLITICAL SCIENCE

1. *Jellinek*: The task of political science is to study in their fundamental relations the public powers, to examine the conditions under which they manifest themselves, their end and their effect, and to investigate the state in its inner nature.
2. *Willoughby*: The science of politics seeks an accurate description and classification of political institutions and the precise determination of the forces which create and control them, while the art of politics has for its aim the determination

18. Michael Curtis, *Comparative Government and Politics*, p. 1.
19. N.P. Guild and K.T. Palmer, *Introduction to Politics*, p. 6.

of the principles which it is necessary to observe if political institutions are to be efficiently operated.

3. *Paul Janet*: Politics is that part of social science which treats of the foundations of state and the principles of the government.
4. *Gareis*: Political Science considers the state as an institution of power (*Machtwesan*), in the totality of its relations, its origin, its setting (land and people), its object, its ethical signification, its economic problems, its life conditions, its financial side, its end, etc.
5. *Seeley*: Political Science investigates the phenomena of the government as political economy deals with wealth, biology with life, algebra with numbers, and geometry with space and magnitude.
6. *Fairlie*: Political Science deals with the life of men as organised under the government and law in what is known as the state. It includes a study of the organisation and the activities of states, and of the principles and ideals which underlie political organisation and activities. It considers the problem of adjusting political authority to individual liberty, the relations among men which are controlled by the state, and the relations of men to the state. It also deals with the distribution of governing power among the several agencies by which the actions of the state are determined, expressed, and exercised and with the problem of international life.
7. *Maurice Duverger*: Ever since men have been reflecting on politics, they have oscillated between two diametrically opposed interpretations. According to one, politics is conflict, a struggle in which power allows those who possess it to ensure their hold on society and to profit by it. According to the other view, politics is an effort to bring about the rule of order and justice, in which power guarantees the general interest and common good against the pressure of private interests.
8. *H.R.G. Greaves*: Politics is concerned among other things with conflicts — conflict over the proper use of force, power and authority.
9. *Pennock and Smith*: Politics, then, refers to all that has to do with the forces, institutions and organisational forms in any society that are recognised as having the most inclusive and final authority existing in that society for the establishment and maintenance of other, the effectuation of other conjoint

purposes of its members, and the reconciliation of their differences.... When we speak of political science, however, we refer to the study rather than to the practice of the government.

10. *S.L. Wasby*: As an academic field, political science includes the study of politics or government on matters which governments consider relevant, and the teaching of the material produced by this study.
11. *David E. Apter*: Taken as a whole, political science is about the relations between the rulers and ruled, and the means and the ends each employs.
12. *Bertrand de Jouvenel*: We call 'political' the pressures exerted upon the public authorities to bring about this or that decision desired by this or that private interest; we also call 'political' the stands taken on the matter by the parties, with a view to attaining or retaining popularity and power.

Thus, political science includes the attempts made since ancient times "to draw inferences, state valid generalisations, and arrive at tentative conclusions about the state, government, law, and political behaviour — conclusions which could serve, at least, as working, hypotheses on which future study and research might be based."[20] Treating politics as both a science and an art, Treitschke states the problem of political science in these words: "First, it should aim to determine from a consideration of the actual world of states the fundamental idea of the state; second, it should consider historically what they have attained in political life, and how; and, third, through this means, it should determine historical laws and moral imperatives. As such, it is applied history."[21] Willoughby says that "there are three great topics with which political science has to deal — state, government and law."[22]

NEW MEANING OF POLITICAL SCIENCE

The above discussion refers to the traditional view of the meaning and nature of political science in which it is a body of knowledge relating to the study of state and government. In the new or modern view, political science is identified with 'politics' and, more than that, the latter is preferred to the former. Its main focus is on the 'power' that plays a crucial part in the struggle in which the individuals and their groups may be found involved according to their capability and degree of interest at

20. Rodee, Christol and Anderson, *op. cit.*, p. 5.
21. Treitschke, *Politics* (Eng. Translation by Dugdale and T. de Bille), Vol. I, p. xxxii.
22. W.W. Willoughby, *The Nature of the State*, p. 382.

all levels — local, regional, national, international.[23] Hence, Lasswell and Kaplan define politics as the 'study of the shaping and sharing of power.'[24] According to Lindsay Rogers, "The lexicographers usually define politics as the 'science of art of government'. The term covers the entire field of political life and behaviour. It embraces the relations between the .states and the individuals and in this sense is practically synonymous with political philosophy. It comprehends the forces at work which form the anatomy and determine the physiology of states. It includes relations between the states and their political sub-divisions and between states and other states. Thus, politics can be domestic, national, federal, municipal, imperial or foreign. The relations thus comprehended and the regulations which they necessitate are inter-governmental." David Easton defines politics as 'the authoritative allocation of values that are binding on the society.'[25]

Three Connotations of Politics

Viewed thus, politics has three connotations — political activity, political process, and political power.

1. Political activity: It consists of the efforts by which conditions of conflict are created and resolved in a way pertaining to the interests of the people, who play their part in the struggle for power. Political activity emanates from a situation of 'predicament'. It begins in a form of human behaviour in which the interests of persons clash or interact for the purpose of having an allocation of binding values in their respective favours. This process goes on. The stage of the resolution of conflict is achieved either by peaceful means of reasoning, persuasion, adjustments, diplomacy or compromise, or by the violent means of force and coercion. As Michael Oakeshott says: "In political activity, then, men sail a boundless and bottomless sea; there is neither harbour for shelter nor floor for anchorage; neither starting point nor appointed destination. The enterprise is to keep afloat on an even keel, the sea is both friend and enemy...."[26]

2. Political process: It is an extension of the sense of political activity figuring the case of all those agencies which have their role in the decision-making process. The 'non-political' associations also engage our attention. They play a part in the political process of the country. Numerous groups made for the protection and promotion of specific interests, compete in the struggle for power. They influence the decision-

23. Rogers, "Politics" in Seligman (ed.), *Encyclopaedia of the Social Sciences*, Vol. XI, p. 204.
24. Lasswell and Kaplan, *Power and Society*, p. xiv.
25. Easton, *The Political System*, p. 119.
26. Michael Oakeshott, *Political Education*, p, 15.

makers. They fight amongst themselves. Hence, the government has to play the role of a co-ordinator or adjustor of group relations. In short, the 'political process' is the set of procedures whereby private associations existing in a state seek to influence the government, or participate in policy-formation by the government, or become the government.[27]

3. Political power: It is described as a certain kind of human relationship'.[28]

Political Science

State has diverse aspects and each social science deals with one of its particular aspects. Hence, it is suggested by some French writers like Du Sablon, Von Mohl and Lewis that instead of using the term 'political science' (in a singular sense), we should use the term 'political sciences' (in a plural sense). According to this view, political science is one which is concerned, not necessarily with the state in all of its aspects of relations, but with any particular phenomenon of the state or any class of phenomena either as a whole or incidentally, directly or indirectly. Thus, there "may be as many political sciences as there are conceivable aspects or forms of manifestation of the state."[29]

POLITICAL SCIENCE AND POLITICS: DISTINCTIONS

The two terms 'political science' and 'politics' have been used interchangeably, though a line of distinction may be drawn between the two.

1. It may be said that politics conveys the sense of political science in its practical form. According to Garner while the term 'politics' is used to describe the activities by which public officials are chosen and political policies promoted or, in a wider sense, the sum-total of the activities which have to do with the actual administration of public affairs, the term 'political science' is used to describe the body of knowledge relating to the phenomena of state.[30]
2. Again, the term 'political science' "has come to be more generally employed by the best writers and thinkers to describe the mass of knowledge derived from the systematic study of the state", while the meaning of the term 'politics' is confined to that of "the business or activity which has to do with the actual conduct of affairs of state,"[31]

27. S.E. Finer, *Comparative Government*, pp. 25-26.
28. Carl J. Friedrich, *Constitutional Government and Democracy*, p. 12.
29. *Ibid.*, p. 6.
30. *Ibid.*, pp. 2-3.
31. *Ibid.*, pp. 4-5.

3. Thus, while political science is a body of knowledge about the state in its various manifestations, politics refers to the actual operation of a political system. While politics is related to the art of statesmanship and diplomacy and, as such, is an art, political science is concerned with the fundamental principles of state and government and, as such, it is more of a science.
4. The term 'politics' "now-a-days refers to the current problems of the government which is often as not are more economic in character than political in the scientific sense. When we speak of a man as interested in politics, we mean that he is interested in the current problems of the day, in tariff questions, in labour questions, in the relations of the executive to the legislature, in any question, in fact, which requires, or is supposed to require, the attention of the lawmakers of the country."[32]

Conclusion

To conclude in spite of the problem of its precise nomenclature, the use of Political Science in theoretical and applied forms, its connotation in singular and plural senses, and above all, its distinction with politics, is a science of the state. It is a branch of social sciences dealing with the theory, organisation, government and practice of the state.[33] To quote Garner: "In short, political science begins and ends with the state. In a general way, its fundamental problems include, first, an investigation of the origin and nature of the state; second, an inquiry into the nature, history and forms of political institutions; and, third, a deduction therefrom, so far as possible, of the laws of political growth and development."[34] As Rodee, Christol and Anderson put it, "It is also desirable that the term political science should be viewed in a broad way so as to include 'political' (power-seeking) behaviour in or by groups, organisations and institutions which are more or less distinct from the state but which seek to influence public policy and the direction of social change."[35]

SCOPE OF POLITICAL SCIENCE

In view of the fact that there is no aspect of our common life which may not sometimes and somehow become political, it is not an easy job to determine precisely the boundary lines of political science.[36] Political Science covers a very comprehensive field that makes its character

32. Gilchrist, *op. cit*, p. 2.
33. E.C. Smith and A.J. Zurcher (eds.), *A Dictionary of American Politics*, p. 238.
34. Garner, *op. cit.*, p. 9.
35. Rodee, Christol and Anderson, *Introduction to Political Science*, p. 4.
36. R.H. Soltau, *Introduction to Politics*, p. 1.

dynamic. It studies the state and the government in relation to their past and present. It throws light on their probable development in time to come. The 'power theorists' like Hobbes of England, Weber of Germany and Merriam of America have made significant addition to the scope of political science. The discussion about the sources and purposes of power is as important as a study of its exercise. However, in the study of political science, power is not taken only in its coercive form. Its moral basis and the influence of such ideas over men loom large in the philosophy and psychology of politics. It informs a student of political science to make an examination of other institutions such as trade unions, churches, business corporations etc. that play an important role in the struggle for power.[37]

The Traditional View

According to the traditional view, political science is a study of the state in its past, present and future aspects. In it we study state as it has been, as it is, and as it may be (or should be) in time to time. First of all, we take up the case:

1. The study of state as it has been in the past: Here a political scientist, like an historian, is concerned with the origin and evolution of authority. He makes a survey of the beginning of organised political life. He makes a consideration of the evolution of political forms from simple to complex as well as a study of constitutional history. It involves a study of various currents of political thought as well as an understanding of the role of groups and organisations striving for power and influence in society. The study of political science in this connection may not be historically authentic. It may be based on speculations on account of the obscure origins of state.

2. The state in relation to the present: Here one's main concern is with political institutions as they are in existence and operation with focus of study on the present, a study of the evolution of authority and political institutions is of great help in understanding the present institutions, ideas and processes. The nature, functions and ends of state are studied in the light of empirical observations. The forms of governments are discussed their merits assessed. The scope of inquiry covers the study of extra-political institutions like political parties and interest groups, the issues of liberty and equality and the relationship between the two, the question of liberty of the individual *vis-a-vis* the authority of the state, the development of the state as a member of the international community. As R.A. Dahl says: "Whether one likes it or not, virtually

37. William A. Robson, *The University Teaching of Social Sciences: Political Science*, P. 17.

no one is completely beyond the reach of some kind of political system. A citizen encounters politics in the government of the country, town, school, church, business firm, trade union, club, political party, civic association and a host of other organisations from the United Nations to the PTA. Politics is one of the unavoidable facts of human existence. Everyone is involved in some fashion at the same time in some kind of political system".[38]

3. The ideal form of the state in future: Politics is a goal-oriented discipline, therefore, its scope also covers a study of the state as it may be in time to come, or as it ought to be in its ideal form. Political science becomes speculative, even utopian in this direction getting away from the world of reality. But it also adds to its goal-oriented or normative character.

4. Nature of future politics: The scope of political science also throw some light on what kind of political science would or should be in time to come. What should be the ideals before human beings so as to improve their institutions? Gettell says that political science is a historical investigation of what the state has been, an analytical study of what the state is, and a politico-ethical discussion of what the state should be.[39]

5. The 'study of powers': Some of the crucial questions that engage the attention of recent political scientists are: What is power? What is struggle for power? What are the causes of this struggle for power? The power makes state different from all other associations. Power alternates from one party to another in the battle of the ballot box; power enhances or reduces the status of a state. Recent writers like Lasswell, Kaplan, Morgenthau and Russell have thrown much light on the study of politics from this angle. As William Robson puts it, "It is with power in society that political science is primarily concerned — its nature, basis and results.... The focus of interest of the political scientist is clear and unambiguous, it centres on the struggle to gain or retain power, to exercise power or influence over others, or to resist that exercise."[40]

6. Policy science: In recent times, the scope of political science has widened by converting it into "policy science'. It aims to understand political phenomena to arrive at practical decisions about the policy that may be adopted. It studies the prevailing developments and tendencies to discover the likely direction of the course of development. It examines

38. Dahl, A.R., *Modern Political Analysis*, p. 7.
39. Gettell, *Political Science*, p. 4.
40. William Robson, *op. cit.*, p. 17.

the existing political processes in the light of the purposes they seek to achieve. To quote G.C. Field, "It must be remembered that most political discussions have as their final aim to arrive at practical decisions about the policy that is to be adopted or supported."[41]

VALUE OF POLITICAL SCIENCE

1. Careers: According to Rodee, Christol and Anderson, the primary objective of the political science curriculum is education for citizenship. The preparation of students for careers in politics, law, teaching, civil services and foreign services (though vitally important) is secondary to the task of equipping them to discharge the obligations of democratic citizenship, which grows constantly heavier in the modern world.[42]

2. Eternal vigilance: While intelligent and responsible citizenship can save democracy; ignorance and neglect can lost it. Hence, eternal vigilance is the price of liberty. The study, information and understanding of the complexities of modern government and politics are necessary for eternal vigilance.

3. Knowledge and understanding of good citizenship: The 'good' citizen who behaves himself and votes regularly must know how his government really operates, what interests and forces are behind particular policies, what the results of such policies are likely to be, who his elected representatives are, and what they stand for. Political science seeks to gather and impart this knowledge and understanding.

Therefore, the report of the American Political Science Association's Committee for the-Advancement of Teaching not only stresses education for citizenship but further states that there "is a widespread feeling amongst political scientists that (political theory) should be made the heart of the subject."[43]

On uses or relevance of Political Theory/Philosophy in the light of classics Germino has made the following points ;[44]

1. It is the attempt to achieve a noetic, as distinct from a non-noetic, interpretation of political reality.

---

41. G.C. Field, *Political Theory*, p. xviii.
42. Rodee, Christol and Anderson, *op. cit.*, p. 17.
43. *Ibid.*, p. 18. Politics, as a matter of fact, is an activity, a study of this activity, and a social science concerned with the theory and practice of political phenomena. We may remember these words of a Chinese leader: "Practice, knowledge, again practice, and again knowledge. This form repeats itself in endless cycles, and with each cycle the content of practice and knowledge rises to higher level." See Mao's paper 'On Practice' (1937) in his *Selected Works*, p, 655.
44. Dante Germino: "The Contemporary Relevance of the Classics of Political Philosophy" in Greenstein and Polsby (eds.), *Political Science: Scope and Theory.*

2. It is the realm of 'sciences of the person' rather than that of the sciences of phenomena and its methods must be appropriate to the investigation of the multi-dimensional participation in political reality experienced from within by the philosopher-theorist-scientist himself.
3. The philosopher exists not in a vacuum but within a specific political culture and civilisation whose collective cultural memory he shares. Thus, he gives a time-dimension to political reality that must be explored in depth through the process of self-conscious historical recollection.
4. The political philosopher (or noetic participant in political reality) is one who 'descends' to the depth of the consciousness and his return antidates symbols designed to illuminate the character of political reality within the structure of existence.
5. It is a science of the whole man and reductionist theories which pretend to explain all of man's behaviour on the basis of only a part of his experience must be rigorously examined and played in a broader context before they may be regarded as contribution to the subject.
6. A major function of a critical science of politics is to speak "truth' to power, however unpalatable that 'truth' may be to the powers that be at that times.
7. There are certain intellectual and existential virtues to be gained from the study and practice of philosophy, such as increased critical awareness, a distrust of single-vision, a political argumentation, a love of philosophical reflection as a means of experiencing dimensions of reality absent from contemporary historical existence, intellectual integrity, openness to the perspectives beyond those of one's immediate practical concerns and predilections, and respect for the inquiring human person behind the labels (or masks) conventionally attached to their political life.
8. Technique is only a tool of thought, despite the seeming assumption of advanced industrial society to the contrary, and decision-makers who remain ignorant of philosophy cut themselves off from a vital source of the intellectual and existential virtues so necessary to making tolerance, let alone wise decision.

RANGE AND VARIETY OF POLITICAL SCIENCE

According to Sir Fredrick Pollock: *An Introduction to the History of the Science of Politics* (London Macmillan, 1923), pp. 99-100:

Theoretical Politics	Applied Politics
A. Theory of the State Origin of Polity (a) Historical (b) Rational	A. The State Existing forms of Government Confederations and Federal State
Constitution Classification of forms of government Political Sovereignty	Independence Protectorates and extra-territorial jurisdiction
B. Theories of Government Forms of institutions	B. Government
Representative and Ministerial Government	Constitutional law and usage Parliamentary systems
Executive Departments	Cabinet and Ministerial responsibility
Defence and order Revenue and Taxation Wealth of Nations Province and Limits of Executive Law	Administrative Constitutions Army, Navy, Police, Currency, Budget, Trade State regulation or non-interference
C. Theory of legislation Objects of legislation, General Character and Division of Positive Law (Philosophy of Law or General Jurisprudence)	C. Laws and Legislation Legislative procedure (Embodiment of theory in legislative forms: memorandum, *expose des motifs etc.*) Parliamentary drafting.
Method and Sanction of Laws	Jurisprudence of particular States
Interpretation and Administration Language and Style (Mechanics of Law-making)	Courts of Justice and their machinery Judicial precedents and authority
D. Theory of the State as Artificial Person	D. The State Personified
Relation to Other States and Bodies of men	Diplomacy, Peace and War, Conference, Treaties and Conventions
International Law	International agreements for furtherance of justice, commerce, communications etc.

SCOPE OF POLITICAL SCIENCE

According to the Report of the UNESCO Committee for the Constitution of the International Political Science Association, W.A. Robson: *The University Teaching of Social Sciences — Political Science*, Appendix III, p. 183:

Broad Themes	Main Topics
1. Political Theory (i) Political Theory	1. Origin and Development of States
(ii) History of Political Ideas 2. Government (i) Constitution	2. Description, analysis and comparison of their present constitutions.
(ii) National Government (iii) Regional and Local Government	3. Governmental structures, poli-tical processes and systems of law.
(iv) Public Administration (v) Economic and Social Functions of Government	4. Regulations imposed by states upon individuals and groups, including the regulation of business, social relations and education.
(vi) Comparative Political Institutions 3. Parties, Groups and Public Opinion (i) Political Parties	5. Technical processes and agencies through which laws are enacted, administered, enforced and adjudicated.
(ii) Groups and Associations (iii) Citizen Participation in Government and Administration	6. Organisation and activities of political parties and pressure groups.
(iv) Public Opinion	7. Nature of public opinion and propaganda.
4. International Relations (i) International Politics (ii) International Organisation and Administration (iii) International Law	8. Relations (political, economic, cultural, ideological) between states and the attempts to regularise and control such relations by means of international law and organisations.

*C.C. Rodee, C.Q. Christol and T.J. Anderson, *Introduction to Political Science*, p. 5.

QUESTIONS FOR EXERCISE

1. Discuss politics as the study of power. What are the various sources of political power?
2. Discuss politics as the study of power with due reference to political, economic and ideological dimensions of power in modern society.
3. Define political science and discuss its scope.
4. Explain the value of political science.
5. What is politics? What are the various views — traditional and modern — regarding the nature of politics?
6. What is politics? Discuss the Liberal and the Marxist view of politics.
7. Define politics. Do you agree with the view that politics is struggle for power? Give reasons for your answer.
8. What do you understand by politics? Compare conventional and, modern views of politics.
9. "Politics is an analysis of the whole political system". Discuss.

2

Political Power

Political science deals with political power, its influence and distribution. A person in modern society is resourceful to the extent he influences the behaviour of other persons. Thus power is judged by the exercise of influence. Influence is a person's capacity to effect the behaviour of others. This is not only in keeping with their choice but mostly, even against it. Defining the nature of influence Harold De Lasswell and Abraham Kaplan point out, "The weight of influence is the degree to which policies are affected; the domain of influence, the persons whose policies are affected; the scope of influence; the values implicated in the policies."[1] Thus the weight of the influence is judged by the amount of change in the position of the actor influenced. Sometimes the compliance on the part of the influence is very high. In such situations, the power holder requires little effort to exercise influence. An example of such an influence may be seen in the power of the father in the family. This is an example of spontaneous influence. On the other hand, in other instances the compliance may be very low requiring force to impose power. This is known as coercive influence. Generally, political power has been termed as coercive influence. It is the use of threats or sanctions to influence others. These threats may be accompanied by possibilities of injuries and rewards. While penalties or punishments are negative sanctions to power, rewards are positive sanctions. Thus, power may be defined as the capacity to affect other's behaviour by the use or the threat of the use of negative or positive sanctions.

Power, therefore, is basically relational, it is not a personal property. Power is exercised only in relation to others. It has been defined as the capacity to affect other's behaviour. Secondly, power is behavioural. It consists in the behaviour of the two actors towards one another. Being

1. Harold D. Lasswell and Abraham Kaplan: *Power of Society*, New Haven: Yale University Press, 1961, p. 73.

behavioural, power is subject to measurement and comparison. It is measured and assessed on the basis of its influence. Thirdly, power is situational. In order to know it one must relate it to a specific situation. Power is known by the specific role of the power holder in a specific situation.

WAYS OF DETECTING POWER RELATIONS

Robert A. Dahl, in his book *Modern Political Analysis* pointed out to the following four different ways of detecting power relations in a particular situation. In other words, these are the symptoms of the presence and exercise of power. Power is known by them.

1. Office: Power is measured by relating it to an office. It operates within the framework of a formal office. No office no power. On the other hand, higher the office, more the power attached to it. This method of detecting power relations is simple since the hierarchy of the offices is easily noticed. However, power is not necessarily linked to formal offices. One finds king makers and invisible bosses who hold no office. Therefore, measurement of power by necessarily relating it to an office is inadequate.

2. Observations of well-placed judges: Well-placed judges are those who have the opportunity of being in close touch with the formal office holders. They could therefore, watch and note the process of the operation of power in and around a formal office. This technique suffers from the defect that it is impossible to evolve a reliable criterion for selection of well-placed judges. Again, as has been pointed out by Lasswell and Kaplan, "Even seemingly well-placed observers can be misled by false reputation: they may attribute great power where little or none exists. Do we need more judges, then, to judge the judges?"[2] Thus the technique leads to a vicious circle.

3. Analysis of actual decision-making process: The analysis of actual decision-making process shows what people actually do and what is the nature and level of their participation. Clearly, one who is most influential in the decision-making process is the most powerful. However, mere participation in the decision-making process cannot be taken as an index of power. The executive and his personal secretary both participate in the decision-making process, but the power of both is clearly different.

4. Comparison of activities of the participants: Thus, instead of a mere observation of the participants in the decision-making process, their activities should be weighed and compared to find out the nature and extent of their power. This method also has its own difficulties. For

2. *Ibid.*, p. 71.

example, it is difficult to find out the relative power of the two participants of which one initiates a proposal and gets it passed easily, while the other gets it adopted in the face of stiff opposition.

The above discussion of the advantages and disadvantages of the four ways of detecting power relations in a particular situation, shows that each of the technique has its own advantages. In order to measure power one has to note its weight, scope and the domain. The weight of power means the degree of participation in the decision-making process. The scope of power means the values at stake. The domain of power means the number of persons upon whom power is exercised. Therefore, a combination of all the above mentioned techniques is required to measure power.

Definition of Power

According to Robert Dahl, "A has power over B to the extent that he can get B to do something that B would not otherwise do."[3] Here the main focus is not on the actions and intentions of the power holder but upon the actions and intentions of the power addressee. There cannot be a power relation unless there is opposition from the other side. Sanction is the most important attribute of power. Affectivity of sanction is the real test of power. Sanction is sensible only when it brings a change in the position of the power addressee. This definition of power however, is applicable only in ideal conditions. For example, a nation accepting a change in its course of actions under the influence of a powerful nation will hardly acknowledge this and go on claiming that this change is the result of its own free will. In such situations it is, no doubt, extremely difficult to apply Dahl's definition.

Another significant definition of power has been advanced by Herbert Goldhamer and Edward A. Shils according to whom, "A person may be said to have power to the extent that he influences the behaviour of others in accordance with his own intentions."[4] This definition lays emphasis upon the power holder and his intention. Thus, it is different from the earlier definition in which emphasis has been laid on the power addressees. According to the definition advanced by Goldhamer and Shils, one must first determine the intentions of the power holder to know the type of power. It is unnecessary to enquire whether the power addressee openly acknowledges power. This definition of power is certainly free from difficulties. For example, in the case the power holder does not communicate his intentions; it will be difficult to constitute a

3. Robert A. Dahl, "The Concept of Power" in S. Sidney Ulmer (ed.), *Introductory Readings in Political Behaviour*, Chicago, Rand McNally, 1962, p. 344,
4. Herbert Goldhamer & Edward A. Shils, "*Types of Power and Status*" in Ulmer, *op. cit*, p. 334.

power relation. This definition insists on some sort of communication between the power holder and the power addressee to make the former powerful. This act of communication involves coercion which may assume any form such as force, domination and manipulation.

Thus power involves coercion which may be of the following three types:

1. Force: It is a physical activity employing visible resources.

2. Domination: It takes place whenever an actor clearly communicates his intention to the power addressee.

3. Manipulation: It is an attempt to influence other's behaviour without communicating the actual intention. It is often used in political situations to avoid direct communications between the most powerful and the actual power addressee.

In the above mentioned three forms the first is the most normal, since a power relation requires the identification of power basis in order to be known.

POWER BASES

Thus, power relation depends upon power bases. The power bases differ from one culture to another and also from one level to another in the same culture. These power bases may be as follows:

1. Wealth: Power due to possession of wealth shows that wealth has the power base. This is particularly found in capitalist societies.

2. Control over means: The power basis in the military states is the control over the instruments of violence.

3. Skill: Personal skill is a power basis observed in the case of powerful individuals in different societies.

4. Power itself: Power over one issue area itself helps in its extension to other issue areas. Therefore, in such cases power itself serves as a power basis.

Besides the basis of power, there should be ability to use it so that a power relation may be established. Thus, the power situation involves power basis, ability to use it and the power relation. Some power actions establish asymmetrical relation between the power holder and the power addressee. This asymmetrical power relation defies measurement and comparison. In such a situation Herber A. Simon has given a solution, "This difficulty can be handled in either of two ways : (i) We can give-up the idea that the relation is asymmetrical; or (ii) We can add an asymmetrical relation operating in the opposite direction from the first. If the processes of influence take time and particularly if the time lags associated with the two asymmetrical relations are different, there is atleast the possibility that we can make separate empirical observations of the two relations. Thus, taking power as an asymmetrical relation, we may take the two power relations between A and B separately and this is quite justified since in the most cases there is a time lag between the operation of these two sets of power relations."[5]

Power Limits Power

Power is not only power seeking. Power seeking becomes power after success. This also requires capability and will. Once the power is acquired, the powerful tries to expand its limit. This is so since power brings with it fame, reverence, security, respect, affection, wealth and many other values. The search for power however is counteracted by the power addressee and also by other power holders. In each case only the power limits power. This however, is partially true since power is also limited by the personal characteristics of the power holder and the traits of the situation. As Lasswell and Kaplan have pointed out, "The social order is equally important as a limitation on power. The mores at any given time may put outside the scope of power such practices as those of religion or sex. In some societies mores directly concern power itself, sanctions being applied, for example, to any sort of personal ambition or aggressiveness."[6]

NATURE OF POLITICAL POWER

Political power is essentially relational. It presupposes social relation between the power holder and the power addressee. The type of social order in which power relation exists, besides the power basis, the power sanctions the reaction of the power addressee etc. For example, these may be found to differ essentially in rural and urban societies. Political power is the power which operates within the periphery of the state and its institutions. It is based upon the power of the state. The state wields the strongest power sanctioned by prison and punishment. However, the essential nature of the power of the state is not different from the power found at any level of society. Therefore, power is judged in the perspective of social variables. Political power is conditioned by the social process. It changes according to the variations in the nature and working of the social process. The political institutions in their turn, influence social environment.

5. Herbert A. Simon, "Notes on the Observation and Measurement of Political Power" in W.D. Hawley & F.M. Wirted, *The Search for Community Power*, Prentice Hall, Inc. New Jersey, 1968, p. 25.
6. Lasswell & Kaplan, *op. cit.*, p. 96.

DISTRIBUTION OF POWER

The nature of political power cannot be fully understood without the study of its distribution. The distribution of political power determines the identity and the role of the power holder. Therefore, political sociology investigates the pattern of the distribution of political power.

Theories of Distribution

Several theories have been advanced to explain the distribution of political power, and the causes behind it. These theories may be classified into Elitist and Non-Elitist theories. The Elitist theory was advanced to refute the Non-Elitist theory of Karl Marx.

TYPES OF POWER

Class Power

Marxist theory represents one of the earliest attempts to explain distribution of political power in a society. According to Karl Marx, political power in every civilised society is unevenly distributed. The ruling class monopolises the political power by the ownership of the means of production. Thus, the political leader represents the dominant class. Socio-economic factors are the determinants of the distribution of political power. The social order however, is marked by a perpetual conflict between the ruler and the ruled classes. This conflict is conditioned by the development of productive forces. This conflict is the basic reason behind the polarisation of classes between the capitalist and the working class. The nature of conflict determines changes in the distribution of power. Thus the Marxist theory is economic determinism. It seeks to intensify class conflict. It preaches violent revolution. Therefore, it was natural for the thinkers of the other world to challenge Marxist theory.

Power of the Elite

The elitist theories challenge the following presumptions of Marxist theory:

1. Political structures are mere reflections of socio-economic relation: As against this assumption, the elitist thinkers maintain that economic factors are not the sole determinants of power structure.

2. Inaccessibility of the ruling class leads to the polarisation between the ruler and the ruled: Challenging this assumption the elitist propound the theory of continual circulation of elites. The ruling class is not stable and fixed.

3. Marx believed in a future classless, egalitarian society: The elitist thinkers, on the other hand, believe in the hierarchical structure of society as the inevitable order.

In spite of the above fundamental differences, some thinkers have tried to arrive at some sort of synthesis between the Marxists and the Elitist view. An example of such theories is the theory of Raymond Aron published in March 1950 and June 1950 in British Journal of Sociology, in the form of two articles with the title, "Social Structure and the Ruling Class". In this attempt has been made to work synthesis between Marx and Pareto. This synthesis is based on the fundamental agreement between the Marxists and the Elitists that political power in a society always rests in the hands of a few.

4. The economic approach of James Burnham: In his book *The Managerial Revolution*, Burnham rejects the Marxist conclusion and maintains that egalitarian society is impossible and there will always be a rule of the elite. He, however, utilises Marxist principle of economic determinism to explain the source of the power of elite. The elite group, according to Burnham, controls the means of production and thus enjoys preference in the distribution of goods. This economic control gives them political power and social prestige, the two pillars of the foundation of elite class. The elite class however, faces a crisis in the capitalist society, the capitalist class gradually becomes only a leisured class divorced from the actual production process which therefore, gradually passes into the hands of a managerial class. Ultimately, this managerial class takes the control of the means of production and thus receives preferential treatment. Thus, the capitalist class is gradually replaced by the managerial elite. According to Burnham, the government in the modern declining capitalist societies will be ultimately run by the managerial elite.

5. The institutional approach of C. Wright Mills: Political power, according to Mills, tends to be institutionalised. The political elite is the product of the institutional landscape of the society. In his book *The Power Elite*, Mills defines the power elite as those who occupy the command posts of the social structure. These persons are placed at the top most ranks of the institutions holding a pivotal position in society, such as the military, the big corporations and the political executive in the American society. The power elite is so-called due to its status at the top of the hierarchy of these key institutions in the society. The elite class is formed only in the context of these vital institutions. These leaders again, form a cohesive group. Power elite is a conscious and conspiratorial group.

According to all the elite theories the following principles are applicable to the distribution of political power in a society:

1. Political power is always concentrated in the hands of a minority who are the political elite. This minority has organising ability and the requisite psychological qualities to guide the masses. It controls the means of production and occupies command positions in the key institutions of society.
2. Political elite rules as a self-conscious, cohesive and conspiratorial group. It has all the characteristics of a powerful minority.
3. Political elite consider power as cumulative. Power brings in more power. The political elite can fully regulate the entry of the non-elite into it.

In spite of sufficient popularity of the elitist theory it has been subject to a lot of criticisms. No theory has been applicable on a national scale. Most of the theories have been applicable on the community level. The community studies have also sometimes refuted the elitist theory. The pluralists have challenged the elitist contention that a society is always ruled by a minority political power. They argue that decision-making cannot be understood without the context of a continuous bargaining process among the elites and the mass approval. Robert Dahl has advanced the following criticisms against the elite theories in his article entitled *A Critique of The Ruling Elite Model*:

1. The elite theory confuses potential control with actual control and forgets their difference.
2. Absence of political equality does not necessarily prove the existence of ruling elite.
3. There may be different scopes of power and a group having a high degree of influence over one scope may not necessarily have the similar degree of influence over another scope within the same system.

In his book *Who Governs*, Robert Dahl examines the process of decision-making in New Haven in USA. On the basis of his examination he shows that power is actually distributed pluralistically. He selects three distinct decision areas covering urban development, public schools and political nominations. He picks up three categories of potential leaders — politicians, social notables and economic notables. After examining all the available data he comes to the conclusion that decision-making is essentially pluralistic. In New Haven he finds not one elite but many elites. These elites never form a cohesive, conscious and conspiratorial group. Resources are unevenly distributed. But this inequality did not always make power cumulative. Thus according to Dahl society is basically a polyarchy. Political power is determined not by hierarchical but by horizontal leaderships. The following arguments have been advanced against Dahl's pluralist model:

1. It wrongly locates power in concrete decisions, or in activities having direct bearing upon their making. Power is not only exercised through decision-making but also through the ability to confine the scope of decision-making to relatively safe issues.
2. Dahl's model fails to differentiate the unimportant issues from the important issues arising in the political arena.

In the midst of the above polemics between the elitist and the pluralist we should remember that they agree that political power is always unevenly distributed. Secondly, political decisions are made only by the few and not by all. However, the elitists and the pluralists disagree on the questions as to who exactly constitute the powerful minority and how do they actually operate it.

Organisational Power

According to Mosca society has always been found to be divided between the ruler and the ruled. To quote his words, "In all societies from societies that are very meagerly developed and have barely attained the dawning of civilisation, down to the most advanced and powerful societies — two classes of people appear —- a class that rules and a class that is ruled. The first class, always the less numerous, performs all political functions, monopolises power and enjoys the advantages that power brings, whereas the second, the more numerous class, is directed and controlled by the first in a manner that is now more or less arbitrary and violent."[7] According to this view the society is ruled by the 'political class' the elite or the minority which is composed of superior individuals occupying economic, military or religious possessions. Due to its organised nature the elite minority tends to maintain its power. The contact and communication within the minority group is simple and speedy. It achieves a high-level of solidarity. It presents itself a group having a communication. Therefore, as Mosca has rightly pointed out, "The power of any minority is irresistible as against each single individual in the majority, who stands alone before the totality of the organised minority."[8] However, in order to rule, the elite depends on 'political formula' which means an attempt by the political elite to represent it as a moral and legal power. In fact, the rule may not be morally sound and yet it may be accepted so by the people. Thus, the

7. G. Mosca, *The Ruling Class*, McGraw Hill, New York, 1939, p. 50.
8. *Ibid.*, p. 51.

elite cannot rule by mere physical force. They are constantly under the necessity of taking account of the desires of the majority.

The position of the political class, according to Mosca is never permanent. As he puts it, "The established elite would be renewed and invigorated by the ablest representatives of the new forces in the new society. At the same time the new elements in turn become imbued with certain of the values of the elite."

In his book *Political Parties*, Roberto Michels maintains organisational approach like Mosca, concerning elite control. Michel's view is however, different from Mosca. According to Mosca the elite maintains its control by virtue of its organisational ability, flowing from its being a minority. On the other hand, Michels maintains that the structure of modern organised society itself gives birth to elite rule. No party in modern society, can be successful without organisation. The organisation, in its turn, requires the power of the leaders. Therefore, concludes Michels, "Who says organisation says oligarchy." To explain this phenomenon, he advances the following two arguments:

1. Organisational reason: As a party grows in organisation it requires an inner circle of officers and leaders to provide technical expertise. These leaders in their turn, develop vested interests, leading to the formation of oligarchy.

2. Psychological reason: The majority of the human beings are apathetic, indolent, ignorant, slavish and incapable of self-government. Therefore, they gladly hand over responsibilities of government to an oligarchy. This oligarchy is stable and cannot be removed. The class at the bottom can never absolutely substitute the class at the apex, though some interchange always goes on. According to Michels even in the case of successful revolution the elite rule does not end, since the revolution is led by leaders, who after achieving power, transform themselves into a closed class apart from the masses. They become completely 'bourgeoisified'. Thus a revolution only means the replacement of the elite rule by a 'proletarian elite'.

Power of Unorganised Masses

In his book, *The Mind and Society*, Pareto explains the elite control in terms of fundamental psychological factors, which according to him, determine human history. According to Pareto, elite is the class of persons having the highest indices of abilities in different branches of activity. The elite class may be further sub-divided into a governing elite and a non-governing elite. The governing elite includes persons directly or indirectly forming the government elite it includes those whose activities are not politically important. However, in actual practice too many factors play important part in determining the elite, besides special abilities. According to Pareto the history of human society is the history of the relationships between the ruling elite and the ruled non-elites.

As has been already pointed out, Pareto gives a psychological explanation of the elite control. According to him, human actions may be divided into two types — logical and non-logical actions are those which are directed to attainable ends, employing appropriate means. Non-logical actions have neither proper ends nor means. Most of the human actions are non-logical though they are often presented as logical actions. The attempt in this tendency is composed of two elements — derivations and residues. Residues are the manifestations of sentiments on instincts. Derivations are the rationalisations of these residues. These residues according to Pareto may be classified into the following six types: (i) Residues of combinations, (ii) Residues of persistence of aggregates, (iii) Residues of sociability, (iv) Residues of the integrity of the individuals, and (v) Residues of Sex.

Of these the first two are relevant in elite control The residues of combination represent tendencies to originate, manipulate and combination represent tendencies to originate, manipulate and combine institutions and ideas by the use of imagination, all these requiring cunning. The residues of the persistence of aggregates represent permanence, stability and order. Pareto calls men having attributes of class first as foxes and those of class second as lions. The style of a government depends on the proportion of the foxes and lions in it. While the foxes are bold, adventurous, cunning and clever, the lions are solid, conservative, tradition loving, relying on forces and loyal to family, church and nation. If the class 1st dominates the foxes will rule, if the class 2nd dominates, the government will be a rule of the lions.

History, according to Pareto, reveals a constant alteration between the dominance of foxes and lions in the elite class. This is what he calls, the circulation of elite or the replacement of one elite by another or the circulation of the individual between the elite and non-elite. The process of replacement of one elite by another, according to Pareto, may be either by gradual process of infiltration or by a violent revolution. The circulation of elites brings change in the psychological characteristics of the members of the elite and as the non-elite looses desired characteristics it restores its vitality by recruitment from the non-elite class. On the other hand, if the elite fails to do so, it is overthrown by the stronger elements in the non-elite section, who now becomes the new elite. In all this process there is no real transformation of the social structure.

Power in Democracy

In the words of Bryce, "The word democracy, ever since the time of Herodotus, has been used to denote that form of government in which the ruling power is vested not in a particular class or classes but in the members of the community as a whole." Thus, mass participation is the greatest characteristic of democracy. In the words of Dicey, "Democracy is a form of government in which governing body is comparatively a large section of the entire nation." The most important characteristics of democratic form of government have been summed up in the famous words of Abraham Lincoln in calling it, "Government of the people, for the people and by the people." Democratic form of government show a new way of life based upon the *triune traits* of equality, liberty and fraternity. It is distinguished by the following characteristics as a form of the government:

1. The political power rests in the hands of people or their elective representatives.
2. People are the final judges in the field of administration.
3. The executive is responsible to the representatives of the people.
4. The legislature is responsible to the masses.
5. The judiciary takes care of the rights of the people.
6. The people control the government. They can even remove it or change it.
7. The constitution of the state takes due care of the rights of different sections of the people.
8. The government remembers the values of equality, liberty and fraternity. Every citizen is given equal rights before the court of law. The state is a welfare state, looking after the welfare of every section of society.

Democracy has been classified as direct and indirect. In the former the entire public directly participates in carrying out the forms of administration. This is possible only in a very small state such as the ancient Greek city states. Since modern states are rather too big, it is generally indirect democracy in which political decisions are taken not directly by the electorate but by their elected representatives. Since this form of government is now present in most of the countries of the world, therefore a huge literature has gathered about the advantages of democracy. Alongwith its obvious advantages such as the expansion and fulfilment of the humanistic values and the establishment of an egalitarian society etc., some of its difficulties have also become rather glaring. It is often observed that democracy becomes in practice aristocracy or the government of particular political party or of a political section or of a dominant political leader. Most of the difficulties of democracy can be removed by proper political education of the masses, organisation of public opinion, growth of national character and the evolution of leadership at different levels of society.

Of the two most well-known forms of democracy in big countries one finds the Presidential form and the Parliamentary form of government. In India there is a parliamentary form of democratic government. U.S.A. is an example of presidential form of democracy. Both these forms have their obvious advantages and disadvantages and they suit different types of nations. In the presidential form of government the President holds all the powers and distributes them to different constituents of the government. Its chief advantages are: separation of political powers, stability, division of labour, able administration, encouragement to national unity and quick adjustment in the periods of crisis. The advantages of parliamentary form of government are: respect to public opinion, responsible government, flexibility, lack of autocracy, political education to citizens and the administration by able persons. The debate about the advantages and disadvantages of the two systems is however unnecessary, they suit to different types of people in different countries. With the increase of political consciousness among the masses everywhere aristocracy, like monarchy, has given place to democratic forms of government.

Power in Totalitarian Society

In the words of Mussolini, "If the 19th century was an age of socialism, liberalism and democracy, the 20th century is to be a century of authority, collectivism and the totalitarian state." Thus Mussolini advocated dictatorship. The same was done by Hitler in Germany who said, "Any one who wants to live in Germany with Germany and through Germany is obliged to submit to the nation and to adapt himself to the totalitarian state." The totalitarian state, as is clear by the term itself, monopolises all power in the hands of the state, who is generally represented by a dictator. The Fascist party in Germany pleaded for authority, discipline and subordination. Mussolini asked the Italian youth to believe, to obey and to fight. The worst commentary on dictatorship, was its fate in the last two World Wars. Today no sane individual supports dictatorship.

Some people point out to its advantages such as good administration, less expenses, growth of national consciousness and fast progress of the nation etc.

However, its disadvantages are more glaring. These are: autocratic government, supremacy of the state, elimination of fundamental rights, narrow and aggressive nationalism, lack of international consciousness, racism, moral degeneration, opposition to public welfare and based upon false propaganda. Therefore, this form of Government has been challenged everywhere and given place to more democratic forms of government.

QUESTIONS FOR EXERCISE

1. What is power? Explain the nature of political power.
2. Explain different types of power in different organisations.

3

Behavioural and Post-behavioural Revolutions

In the period following the second World War many important changes have taken place in the field of political science. The new generation of political scientists realised that their discipline aims at explaining life in relation to the struggle for power. It must come out from the nucleus of the study of the government. It must take into account sociological, psychological and economic factors. Prof. Charles Merriam of the Chicago University maintained that the study of politics should be done in empirical terms. The pioneering contribution of Merriam was enriched by a galaxy of his students and faculty members like V.O. Key, Jr., D.B. Truman, Herbert Simon, David Easton and G.A. Almond, who came to be known as the leading lights of the Chicago School. G.E.G. Catlin did the same at the Cornell University. Besides, a good number of European scholars who shifted to the United States after 1920, brought with them the messages of a psychologist like Sigmund Freud and a sociologist like Max Weber. In this direction, one may refer to the names of Franz Neumann, Paul Lazarsfeld, Hans Speier, Hans Gerth, Reinhard Bendix etc. After 1950 the new trend became so powerful that it represented "a new approach, and a challenge, a new orientation and a reform movement."[1]

Protest Movement

The new generation of American political scientists launched a sort of 'protest movement' against the line of traditionalists who had underlined the significance of normative political theory. The American government as well as by philanthropic institutions of the Ford, the Carnegie, and the

1. E.M. Kirkpatrick, "The Impact of the Behavioural Approach on Traditional Political Science" in Austin Ranney (ed.), *Essays on the Behavioural Study of Politics*, p. 11.

Rockfeller gave huge financial assistances to remodel the disciplines of social sciences in the light of actual human behaviour. Advanced study centres of behavioural research came into being at Palo Alto and at the university of Michigan. Other universities like the Princeton and the Yale followed suit. It showed that the "young turks' of the community of American social scientists "needed new approaches, new techniques of research and new concepts for which they-had to borrow from other social sciences."[2]

BEHAVIOURAL REVOLUTION

The American writers termed it, "behavioural revolution. Its most outstanding characteristic was that political science moved closer and closer to the worlds of psychology, sociology and economics at the hands of eminent figures like David Easton, David Apter, G. A. Almond, G.B. Powell, Harold Lasswell, Robert A. Dahl, Karl Deutsch etc. These writers sought to study political matters in the context of non-political phenomena in a variety of ways.

Characteristics of Behavioural Movement

E.M. Kirkpatrick underlined four characteristics of the behavioural movement as:[3]

1. Rejection of political institutions as the basic conceptual units and a substitution of individual and group behaviour;
2. Emphasis on the unity of social sciences, hence an increased willingness to cross-disciplinary lines;
3. Greater attention to precision, measurement and quantification techniques, and
4. Development of systematic political theory.

Intellectual Foundations

A better representation of the behavioural revolution in political science and its key features is contained in Easton's description of its eight 'intellectual foundations'. There are :[4]

1. Regularities: There are certain discernible uniformities in the political behaviour of human beings that can be expressed in generalisations as they are capable of explaining and predicting social phenomena.

---

2. See R.A. Dahl, "The Behvioural Approach in Political Science, Epitaph for a Monument to a Successful Protest" in *American Political Science Review* (December, 1961), pp. 763-72,
3. *The American Political Science Review*, 1963, No. 1, p. 162.
4. Easton, "The Current Meaning of Behaviouralism" in J.C. Charlesworth (ed.), *Contemporary Political Analysis*, pp. 11-31.

2. Verification: All knowledge must be based on observation and verification. That is, in order to be valid, knowledge should consist of the propositions that may be subjected to empirical investigations.

3. Techniques: Correct techniques should be adopted for acquiring and interpreting data, use of research tools or methods which generate valid reliable and comparative data.

4. Quantification: Data should not only be collected, it should also be measured and quantified so that the conclusions of a researcher may be verified on the basis of quantified evidence.

5. Values: The research should be value-free so that the researcher may not be in a position to examine a political issue from his own subjective standpoint of valuational judgement. Moral and ethical questions should be discarded in order to give a scientific explanation.

6. Systematisation: It is on the basis of well-organised, logically interrelated structure of concepts and propositions that hypotheses have to be advanced, and that hypotheses, in their own turn, have to be capable of undergoing rigorous testing.

7. Pure science: Research should be of a pure type or perfectly verifiable by evidence irrespective of the fact that it may, or may not, apply to a specific social problem. The ultimate aim should be to make social sciences like natural sciences.

8. Integration: Since the behaviouralists subscribe to the interdisciplinary approach, they do not treat political science as a separate or a distinct discipline. To them political science is one of the social sciences and, for this reason, it should be integrated with other social sciences like sociology, psychology and economics and even with natural sciences like biology and anthropology. Knowledge should be unified, because it is indivisible.

Thus behavioural political science rejects the place of norms, values and goals. It sticks only to the side of 'facts' in the study of this discipline. It likes to follow the new techniques of mathematics, statistics, engineering (like sample survey, multi-variate analysis, game theory, content analysis etc.) for presenting conclusions in a 'scientific' way.

CREDO OF RELEVANCE

In 1969 David Easton delivered his presidential address at the annual session of the American Political Science Association. He heralded a 'new revolution' that is now known by the name of 'post- behaviouralism.' He presented following new points (what he called 'credo of relevance') to revise the political science of the behavioural phase on these lines:[5]

5. Eston, *Political System*, pp. 324-25.

Traditional Behavioural and Post-behavioural Political Science

Traditional	Behavioural	Post-Behavioural
1. Inter-relates facts and values	1. Separates facts and values	1. Facts and values tied to action and relevancy
2. Prescriptive and normative	2. Non-prescriptive, objective and empirical	2. Humanistically problem-oriented
3. Qualitative	3. Quantitative	3. Quantitative and qualitative
4. Concerned with irregularities and regularities	4. Concerned with uniformities and regularities	4. Concerned with regularities and irregularities
5. Focus on European countries	5. Focus on Anglo-American ountries	5. Focus on Third World countries

1. Substance must precede technique. It is more important to be relevant and meaningful for contemporary urgent problems than to be sophisticated in the tools of investigation.
2. Research in social sciences must not lose touch with reality. Study should not be made abstract or hypothetical.
3. Study should not be based exclusively on 'facts,' it should also accord some place for 'values' to the possible and desirable extent.
4. Mad craze for scientism should be discarded, because social sciences cannot be converted into pure or natural sciences.
5. The study should be related to the past and present, it should also be future-oriented.
6. While sticking to the way of borrowing necessary material from different sources, the perspective should be as wide as possible so that a student may borrow from any source like Platonism, existentialism, liberalism, and Marxism.
7. The political scientists should present the knowledge of their discipline in a way that it is useful to the administrators of the country.

Distinction of Behavioural Political Science

1. It discards *values* and lays emphasis on *facts* alone so that political science may be converted into a science.
2. The area of politics has widened to include non-political phenomena in the study of politics they have their role in the struggle for power.

3. A mad craze for borrowing from other social, even natural, sciences is appreciated.
4. The writers prefer to discard the old descriptive and prescriptive method. Instead they take to the ways of mathematics, statistics, engineering etc. to present their research in a 'scientific' form.
5. In a very cryptic manner the behaviouralists try to eulogise the politics of 'western' countries and thereby reject or undermine the politics of the communist countries.

POST-BEHAVIOURALIST TREND

The post-behaviouralists depict a trend of return to the past. They includes the following deviations from the past:

1. Reaffirming the place of norms and values in the study of politics.
2. Laying more emphasis on the substance than on the exhibition of facts.
3. Advising us to abandon mad craze for scientism.
4. Insisting on giving a correct turn to the inter-disciplinary approach so that material may be borrowed from diverse sources ranging from the ideas of Plato to those of Dewey, Sartre and Marx. Thus, political science in the phases of behaviouralism and post-behaviouralism marks the degrees of break, continuity as well as continuing differences with its form in the phase of traditionalism.

Criticism of Behavioural Political Science

1. Pseudo politics: The behaviouralists have expanded the scope of this discipline by giving a new definition of the term 'politics.' To them it is identifiable with power and a struggle for its sake. Politics is everywhere from the office of the head of the state (and government) to that of a local council. Therefore, a student of this subject is at a loss to know as to what is 'political', and what is not. Political science is now everything or nothing. Much has been dragged into the domain of politics that was once regarded as falling within the domains of other sciences like sociology and psychology. Therefore, a critic like Christian Bay has called behavioural politics as 'pseudo politics' or 'counterfeit politics.[6]

2. Mad craze for scientism: As political science is a social science, it cannot be converted into a natural science. The behaviouralists showed something like 'mad craze for scientism'. A leading light like Easton had to admit this mistake of the champions of the behavioural orthodox. He

6. Bay, "A Critical Evaluation of Behavioural Literature" in *The American Political Science Review*, March, 1965, pp. 39-51.

also admitted that much work done during the phase of 'behaviouralism' was like more of a show than that of a reality, What the behaviouralists contributed failed to perform the functions of a theory.[7]

3. Discarded values: The behaviouralists committed the mistake of discarding values from the study of politics. By depending only on facts, and facts of their own preference, they demonstrated their inherent bias in favour of a particular kind of political science. They made political science valueless by making it value-free. Mulford Q. Sibley has condemned them for presenting a dull and monotonous kind of political science. Leo Strauss described them as being 'biased' in favour of a political science in defence of the American model of democracy. Despite its insistence on the reaffirmation of values to some extent even post-behaviouralism tilts heavily in favour of a value-free political science and now looks like a raving, rumbling structure without any ultimate destiny.[8]

UNION OF NORMATIVISM AND EMPIRICISM

To conclude, a proper study of politics should be based on both facts and values. Neither should be discarded or sacrificed. Then alone a study of politics shall be satisfying to the human mind. A union of normativism and empiricism would enrich politics by all means and in all respects. To quote W.T. Bluhm, "In a political science created by the union of noumenalism and naturalism political ethics would not swallow up descriptive science, nor would ethical questions be reduced to behavioural ones. Each part of the discipline would proceed autonomously, but in co-operation with the other. As in any happy marriage neither partner would be destroyed, but would be rather enriched by the other. Ethical speculation about virtue and freedom would be grounded in any awareness of the facts of process, which specify the limits of the freedom the notion of ethics presupposes, limits, however, which are also the laws by which purposes are achieved. But the logic of ethical inquiry, as a logic of man's freedom and virtue, would continue to be a discipline in some sense different from scientific inquiry."[9]

QUESTIONS FOR EXERCISE

1. What are the characteristics of behavioural movement? What are its intellectual foundations?
2. Critically evaluate Post-behavioural Revolution in modern political science.

7. Eugene Meehan, *The Theory and Method of Political Analysis*, p. 162.
8. L.S. Rathore, "The Conflict of Modernity and Tradition in Contemporary Political Theory" in Bains and Jain (eds.), *Political Science in Transition*, p. 25.
9. W.T. Bluhm, *Theories of the Political System*, pp. 503-504.

4

Nature of Political Science

It is said that the nomenclature of political science owes its origin to William Godwin and Mary Wollstonecraft. It was also preferred by Vico, Hume, Pollock and Seeley. The new name political science became popular in the present century. A very large number of scholars preferred to use it in place of its old nomenclature. But some leading scholars of this subject have used the two names interchangeably.[1] R.H. Soltau quotes with approval the opinion of a British publicist (Spender), who regards the "belief in the existence of a science from which rules and principles may be deduced for the government of mankind" as "one of the most disastrous of the many political myths of recent years" and it is for this reason that he prefers the term 'politics' or 'government' to 'political science' which, as he concedes, is so widely used that we cannot altogether avoid it. "It appears that he is still very definite in his mind that political study has achieved 'a number of strictly limited conclusions."[2] Though some American writers have preferred to use the new term 'political system' instead of state and government and thereby defined it as study of 'power' and struggle for its sake that affects the operation of a political system the behaviouralists have once again preferred to call it by its old name.

There are contradictory views on the subject whether political science is a 'science' or not, science "is a branch of knowledge or study dealing with a body of facts or truths systematically arranged and showing the operation of general laws."[3] A science is a systematised study of facts linked together in their causal sequence with a view to

1. For instance, Laski a professor in the London School of Economics and Political Science, calls his books as *A Grammar of Politics and An Introduction to Politics.*
2. Soltau, R.H., *An Introduction to Politics*, p. 6.
3. The *American College Dictionary*, p. 108.

draw valid inferences that may be subjected to empirical verification or experimentation. Hence, scientific knowledge is taken as based on facts and experimentation.

Characteristics of Science

The chief characteristics of a science are:

(i) the possibility of a concise, consistent and connected formulation;
(ii) the capacity to form generalisations and make predictions;
(iii) the possibility of the verification of data as well as of generalisations;
(iv) an agreement on methods or methodology, and
(v) the adequate training of those who are engaged in a scientific work.

Carl Friedrich says : "It is the *new evidence* or the *new* generalisation which occupies the fellowship of scholars in the particular field, receives detailed criticism and either wins out or is discarded."

What is Science?

A science is a branch of knowledge which has been systematised without any ulterior motive or any idea of its being put to any practical use. It is acquisition of knowledge for knowledge's sake. Facts regarding science are collected impartially without any practical bias. They are arranged and classified according to their characteristics or similarities and differences, without any practical bias. Generalisations are made strictly on the basis of their behaviour. Finally, laws are formulated regarding them. According to William Esslinger, what distinguishes a science is that it is exclusively and methodically based on reason. Experimentation and prediction are not its requirements. It only signifies the existence of systematic methods of enquiry. An Italian writer Gaetano Mosca says : "A science is the product of a system of observations made on a given order of phenomena, with special care to appropriate methods, and so co-ordinated as to raise them to the level of an indisputable truth not apprehensible by ordinary, superficial observation.... We do not think that political science in its present condition has as yet genuinely entered upon the scientific stage."

Kinds of Sciences

According to G.N. Singh, sciences may be of four kinds:[4]

1. Abstract or mental sciences: Such as mathematics and logic which deal with mental concepts.

4. Singh, G.N., *Fundamentals of Political Science and Organistion*, p, 5.

2. Physical sciences: Such as physics, chemistry and geology which deal with inanimate material, capable of study under controlled conditions and admitting the use of experimental method.

3. Biological sciences: Such as botany and zoology which deal with plant and animal life respectively, and which also have the use of experimental method.

4. Social sciences: Such as sociology, economics and politics which deal with man as a social being.

ARGUMENTS AGAINST POLITICAL SCIENCE AS A SCIENCE

1. Term with precise definitions: A science has a set of its own terms and their precise and standard definitions. Political science has a set of its own terms like liberty, equality, rights, justice, democracy, rule of law, socialism, ideology etc. But no term has a precise and standard definition of its own. Different writers take different meanings of these terms that creates a lot of confusion.

2. The complexity of political phenomena: The habits, sentiments, moods and temperament of the people differ from place to place. Hence, we cannot lay down certain fixed rules of their behaviour. For example, the electoral behaviour of the voters is determined by various factors like religion, caste, community, social and economic conditions and the like. Hence, the working of a democratic system of a country like the United States is different from that of a country like India.

3. False generalisations: Most of the statements of a political scientist are based on false generalisations. For example, it is a generalised statement that democracy is the best form of government. Political scientists make a comparative study in order to strengthen our generalisations. In doing so they pick up only those facts which substantiate or strengthen their impressions. Therefore, their statements lack objectivity that is a necessary condition of a scientific investigation. Their comparisons may not be accurate in their systematisation.

4. Subjectivity: A study of political events should be done in a particular context. But great thinkers and theorists either laud or denounce some event in the light of their own impressions as the people have different notions about the 'environment' in which political developments take place. For a revolution which is a glorious happening to some, example may be dubbed as a counter-revolution by others.

5. Difficulty of experimentation: The conclusions of a political scientist cannot be put to experimentation. There are no instruments, no machines, no laboratories and the like where the theories of a writer may be subjected to thorough examination, and predictions may also be made therefrom. Keeping such limitations in their view, a good number of writers have either hesitated in calling political science as a science or have accepted the fact of its limitations. For example, in the mid-nineteenth century J.S. Mill expressed doubts about the scientific character of political science.[5] Buckle said that "in the present state of knowledge, politics, far from being a science, is the most backward of all arts."[6] F.W. Maitland expressed his surprise not at the set of questions but at the heading of the question paper.[7]

6. Criticism by Auguste Comte: In France, Auguste Comte rejected the case of politics as a science on these grounds:

(i) Disagreement among the writers about the use of methods and methodologies.
(ii) Lack of general acceptance on the principles and conclusions of this subject.
(iii) Want of continuity in its development.
(iv) Its failure to provide material on which accurate predictions may be made.

Continued Trend

This trend continued even in the present century.

1. In 1920 Lord Bryce endorsed : "However widely and carefully the materials may be gathered, their character makes it impossible that politics should ever become a science in the sense in which mechanics or chemistry or botany is a science."[8]
2. In this presidential address delivered at the American Political Science Association in 1926 Prof Charles A. Beard said that it was neither possible nor desirable that there is a science of politics.[9] So G.E.G. Catlin thought that there "is no such thing as political science in any admissible sense."[10]
3. In his inaugural address delivered at the Cambridge University in 1946 D.W. Brogan observed: "We may doubt today whether any such academic discipline as political science exists, a doubt practically unknown to earlier ages...."[11]

5. Mill, J.S., *A System of Logic*, Book VI.
6. Buckle, *History of Civilisation in England*, Vol. III, p. 301.
7. Maitland, *Collected Papers*, Vol. I, p, 302.
8. Bryce, *Modern Democracies*, Vol. I, p. 16.
9. Beard, *Research in Social Sciences*, p. 271.
10. Catlin, *The Science and Method of Politics*, p. 147.
11. So a great political scientist like E. Barker expressed his reservations about the term 'science' associated with political studies. *The Study of Political Science and Its Relation to Cognate Studies*, p. 3.

DEVELOPMENTS IN FAVOUR OF SCIENTIFIC NATURE

More and more efforts are being made to put political science into the form of a social science. The character of political science has changed in the present century, particularly in the period following the Second World War. Following important developments have made it more and more scientific:

1. Empirical political study: An astonishingly large number of studies based on *facts* have led to the emergence of a very wide stock of empirical political theory. Generalisations based on them have led to the laying down of some irrefutable conclusions. For example: democracy is the best form of government. Separation of powers is necessary to ensure liberty of the people. An elective office is better than an appointive office. Judges should have a fixed tenure for the sake of enjoying independence in their working. Elections are the best educators of a democratic system. As A. Appadorai says: "The larger the number of facts studied, the wider the area from which these facts are observed, and the greater care with which they are studied in relation to their environment, the greater the possibility of the precision and value of the generalisation obtained."[12]

2. Inexact science: Some sciences are an exact nature like physics and biology. But there are also some 'inexact' sciences like meteorology. While political science cannot be likened with physics, it can certainly be likened to meteorology. While some laws of this discipline may not be put to empirical investigation, some may be experimented with. While the law of Aristotle that the aim of state is to ensure 'good life' to its people may not put to an empirical test but one may certainly test his law that 'inequality is the cause of a revolution'. For example, in his presidential address at the American Political Science Association in 1909, Lord Bryce could establish the nature of political science as an inexact science like meteorology. He emphatically asserted that political science is a science in the same sense that there "is constancy and uniformity in the tendencies of human nature which enable us to regard the acts of men at one time as due to the same causes which have governed their acts at previous times."[13]

3. Prediction as in social sciences: It is said that a science has the quality of making predictions and political science has no such quality, it cannot be ranked as a science. This argument is correct, but it may be studied in a different way also. Social sciences cannot predict like the natural sciences, because they deal with human behaviour in its diverse

12. Appadorai, A., *The Substance of Politics*, p. 7.
13. Bryce quoted in Garner, *op. cit.*, p. 12.

manifestations. Since human mind is always changing, predictions cannot be made on that basis. A natural scientist on the other hand, can do so, because he deals with the objects of nature like heat and sound. However, recent studies have shown that even the element of prediction can be created in social sciences. Marx and Engels could predict the emergence of socialism at the fall of capitalism in the present century on the basis of certain laws of social development. Therefore, the Marxists laud their socialism as 'scientific'. Some American writers like Lasswell and Dahl have their own claims in this direction. As Wilson maintains, "prediction by statistical analysis is possible in the realm of political science."[14]

POLITICS IS A SCIENCE

Some writers have preferred to describe politics as a science. Holtzendorff asserts: "With the enormous growth of knowledge, it is impossible to deny that the sum total of all the experiences, phenomena and knowledge respecting the state may be brought together under the collective title of political science."[15] Political science is not a natural but a social science and if it seeks to be scientific, it must spell out its assumptions in clear-cut scientific terms."[16]

Arguments in Favour of Scientific Nature

Every social science is integrally bound with a normative aspect. It cannot be converted into a pure and exact science. When the behaviouralists tried to scientise the study of political issues, they exhibited their 'mad craze for scientism'. The post-behaviouralists veered round to the view that the study of politics should have some room for the values, goals and norms of human life. D.D. Waldo justly points out: "Political Science by historical development, institutional involvement, and public expectation is deeply rooted in the normative — more so than psychology, sociology and anthropology, probably more so than economics, though here comparison becomes very complex. My point is that Political Science is deeply involved both in the processes of defining and inculcating civic loyalty and of shaping and executing public policy. Obviously, any request to be value-neutral about the moral imperatives of patriotism, of constitutionalism of democracy, of traditional values associated with liberty and equality, and drive to abandon the *ought* in favour of the *is*; any push to make Political Science a value-free descriptive enterprise, is bound to create confusion, raise tension, cause controversy."[17] Political

14. F.G. Wilson, *The Elements of Modern Politics*, p. 4.
15. Gamer, *op. cit.*, pp. 13-14.
16. S.M. Lipset, *Politics and the Social Sciences*, p, xv.
17. Refer to his paper "Comparative Public Administration" in *The Indian Journal of Political Science*, 1963, No. 3 (July-September).

science is a social science. Hobbes and Marx raised the study of politics to the level of a 'science'.

Von Mohl, Bluntschli, Jellinek, Ratzenhoffer, Treitschke, Lewis, Sidgwick, Lieber, Pollock, Woolsey, Burgess, Willoughby, Michels, Weber, Merriam, Easton and Lasswell etc. emphatically preferred to call politics a science. To quote Pollock: "Thus, political science must and does exist, if it were only for the refutation of absurd political theories and projects."[18] To conclude with Garner, "We must conclude, therefore, that the weight and authority justifies the claim of politics to the rank of a true science. It renders practical service by deducing sound principles as a basis for wise political action and by exposing the teachings of a false political philosophy. As a science it falls short, of course, of the degree of perfection attained by the physical sciences, for the reason that facts with which it deals are more complex and the causes which influence social and practical phenomena are more difficult of control and are perpetually undergoing change."[19]

QUESTIONS FOR EXERCISE

1. Is Political Science really a science?
2. "When I see a good set of examination questions headed by the words 'Political Science' I regret not the questions but the title." Discuss and point out whether Political Science is a science or not in light of above statement of Maitland.

18. Pollock, *op. cit.*, p. 4.
19. Gamer, *op. cit.*, p. 14.

5

Methods of Studying Political Science

All natural or social sciences have their methods for studying the phenomena within their scope. As Ellwood said, "what the microscope is to biology, or the telescope to astronomy, a scientific method is to the social sciences." Since ancient times, there have been many thinkers and theorists, who gave their attention to the methodology of political studies. One may refer to the names of Aristotle, Machiavelli, Bodin, Hobbes, Vico, Montesquieu, Mill, Marx, Lewis, Comte, Bryce, Weber, Pollock, Dewey, Kaufmann, Leo Strauss, Vogelin and Karl Popper.

Notable Developments

1. Marx is the only social scientist, who invented a methodology of his own for the study of social evolution. On that basis, he could make certain predictions which have proved true in time to come.
2. The issue of methodology has assumed an unprecedented significance in the present century at the hands of those, who have taken upon themselves the task of converting this subject into a 'science'. As Arnold Brecht said, "It is not saying too much that ours has become the methodological century in the social sciences."[1]
3. According to F.G. Wilson, it "should be borne in mind that no method, however scientific, is entirely free of metaphysics. The philosophical method flaunts its assumptions and uses logic to support them, but the assumptions of the scientists are not so carefully recognised and are, therefore, much more dangerous than those made by philosophers."[2]

---

1. Arnold Brecht, *Political Theory*, p. 5.
2. Wilson, F.G., *op. cit.*, p. 43.

METHODS OF POLITICAL SCIENCE

The term 'method', according to Massino Salvadori, is the rational working of the mind in quest for knowledge of political reality. Following are the recognised methods of study in the field of political science:

1. HISTORICAL METHOD

Historical method is associated with the names of Machiavelli, Vico, Montesquieu, Savigny, Maine, Seeley and Freeman. This method lays stress on the use of historical evidence for a proper study of the political phenomena. It is useful because all political institutions have a long record of their rise and growth and their present form may be well-understood in the context of their past history. As Sir Fredrick Pollock says, it "seeks an explanation of what institutions are and are tending to be, more in the knowledge of what they have been and now they came to be what they are, than in the analysis of them as they stand."

Advantages

1. The advantage of historical method lies in the fact that it explains the past and enables us to draw dependable conclusions.
2. It also supplies us with basic principles for interpreting the future. In the later part of the eighteenth century Edmund Burke condemned the philosophy of the French revolution in establishing new political institutions in a hurry. Instead he eulogised the greatness of the English constitution inherent in its prescriptive character. Today, an English theorist Michael Oakeshott is of the view that genuine historical study is an indispensable part of political education.[3]
3. The historical method enables us to make certain sound generalisations. Then may be called authentic by virtue of being based on past evidence.
4. Such a study is always open to verification. On the basis of gathered facts of history, we may test the validity of excogitated ideas.
5. It gives a sense of history that warns us against repeating blunders of the past and instead correcting them for the future.
6. History, in this way, becomes like a great teacher of wisdom. It enlarges mental horizon, improves the perspective and builds up an attitude towards events that may be termed 'sense of history'.[4]
7. It is contact with the past which equips men and communities for the tasks of the present. The more bewildering the present, the greater the accumulation of material goods and material cares, the

3. Oakeshott, *Political Education.*, p. 18.
4. E.M. Sait, *Political Institutions: A Preface*, p. 49.

greater the need for inspiration and refreshment from the past.[5] So Laski says: "The study of politics must be an effort to codify the results of experience in the history of states.'[6]

1. **Limitations and shortcomings:** Lord Bryce has warned against the tendency of making superficial resemblances. Historical parallels may be interesting and sometimes illuminating, but they may-be misleading also.
2. The element of subjectivity in seeking historical facts and then using them for the purpose of a political study may stand in the way of an objective assessment. The historical investigator may be consciously or unconsciously influenced by his religious beliefs, his political partisanships, his racial prejudices, or his philosophical doctrines.[7] As Sidgwick says, "I do not think that the historical method is the one to be primarily used in attempting to find reasoned solutions of the problems of practical politics.'[8]
3. In the view of Barker, the state is concerned less with historic processes than with the fundamental realities — essence, purpose and value — which transcend the category of time."[9]

2. OBSERVATIONAL METHOD

This method as its name suggests, lays stress on close observation of facts under study. Seeing is believing. An investigator should first see things himself and then frame his generalisations. The use of observational method leads to an immense supply of trustworthy observations.[10] A.L. Lowell says: "The main laboratory for the actual working of political institutions is not the library but the outside world of political life."[11] But its best advocate is Lord James Bryce. He first visited some countries, saw things with his own eyes and then wrote chapters on the working of democracy in countries like USA, Canada, Switzerland and Britain. He maintained that the observations of a researcher must not be superficial or based on his subjective assessment, rather they should be profound, critical and objective. In his presidential address delivered at the American Political Science Association in 1909 Lord Bryce said, "Make sure of it (fact). Get it perfectly clear. Polish it till it sparkles and shines

5. Alfred Zimmern, *Nationality and Government*, p. 100.
6. Laski, *The Danger of Being Gentleman and Other Essays*, Ch. 2.
7. Bryce, *Modern Democracies*, Vol. I, p. 15.
8. See Garner, *op. cit.*, p. 24.
9. Barker, *The Study of Political Science and Its Relation to Cognate Studies*, p. 18.
10. Seeley, *op. cit.*, p. 23.
11. *American Political Science Review*, Vol. IV, 1910, p. 8.

like a gem. Then connect it with other facts. Examine it in its relation to them, for in that lies its 'worth and its significance. It is of little use alone. So make it a diamond in the necklace, a stone, perhaps a corner-stone, in your building."[12] Sait says: "A science of politics can be developed only through observation, which is much laborious and far more open to error than experiment."[13]

Limitations and Pitfalls

1. The observer may sees things of his own interest alone and form his impressions accordingly. As such, the element of subjectivity stands in the way of a scientific investigation through observational method.
2. A surveyor may not be in a position to see all facts due to restrictions of diverse kinds, or he may have a partial vision of things and, as such, his generalisations may be partly correct. As Laski holds the processes of a government are very much like an iceberg, what appears on the surface may be but a small part of the reality beneath. It is due to this that in spite of spending much time there for the sake of seeing things with his own eyes even a competent student of comparative politics or constitutional law may not be able to present a correct and universally acceptable picture of the political processes of a fascist or a Communist country.
3. Political issues come very close to human emotions and inherited prejudices. Only a few individuals can undertake an analysis of things calmly, dispassionately and in a completely objective frame of mind.[14]

3. EXPERIMENTAL METHOD

Experimental method is adopted in the field of natural sciences like physics and chemistry.

1. **Limitations:** It is said that it cannot be made use of in a social science like political science. As Sir G.C. Lewis said: "We cannot take a portion of the community in our hands as the king of Brobdignag took Gulliver, view it in different aspects and place it in different positions in order to solve social problems and satisfy our speculative curiosity."[15]

12. *Ibid.*, Vol. III, 1909, p. 10.
13. Sait, *op. cit.*, p. 36.
14. W.B. Munro, *The Government of the United States.*, p. 9.
15. Lewis, *Methods of Observation and Reasoning in Politics*, Vol. I, pp. 165-66.

2. In a subject like political science we deal with man's behaviour as a social and political creature. The method of experimentation cannot be used as behaviour differs from person to person on account of varying emotions, likes and dislikes.
3. The main obstacles to experimentation in the study of political phenomena arise out of the fact that the individual processes of inquiry can hardly be isolated from each other and the conditions can never be exactly reproduced, as Heraclitus says, "that one cannot step twice into the same river."[16]

Possibility of Use

1. The experimental method can be used in the field of political studies in its own way. The whole society is a laboratory in which political actions are put to test every day. If some policies succeed and some policies fail, its reason should be traced in the fact of social experimentation which a social scientist may comprehend.
2. Bacon and Comte well argued that every political change made consciously or unconsciously is a sort of experiment. The fact of social experimentation may be traced in the rise and fall, retention and abrogation, adoption and deletion of official policies. As Prof Charles Merriam holds: "Certainly the state has more material available for such observation than any other institution. The army, the schools, the public personnel, and an array of public institutions are directly under its management, and may be utilised for purposes of experiment if so desired."[17]
3. Catlin is of the view that correct generalisations may be had in the study of politics by means of having experiments after experiments.[18]
4. In relation to the working of the American federal system, Bryce said that its merit has been discovered by the people in the fact that it enables them to try experiments in legislation which could not be tried in a large centralised state.[19]

Two Important Points

1. Laboratory of community: This method cannot be used in political science in a way as it is used in the field of natural sciences. But we may use it in a different way. A natural scientist makes experiments in his

16. Bryce, *Modern Democracies*, Vol. I, p. 14.
17. Merriam, *New Aspects of Politics*, p. 55.
18. Catlin, *The Science and Method of Politics*, p. 114.
19. Bryce, *The American Commonwealth*, Vol. I, p. 353.

laboratory or workshop with the aid of instruments, tools, machines, barometers, computers and the like. A social (political) scientist makes experiments in the vast laboratory of the community. On that basis he tells us as to how a particular statute or a constitution could survive or fail in the midst of such and such stresses and strains. As J.W. Jenks says: "While, of course, we cannot make experiments with the same degree of definiteness and completeness as in the natural sciences, nevertheless by the laws that have a limited application locally or in time, by a variety of laws that are passed in different states, and by various ordinances passed in different cities under similar conditions, we do obtain some conditions remotely like an experiment in natural sciences, and from these experiences we may gather valuable information."[20]

2. Possibility of improvements: In the field of social sciences, experimental method serves the purpose of putting some generalisations to tests. It also enables the investigators to make improvements upon the existing things. As Garner puts it, "By observing the operation of a new law or a new policy and then enlarging or diminishing its scope as experience suggests modification, the legislature is able to adapt its provisions to the needs and desires of the community. The process is in the nature of an experiment whose purpose is not the ascertainment of a general truth but the testing and improving of the institution."[21]

To conclude with G.C. Lewis, "if by an experimental science we mean a science which admits of scientific experiments, then politics is not an experimental science; but if we mean a science founded on observation and experience, politics is an experimental science.'[22]

4. COMPARATIVE METHOD

Comparative method consists in drawing generalisations through comparisons. A student of political science may arrive at certain conclusions after establishing comparisons between different political systems, political institutions, and political ideas. Its essence consists in noting similarities as well as differences in circumstances and conditions of the state under comparison. The comparison may be between apparently similar looking objects. Plato, John of Salisbury, Hobbes and, above all, Spencer drew analogies between natural and social organisms. In the studies of Herman Finer, C.F. Strong and K.C. Wheare it is between different political institutions. Aristotle, Montesquieu and de Tocqueville among others discovered the 'general currents running through the

20. Jenks, J.W., *Principles of Politics*, p. 21.
21. Garner, *op. cit.*, p. 20.
22. Lewis, *op. cit.*, p. 178.

whole body of constitutions and other political institutions upon which experience has set the' stamp of approval.[23]

Three Forms

According to Mill the comparative method may have one of the three forms :

1. Process of difference: One may take up the cases of two identical political systems and then come to a certain conclusion by the *process of difference*. For instance, both the United Kingdom and the United States have democratic models and yet the point of difference is that while Britain is a welfare state, US is a state based on the ideal of free enterprise.

2. Method of indirect difference: One may adopt the method of indirect difference by choosing two quite opposite political systems and then coming to certain conclusions on the basis of a comparative study of the two. For instance, one may compare and contrast the American and the Russian political systems and then come to hold the view that while the former is democratic, the latter is of a totalitarian variety.

3. The course of agreement: Here two polities wholly different from each other may be compared. The points of contrast may be discarded and the broad generalisations may be laid down where the two look like the same. For example, one may ignore the aspect of inner details and come to hold the view that the USA and the USSR have a federal system.

1. **Limitations:** Comparative method is lauded for being 'scientific' as one may draw some valid conclusions on the basis of comparisons. But comparisons may be faulty in some cases.
2. It is likely that the results are affected by extraneous circumstances or by a plurality of causes with an intermixture of effects.
3. The danger of the use of this method also lies in the liability to error to which it is susceptible in practice. In the effort to discover general principles, the diversity of conditions and circumstances, such as differences of temperament and genius of the people, economic and social conditions, "moral and legal standards, political training and experience, are apt to be ignored or minimised."[24]

5. PHILOSOPHICAL METHOD

Deductive in its approach this method starts with self-evident general propositions and then confirms or denies facts. It starts from abstract

23. Garner, *op. cit.*, p. 23.
24. *Ibid.*, p. 24.

view of humane nature and draws conclusions from that view concerning the nature, functions and aims of the state. Conclusions thus drawn are then sought to be harmonised with the actual facts of history and/or political life modifying its conclusions as necessary. Thus, the philosophical method proceeds from general to particular whereas the experimental, observational, comparative and historical methods start from particular to general. Thus, philosophical method is a good antidote to pedestrianism. Philosophic argument develops the intelligence, it imparts resourcefulness and elasticity of mind.

Limitations

1. This method may become purely imaginative and phenomenal. The investigator using this method or cultivating ideas about political may be lost in imaginary ideals and lost sight of actual conditions. History proves that the Plato and Thomas Moore created an ideal of their own imagination and conceived of the idea discovered from reality.
2. The philosophical method has value only if supplemented by sound observation, historical and comparative study.

Conclusion

No precise answer can be given as to which of the above methods is appropriate for the study of political phenomenon, it is so, because the subject matter of Political Science is complex and varied. It may use of all the methods to collect the available data and reach right conclusion. A careful political investigator would seek to make a happy blend of realism and idealism and combine the inductive method with the deductive method. As it is said, "The true philosopher must take the counsel of history. The experiences and phenomenon of history must be illumined with the light of ideas."

QUESTIONS FOR EXERCISE

1. Write short note on Experimental Method in Politics.
2. Explain Historical Method in Politics.
3. What are the limitations of Method of Observation in Political Science.
4. Assess the value of Comparative Method in Politics.
5. Write short note on Philosophical Method in Political Science.

6

Political Science and other Social Sciences

Science about man or nature is a systematised body of knowledge. Man lives in society. There are many aspects of his behaviour in society such as economic aspect, social aspect, political aspect, moral and ethical aspects etc. Subjects dealing with these different aspects of man in society are called Social Sciences as Economics, Sociology, Politics, Ethics etc. Politics is a social science which studies human behaviour concerning his political life. The study of politics cannot be confined to a political system alone. With the increase in the economic functions and social responsibility of the present day governments, it has become necessary to make the scope of politics more and more wide. Sociology, History, Economics, Ethics, Psychology etc. will have to be included in it. Familiarity with these subjects is essential to proper understanding of the nature of political processes and to a genuine application of the basic problems of political life. We study man's political behaviour in association with other men as members of a common society. Political activities of man cannot be isolated from other activities. There is a close relationship of political science with other social sciences.

As all social sciences deal with man as a social creature, a thread of unity binds all. However, each science develops in such a fashion that it grows into an autonomous discipline in course of time. As knowledge is one and indivisible, it should not be compartmentalised. Inter-disciplinary approach should be adopted for avoiding the unnecessary multiplication of efforts. Therefore, contemporary writers are led to the popularisation of studying social, economic and political phenomena in inter-disciplinary perspective. S.M. Lipset is rightly holds that there "is almost no form of human behaviour which is not treated to some extent by each of the social sciences. Each varies only in its primary area of interest."[1] Lipset is so confident of the success of this trend that he says that we "have now reached the point where all social sciences must operate with a common conceptual scheme and vocabulary."[2] The old barriers created by the trend of compartmentalisation of knowledge are crumbling today. The talk of inter-disciplinary studies is very much in the air.

POLITICAL SCIENCE AND HISTORY

Use of History in Politics

History is a record of the past events; it is a treasure house of knowledge about things as they were, or as they have been since times immemorial. Therefore, history is of great use to a student of political science if he wants to know about political institutions as they have originated and developed over the span of time. Important theories of political science cannot be understood and appreciated without a peep into history. For example, a knowledge of the history of the Greeks is required to comprehend the ideas of Plato and Aristotle. The true character of medieval political philosophy may not be understood without a knowledge of the history of the middle ages. One may understand the ideas of Hobbes and Locke only after the knowledge of the Civil War and the Glorious Revolution in England in the 17th century. Many great political theorists adopted historical method to understand the nature of 'political reality' and laid down important conclusions on that basis. Machiavelli used historical material to substantiate as well as to strengthen his theory of statecraft. Montesquieu and Bryce also used it for their own purposes. To quote Lord Acton, the science of politics, "is deposited by the stream of history, like the grains of gold in sands of a river. We endeavour to make use of these 'grains of gold' to bring about some improvement in things as they stand or exist at present. So history may be taken as the 'third dimension of political science.'[3]

Use of Politics in History

While political science takes so much from history, history also takes much from political science. It takes from politics the angle of vision to understand and interpret events. Facts have little significance by themselves. Apart from the truth they contain it is political science which helps history to grasp it. Leacock rightly says that history will lose its

1. Lipset, "Introduction" in his (ed.), *Politics and the Social Sciences*, p. viii.
2. *Ibid*,, p. xviii.
3. W.W. Willoughby, *The Nature of the State*, p. 5.

main significance without at least an unconscious political science. Thus, the two disciplines are closely related. In the words of Leacock, "Political science has no concern with history in its purely narrative aspect; it has no interest in the mere cumulation of instances; nor has it any interest in the military, commercial or economic aspects of history as such; only in so far as these bear upon the evolution of organised social control, only so far as they elucidate the nature of the state, are they of import for the student of political science. The latter must revert to history for much of the matter of his study, but always in an elective or selective fashion, co-ordinating his facts with a view to their special significance."[4]

Distinction between History and Politics

It would be a mistake to treat history and political science as the two similar subjects. Freeman wrongly said that history is past politics and politics, is present history. All history cannot be all politics and *vice versa*. Only some history is relevant for politics as some part of politics is relevant for history. Seeley rightly said that history without political science has no fruit and political science without history has no root. To quote his words, history without political science is "a study incomplete, truncated and political science without history is hollow and baseless. Politics are vulgar when not liberalised by history, and history fades into mere literature when it loses sight of its relation to politics."[5] As Burgess rightly says, "separate them and the one becomes a cripple, if not a corpse, the other a will-of-the-wisp."[6] As F.G. Wilson says: "For the political scientist history is data to be used in sounding the depths of his problems; for the historian the data of politics is part of the development and treatment of historical issues."[7]

POLITICAL SCIENCE AND ECONOMICS

Political Economy

There was a time when economics and political science were one in the form of 'political economy'. In ancient India Kautilya wrote his *Arthasastra* on the subject of practical politics. The Sanskrit term *artha* in those days represented not only wealth but mainly statesmanship and diplomacy. In his *Politics* Aristotle treated economics as the art of managing household that constituted an inseparable part of his political philosophy. In his *Principles of Political Economy* John Stuart Mill dealt with many political issues. The great classical economist Adam Smith said

4. Leacock, *op. cit.*, p. 7.
5. Seeley, *op. cit.*, p. 4.
6. See Garner,' *op. cit.*, p. 32.
7. Wilson, F.G., *op. cit.*, p. 30.

that the political scientists could study economic life in two categories: the first the actual organisation and its probable effects upon political life, and the second, the motives which drive the organisation. Karl Marx interconnected economics and politics and also other disciplines like sociology, psychology, philosophy and history.

Close Relationship

Pointing out the close relationship between the Economics and Political Science Garner says: "Political and social life is obviously intermixed with, and the activities and even the forms of government are profoundly influenced by economic conditions. Conversely, there is a distinct interaction of politics upon economics. The production and distribution of wealth are to some extent determined by the existing forms of government. The solution of many economic problems must come through political action, while, on the other hand, some of the fundamental problems of the government have their origin in economic conditions. Thus, tariff laws and trade restrictive acts, generally are favoured or opposed largely on economic grounds and, to a great extent, the whole question of the relation between government and liberty is at bottom an economic problem. Some of the important questions of present-day politics — government control of public utilities, the reaction of state to corporate enterprise and its attitude towards the whole question of capital and labour — are, at the same time, fundamentally questions of economics; indeed, the whole theory of government administration is largely economic."[8] According to Nicholson, "It is no doubt true that the system of the government "operates on economic facts and that economic history furnished endless examples of the injurious effects of the bad government."[9]

The doctrine of socialism has brought politics and economics very close to each other in recent times. Many social thinkers have studied the questions of production, distribution and exchange of things and their relationship with the system of private property. The liberals have sought to justify the existing state of economic relationship. The socialists have discovered the cause of poverty and exploitation of the many at the hands of the few in the inequitable distribution of national wealth. It has been suggested that the state should impose more and more restrictions on private property system. If necessary, it may go to the last extent of nationalising key private industries in the public interest. Today, public economy has become a subject of politics. As fantastic

8. *Ibid.*, pp. 33-34.
9. Nicholson, *Principles of Political Economy*, p. 11.

inequality in income and wealth, rampant exploitation and occasionally violent fluctuations in national economy constitute a perennial source of friction in the industrial societies, these evoke the necessity of political intervention in the field of economic activities. The concept of 'welfare state' with its planning content emerged and forged a *rapprochement* between economic and political studies to the mutual benefit of both."[10]

POLITICAL SCIENCE AND SOCIOLOGY

Sociology is a subject of recent origin. Universally, recognised as the 'father' of sociology, Auguste Comte, conceived of sociology as all-inclusive social science. Sociology deals with the origin, evolution, structure and activities of society. As state, the fundamental theme of politics, is a part of social structure. Sociology covers within its fold what falls within the domain of political studies. A good number of recent social theorists like Weber of Germany and Merriam of America recognised that the two disciplines are closely related. Their students like Easton, Almond and Apter have taken much from the sociological writings of Talcott Parsons and R.K. Merton to enrich the stock of empirical political theory. In the period following the Second World War a new subject with the name of 'political sociology' emerged in the form of, what Giovanni Sartori says, 'a cross-disciplinary breakthrough.' In this connection Giddings makes an illuminating observation when he says that, "to teach the theory of state to men, who have not learned the first principles of sociology is like teaching astronomy or thermodynamics to men who have not learned the Newtonian laws of motion"[11] F.G. Wilson says: "Sociology is a very comprehensive attempt to organise social science. It is the science of society, but in its approach it considers the individual as associated with others, as a member of a group and as involved in social relations. The state, of course, is sociological as well as purely political, but during its early development the distinction is difficult to make. The state has become distinct by withdrawing itself from other types of associations and functions. But the politics is embedded in the social and they cannot be separated by distinct boundaries except for the purpose of investigation. Political science is interested in men as organised in the state, and the study of historical sociology, which traces the development of social organisation, merely provides data for the conclusion of the political scientist or for the study of politics. Sociology deals with all forms of human associations, but politics deals with only one in its primary manifestation. Both political science and sociology attempt to

10. Leslie Lipson, *The Great Issues of Politics*, p. 80.
11. Giddings, Principles of Sociology, p. 37.

give explanations as to why man is a political being, and they must rely to a great extent on philosophy and psychology for data.[12]

Concerning the close relation of sociology to political science Barnes has written, "The most significant thing about sociology and modern political theory is that most of the changes which have taken place in the political theory in the last thirty years have been along the line of development suggested and marked out by sociology."[13] Actually, knowledge of sociology is necessary for understanding the problems of political science because political problems also have a social aspect. G.E.G. Catlin has remarked that political science and sociology are two facets or aspects of the same figure. According to Comte and Spencer, there is no difference whatsoever between the two. In the opinion of F.G. Wilson, "It must be admitted, of course, that it is often difficult to determine, whether a particular writer should be considered as sociologist, political theorist or philosopher."[14]

The laws of the state have a profound influence upon society. It is by means of law that the government changes and improves society, but it is necessary to keep in view the mores, traditions and customs of the country while formulating laws. For this, knowledge of sociology would be needed. For example, in making the Hindu Code Bill, assistance was taken both from politics and sociology. The problem of deciding upon the form of government is best explained by having recourse to both sociology and political science. The problem of determining the government's policy also is common to both.

Distinctions

But the subjects of politics and sociology have their own boundary lines. Sartori well observes that the formal theory of social system leaves off where the formal theory of political system begins. While political science is concerned with only one form of human association (the state); sociology deals with all forms of human associations. In sociology the unit of investigation is the *socius*. It views individual not merely as an animal and a conscious being but also as a neighbour, a citizen, a co-worker and the like. In political science the unit of study is the state as distinct from the nation, tribe, clan, family, while all these have their detailed treatment in the field of sociology. While sociology deals with all human associations and institutions, political science is concerned mainly with one of them — man as a political creature. As Barker puts

12. Wilson, F.G., *The Elements of Modern Politics*, p. 29.
13. Barnes and others, *History of Political Theories in Recent Times*, p. 899.
14. Wilson, F.G., *Elements of Modern Politics*, p. 37.

it, "Political theory only deals with political associations united by a constitution and living under a government; sociology deals with all associations. Political theory assumes as a datum that man is a political being, it does not explain as sociology seeks to do, how he came to be a political being."[15]

Distinctions between Political Science and Sociology will be clear from the following table:

Sociology	Political Science
1. Science of society.	1. Science of government or political society.
2. Social viewpoint.	2. Attitude of authority.
3. Study of both organised and disorganised communities.	3. Study of organised communities.
4. Study of all kinds of social relationships.	4. Study of political relationships only.
5. Study of all forms of society.	5. Study of the political society only.
6. Study of all means of social control.	6. Study only of government recognised means of control.

Pointing out the close relationship between political science and sociology Garner said: "While their respective fields are largely separate and distinct, political science and sociology are mutually contributory, the one to the other. Sociology derives from political science knowledge of the facts regarding the organisation and activities of the state, while political science derives in large measure from sociology its knowledge of the origin of political authority and the laws of social control. The political scientist, therefore, ought to be at the same time a sociologist and the *vice versa*"[16] To quote Lipset, "No sociologist can conceive of a study of society that does not include the political system as a major part of the analysis. And many political scientists, particularly in recent years, have argued sometimes with others in their own field, that it is impossible to study political processes except as special cases of more general sociological and psychological relationships."[17] By a broad interpretation of sociology, Barnes has contended that the recent developments of political theory have been along the lines indicated by sociological study.[18]

15. Earnest Barker, *Political Thought in England*, p. 159.
16. Garner, *op. cit.*, p. 31.
17. S.M. Lipset, *The Political Man*, p. 9.
18. Barnes, His paper 'Some Contributions of Sociology to Political Theory" in Merriam, Barnes and others (eds.), *History of Political Theories*, Ch. IX.

POLITICAL SCIENCE AND PSYCHOLOGY

Inter-relation

A good number of theorists have sought to integrate the study of political science with psychology, particularly social psychology. *Physics and Politics* of Walter Bagehot appeared in 1873. In it he tried to deal with political issues with the help of psychological formulations. Physics is psychics to him. In his *Human Nature in Politics* (1908) Graham Wallas says: "Politics is only in a slight degree the product of conscious reason, it is largely a matter of sub-conscious processes of habit and instinct, suggestion and imitation." In the same way in his *Psychology and Politics* W.H.R. Rivers and Harold Lasswell in his *Psychopathology and Politics* present a study of politics based on psychological premises. The new trend has become so popular in recent times that a new discipline has emerged with the name of 'political psychology'. Taking note of this fact, E. Barker has observed: "If our fathers thought biologically, we think psychologically."[19]

As F.G. Wilson says: "If we go beyond the state as a concrete organisation of government and a jurisdiction that involves the concept of public law, it is clear that many of the most significant facts about the state are psychological rather than physical; they are subjective rather than objective in character. Psychology tells us of the instincts, emotions and habits of individuals, it reveals to us the manner in which the mind generally works, and it qualifies the older historic conclusions as to the rationality of man."[20]

Use of Psychology in Political Science

To highlight the role of men's habits, nature, moods, instincts, emotions, passions and the like that play a very important part in the expression of political events, the study of politics should be made from psychological angles. The political culture of a people is formed by psychological factors. In the early phase of the present century American publicist Walter Lippmann took note of this fact when he said that "to talk about politics without reference to human beings is just the deepest error in our political thinking."[21] Catlin opined that inter-disciplinary relations between politics and psychology were very important.[22] Bryce said that politics, "has its roots in psychology the study (in their actuality) of the mental habits and volitional proclivities of mankind."[23] In the words of

19. Barker, *op. cit.*, p. 148.
20. Wilson, F.G., *op. cit.*, p. 35.
21. Lippmann, *Preface to Politics*, p. 2.
22. Catlin, *Systematic Politics*, p. 38.
23. Bryce, *Modern Democracies*, Vol. I, p. 15.

F.G. Wilson: "We have suffered also for those who have exploited the prejudices and ignorance of the voters who have employed the findings of the science of psychology. Undoubtedly, the modern development of the art of propaganda has profited much by the revelation of mental processes of men. Those who created 'morale' in the World War were men who understood in the greatest possible degree some of the motivations of conduct."[24]

It is now possible for the political investigator to undertake a study of public opinion and electoral behaviour with the help of psychology. A plausible answer to the rise and fall of governments or frequency of revolutions and violent outbursts has been given by the mood and temperament of the people. To quote Garner: "If we consider the state apart from its concrete organisation and its manifestations through its legally constituted agencies, we shall see that it is essentially psychical rather than physical, subjective rather than objective in character. Consequently, the course of state life is determined in large measure by the psychic factors. Government to be stable and really popular must reflect and express the mental ideas and moral sentiments of those, who are subject to its authority; in short, it must be in harmony with what LeBon calls 'the mental constitution of the race'. Psychology, therefore, contains the key to the problem of the adaptation of particular forms of the governments and laws to the character of the people."[25]

POLITICAL SCIENCE AND ETHICS

Close Relationship

Ethics is concerned with 'good' and 'bad' in human behaviour. Men possess certain moral norms on the basis of which they differentiate between right and wrong, just and unjust, good and bad, and they strive to stick to the former side and discard the latter. Ethics helps us to realise more clearly than we do now what are the nature and content of our moral consciousness."[26] Therefore, social and political theorists since ancient times have tried to integrate their ideas about different facts of man's life with certain ethical standards. Plato and Aristotle presented an ethicised study of state. To them state was like 'a partnership in virtue' or a supreme association having its end in the realisation of 'good life'. During middle ages the standards of ethics were governed by the principles of Christian theology. When a theorist like Machiavelli discarded the place of values in politics, he was accused of vulgarising politics. In modern

24. Wilson, F.G., *op, cit.*, p. 36.
25. Garner, *op. cit.*, p. 38.
26. C.E.M. Joad, *Guide to the Philosophy of Morals and Politics*, p. 170.

times Rousseau, Kant, Hegel, Green, Bosanquet, Nettleship and M.K. Gandhi appreciated the normative aspect of man's life in politics.

However, a large number of recent theorists have sought to present a value-free political theory to convert it into a pure science. Charles Merriam, Lasswell and Morgenthau have sought to make politics free from all ethical considerations. This approach of power theorists has contributed to the enrichment of the stock of empirical political science. But, at the same time, it has made political science value-less. Therefore, in the post-behavioural phase the trend towards the reaffirmation of values has resurfaced. The theorists have once again veered round to the tradition of integrating politics with values and norms. While the *New Aspects of Politics* of Merriam advised to stick only to the side of facts, the *New Science of Politics* of Eric Vogelin pleads for a reorientation of political science through a resuscitation of the efforts of the ancient Greek and medieval Christian philosophers to provide the theoretical orientation of man in this world. It is a great instrument for man's understanding of his own position in the universe. As Ivor Brown well-observed: "Ethical theory is incomplete without political theory, because man is an associative creature and cannot live fully in isolation: political theory is idle without ethical theory, because its study and its results depend fundamentally on our scheme of moral values, our conception of right and wrong."[27]

QUESTIONS FOR EXERCISE

1. What do you understand by inter-disciplinary approach in the study of politics? Do you think that the other social sciences have fruitfully contributed to the development of the study of politics?
2. What do you understand by inter-disciplinary approach in the study of politics? Discuss the usefulness of history and economics for the study of politics.
3. Explain and illustrate the relation of politics with (a) History, (h) Economics, (c) Ethics, and (d) Psychology.

27. Ivor Brown, *English Political Theory*, p. 2.

7

The State

State is the subject matter of Political Science. The present chapter deals with the definition, origin, authority, forms, functions and nature of the state.

DEFINITION OF STATE

Aristotle and some thinkers after him defined state in a number of ways, some of which definitions follow:

1. *Aristotle*: "The State is a union of families and villages having for its ends a perfect and self-sufficing life." This definition by Aristotle applies only to city states. Modern states are not limited to merely villages. Modern thinkers point to four characteristics of a state — (1) Public, (2) Defined geographical areas, (3) Administration or government, and (4) Sovereignty.
2. *Burgess*: "The State is a particular portion of mankind viewed as an organised unit." This definition of state lacks a delimited topography.
3. *Bluntshli*: "The State is the politically organised people of a definite territory." This definition of state does not mention sovereignty.
4. *Garner*: "The State as a concept of political science and public law is community of persons more or less numerous, permanently occupying a definite portion of territory, independently or nearly so, of external control and possessing an organised government to which the great body of inhabitants render habitual obedience." This definition of state can be regarded as one of the best. Thus, in brief, it-can be summed up, "State can be defined as an organised people living in a definite territory which has its own sovereign government."

5. *Cicero*: The commonwealth is the coming together of a considerable number of men who are united by a common agreement about law and rights and the desire to participate in mutual advantages.
6. *Bodin*: A State is an association of families and their common affairs governed by a supreme power and reason.
7. *Grotius*: The State is a perfect association of freemen united for the sake of enjoying the benefits of law and for their mutual advantage.
8. *Woodrow Wilson*: The State is the people organised for law within a definite territory.
9. *R.M. MacIver*: The State is an association which, acting through law as promulgated by a government endowed to this end with coercive power, maintains within a community territorially demarcated by the universal external conditions of social order.
10. *Laski*: By a State I mean a society of this kind which is integrated by possessing a coercive authority legally supreme over any individual or group which is part of the society. An examination of any national society will always reveal within its boundaries not only individuals but also associations of men grouped together to promote all kinds of objects, religious, economic, cultural and political, in which they are interested. Such a society is a state when the way of life to which both individuals and associations must conform is defined by a coercive authority binding upon them all.
11. *T.E. Holland*: The State is a numerous assemblage of human beings generally occupying a certain territory, amongst whom the will of the majority or of an ascertainable class of persons is by the strength of such a majority of class, made to prevail against any of their number who oppose it.
12. *Robert Philimore*: "A State is a people permanently occupying a fixed territory, bound together by common laws, habits and customs into one body politic, exercising through the medium of an organised government independent sovereignty and control over all persons and things within its boundaries capable of making war and peace and of entering into all international relations with the communities of the globe."
13. *Pennock and Smith*: We may summarise by defining the State as a political system comprising all the people in a defined territory and possessing an organisation (government) with the

power and authority to enforce its will upon its members by resort, if necessary, to physical sanctions, and not subject in like manner to the power and authority of another policy.

VARIOUS NOTIONS OF STATE

State has been viewed differently by different political thinkers. The State is a historic entity. During the course of evolution of political philosophy different notions of it have emerged. A brief discussion of these notions of the State follows:

1. Ethical notion of the state: Plato and Aristotle regarded the State as representing the highest form of human life and looked upon it as an institution which made the virtuous life possible. They saw in the State the necessary agent for the ethical and intellectual more than the material element. The ethical notion was further developed by Rousseau, Hegel, Kant and Green. State is a necessary ethical and natural institution. It fulfils our various needs and requirements. It is an association of association and supreme association. It is an ethical institution. It embraces the whole of the human being. Aristotle said, "the State has come into existence for life and exists for the sake of good life. The State is an end itself because it is a perfect institution. The State is the highest morality. It is necessary for all-round development of man. It is within a State that man achieves moral excellence by performing his duties and enjoying his rights." Hegel endowed the State with a real personality and a will. He identified the will of an individual with the will of the State. He regarded the State as a collective person, a majestic being, the march of God on earth.

Criticism of the Ethical Notion

1. All good citizens have to conform to one single pattern laid down for him by the State. But all individuals are not alike.
2. Individuals cannot enjoy liberties in an absolute State.

2. The legal notion of the state: Bodin, Hobbes, Bentham and Austin interpret the State as a legal structure. It was formed for making, interpreting and enforcing law. It creates laws and norms in order to regulate human behaviour. It has coercive powers in the case of violation of laws. The legal notion regards the State as a legal person having a distinctive personality and will of its own. As a legal personality State property, direct economic enterprises, may be sued in the Courts. It harmonises activities of the various members of Society.

Criticism of the Legal Notion

1. It does not conform to the facts of daily life.
2. It is not absolute. There are limitations on the exercise of political power by the State.

3. The power motion of the State: Machiavelli is the main exponent of power notion. When individuals came into contact with one another, it is but natural that conflicts and contradictions may arise in society. To resolve these conflicts and to maintain peace and harmony in society there is a need of power — a power which upholds the common good of the people. The State is the power to cope with the demands of the individuals and to resolve the contradictions in society.

Some thinkers also hold the view that it is not correct to say that the State restricts the freedom of individuals. Freedom in society is born out of the rules which every society maintains. In the absence of the rules the security of the person in endangered.

Criticism of the Power Notion

1. Though force is an essential part of the State, yet it is not the foundation of the State.
2. MacIver observes, "*Coercive power is only the criterion of State and not its essence*".
3. It is the right which lends support to might and not the *vice versa*.
4. Will not the force is the basis of the State.

4. State as a natural institution. The exponents of this theory say that man became civilised only in the State. The Organic theory regards State as a natural institution. The State came into existence for the sake of good life and continues to exist for the sake of good life. It is on this ground that Aristotle called man a political animal. It means that State was their right from the beginning, State is prior to man.

5. State as a divine institution: The medieval thinkers considered State as a divine institution. In the medieval period the Church dominated the monarch. It was thought that God created the State and the monarch was the representative of God on earth. Thus, the King was not responsible to any institution except to God only. The King was representative of God will take care of the subjects as a father takes care of the children. He could rule according to his own will. He alone was capable of deciding good from bad. His word was considered to be the law. Any person who disobeyed him was a sinner. Kingship was hereditary i.e., after his death his son automatically became the ruler of the subjects.

6. State according to liberal thinkers: The Renaissance and Reformation challenged the divine theory. The French Revolution gave a rude shock to the State as a divine institution. It gave the slogan of equality, liberty and fraternity. The views of the liberals about the State can be summed up as follows:

1. State is not a divine institution but man-made institution.
2. The State is only a mean not an end in itself.
3. The State is a necessity evil.
4. All laws framed by the State are opposed to man's liberty.

7. State according to Marxist thinkers: The State is essentially a class structure. It is an organisation of one class dominating over the other classes. The State took birth at a certain stage of economic development, when society was broken into classes — haves and haves-not.

In history, there has been a fierce struggle between these two classes. Even today the State is an agency for exploitation of the poor by the rich. It upholds the interests of the few at the cost of many. According to Karl Marx and Fredric Engels the State is a man-made and artificial body. It is a class organisation. It represents force and oppression. They believe that a stage will come when there will be no classes and consequently the State will wither away. State is thus only a temporary organisation.

Criticism of the Notion of Class Structure

The notion may be true of certain states at certain times. But it is wrong to apply it universally to all states at all times. It applies more to a diseased State than to a normal one.

8. The Totalitarian notion of the State: The modern totalitarian notion of the State regards the whole life of an individual as coming within the jurisdiction of the State. There is no part of a man's life which he can call his own. If he lives, he lives for the State and if he dies, he dies for the State. Mussolini stated the totalitarian view in these words, "*All within the State none outside the State none against the State.*" The motto which he placed before the people was: "*to believe, to obey, to fight.*"

Criticism of the Totalitarian Notion of the State

Totalitarian view means regimentation of the life of the individual. It is wholesale denial of the worth and dignity of man. Individual is regarded just a log in the wheel of the State.

The Pluralists opposed the absolute sovereignty of the State and pleaded for the decentralisation of political power. They regarded State like other association and asked for the division of power between them.

ORIGIN OF STATE: ORGANISMIC THEORY

Ever since the ancient times the organisation of the State is being compared with human body. According to the Purusha Sukta in Vedas, each part of the state organisation has its divine allotted function and each part should do it as its duty. Plato has also compared the State with a human body. According to Cicero, "Just as the soul rules the human body similarly the King rules the body politic state." Herbert Spencer has advanced an organismic theory of the state as has been discussed earlier. The state and the body, according to organismic theory resemble in the following:

Similarities Between Organism and State

1. Body is made of cells and the State of citizens.
2. Both body and the state are born in space and time.
3. Both body and state evolve from simple to complex.
4. Both body and state die through disintegration.
5. The components in a body and state are interdependent.
6. There is an organic relationship among components in the body and also in the State.
7. There is an interdependence of the part and the whole in the body and the state.
8. There is a similarity of organisation between the body and the State.

Distinction Between Body and the State

The organismic theory however forgets that there are following distinctions between the organism and the State:

1. While the cells of the body cannot exist outside the body, the citizens may exist outside the State.
2. While the cells are activated by central nervous system there is no such parallel in the State where the individuals are self-conscious beings.
3. Thus while the cells have no independent life and will or purpose, the citizens in a State have independent will and purpose.
4. The State is not born in the manner a living organism takes birth.
5. The body develops by growth as a whole. The evolution of the State, on the other hand, is the result of combined efforts of all the constituents.
6. While the organism is born and it dies, the State is neither born nor does it die.

Defects in Organic Theory of State

Thus the organic theory of the origin of the State suffers from the following defects:

1. Admitting the individual as a cell in the body politic, it neglects his individuality.
2. According to Garner, "Its chief weakness lay in its exaggeration and in the fact that it rested upon analogies which were often superficial or false." Thus, this theory supplies a base for the exploitation of the individual.

Therefore, Jellinek has suggested, "We had better to reject the theory lest the dangers from the large amount of falsity in the analogy should out weigh the good in the little truth which it contains."

DIVINE ORIGIN THEORY

The theory of divine origin of the state is the oldest theory of the origin of the State. The Jew thinkers supported this theory. The Old Testament in Bible maintained that God is the source of all the rights of the state. Similar ideas may be traced in *Mahabharat*. Manu Smriti maintained that King is the incarnation of God Vishnu. *Artha Shastra* has prescribed that the *k*ing should never be insulted. According to Plato the State cannot be established without faith in God. The king of Egypt was held as God. In Islam the King is the agent of God. Divine right of the King was generally held in the 16th and 17th century England. According to Christianity God appoints the King.

Postulates of Divine Origin Theory

The Divine Origin Theory of the State believes in the following postulates:

1. King is appointed by the God.
2. The right of kingship is hereditary.
3. The King is responsible to God for his actions.
4. It is sin to disobey the command of the King.

Advantages of the Divine Origin Theory

The divine origin theory of the State had the following advantages:

1. The fear of God maintained discipline and peace in the subjects and resulted in spontaneous subordination.
2. This conjoined religious and political institutions. Thus, the Church and the State ruled together.
3. This theory supported obedience, co-operation and the sense of responsibility among the citizens.

4. It helped in the achievement of a welfare state.
5. It provided for a moral basis to the State as the morality in ancient times was derived from religion.

Causes of the Rejection of Divine Origin

However, the following causes led to rejection of the Divine origin theory of State in the 17th century:

1. The social contract theory of the origin of the State generally appealed to the people.
2. The Church and the State were separated in Europe.
3. The rise of nationalism also gave blow to this theory as it was opposed to the autocracy of the King.

Criticism of the Divine Origin Theory

Thus the following arguments have been advanced to criticise the Divine Origin theory of the state:

1. This theory is absolutely baseless.
2. It is against experience and lacks historical evidence.
3. It ignores the human nature of the King, who is not perfect but subject to human failings.
4. In the garb of religious support it sanctions exploitation.
5. Being based on superstition it is not political but a religious explanation of the origin of the State.
6. Supporting autocracy it supports immorality.
7. It is traditionalist and against all progressive ideas.
8. It ignores the rights of the people and supports the King.
9. It is an imaginary theory without foundation.
10. It is, therefore, against the modern consciousness of man. It is against democratic ideas.

THEORY OF FORCE

According to Leacock, the theory of force as origin of the state, means that the State is the result of war. In the words of Voltair, "The first King was a fortunate warrior." War begot the King, as the proverb goes on. Thus, according to this theory, the State does not depend on religion or on logic or reason, but on force. In the word of Triestchke, "State is power, it is sin for a state to be weak. State is the public power of offence and defence." Oppenheimer held that the aim of the State is the economic exploitation of the weak subjects. In the words of Gallicking Brennus, "The most ancient of all laws, which extends from the God to the beasts, gives to the stronger rule over the weaker." Engels has written, "Without force and iron ruthlessness nothing is achieved in history."

Criticism of Force Theory

The following arguments have been advanced against the force theory of the origin of the State:

1. Force may be an important element in the origin of the State but to consider it as the sole cause is a one-sided theory. It is over simplification. As Leacock has said, "The theory of force errs in magnifying what has been only one factor in the evolution of society into the sole controlling force."
2. This theory ignores moral basis of the State. As Gilchrist has rightly pointed out, force in politics is not physical but moral. Force is a factor in State but it is not its basis. In the words of T.H. Green, "Will, not force, is the basis of the State. Might, without right can at the best be only temporary, might with right is a permanent basis for the State.
3. This theory is against the freedom of the individual. Examples of it may be seen in Nazi Germany and Fascist Italy states.
4. This theory supports war. Mussolini said, "As war is to men, so maternity is to women, War was a biological necessity and peace meant decadence."

Value of Force Theory

In spite of the above mentioned criticism, the force theory cannot be rejected down right. The following may be pointed out in its favour:

1. It is true that states have been built by force. No State has been born without force.
2. From practical viewpoint also, force is required by a State.
   In the words of Kant, "Even a population of devils would find it to their advantage to establish a coercive state by general consent."
3. The present wars and cold wars also support the value of force.

The force, however, cannot be considered as the sole and only cause of the origin of the state. These elements such as will of the masses etc., should also be considered.

SOCIAL CONTRACT THEORY

The Sophist thinkers in ancient Greece, supported social contract theory of state. It has been admitted by Plato and Aristotle. But the most important support and explanation of the social contract theory of state, was found in the works of Thomas Hobbes, John Locke and Jean Jacques Rousseau in the 17th and 18th centuries. In the 19th century its following deteriorated. In the present 20th century none seriously believes this theory.

Fundamentals of Social Contract Theory

In spite of differences in details in the theories advanced by Hobbes, Locke and Rousseau the following characteristics may be held as the fundamental principles of the social contract theory:

1. According to this theory the State is based upon a contract between the ruler and the ruled and among the ruled themselves.
2. This theory is against the evolutionary theory of the State. According to this theory men have created the State and men maintain it for the fulfilment of their needs.
3. These thinkers divide human history in two stages. In the first stage, there was no state. It was a natural state variously described by Hobbes, Locke and Rousseau. According to Thomas Hobbes, "The life of man was solitary, poor, nasty, brutish and short." "The general principle was — Kill whom you can, take what you can." Locke, on the other hand, believed that the life in the state of nature was not selfish but co-operative and happy. According to Rousseau also, "The state of nature is a period of idyllic happiness, men being free and equal." The state of nature, however, had no laws and no system of rights and duties. It, therefore, gave place to political state in which laws and system of rights and duties substituted the state of nature.
4. Though Hobbes, Locke and Rousseau equally admit the theory of social contract they have expressed different ideas concerning the nature of this contract. For some writers, the contract was social for others it was legal while for some it was both.
5. All these thinkers admit that authority is a necessary element of State. But they differ about the basis of the State authority. While for some authority rests in the individuals, others base it in masses and still others in people's representatives. While Hobbes held it in the ruler, for Locke it was partly in the ruler and partly in the ruled. Rousseau believed that the people are the basis of authority.
6. These thinkers have interpreted human nature differently. Hobbes considered it as utterly selfish while Locke considered it as altruistic. Rousseau accepted both.

Criticism of Social Contract Theory

The following arguments have been advanced as criticism of the social Contract theory:

1. Historically, there is no evidence of the origin of the state in a social contract. The social contract theory, therefore, is not historical. In ancient times, the unit of society was not individual but family. Therefore, there was hardly any question of social contract.
2. There is contradiction among the state of nature and, social contract. Admitted with Hobbes that men were selfish then how could they arrive at a social contract? Again, if they were co-operative what was the need of social contract?
3. There was no norm or law in the state of nature. Then, how could there be a social contract between human beings? And how could that contract be binding in the absence of any law?
4. As the ruler was not a party to social contract he becomes an autocrat.
5. On the basis of this theory, the State becomes an optional institution. In the words of Barker, "....the state ought not to be considered anything better than a partnership agreement in a trade of pepper, coffee or tobacco or some other such low concern...to be dissolved by the fancy of the partners. It is to be looked on with reverence."
6. The state, according to this theory, is an artificial institution while according to modern thinkers it is the result of gradual evolution.
7. This theory wrongly explains the cause of allegiance to the State.
8. Thus, it is an illogical theory. In the state of nature, in the absence of political consciousness, how can there be social contract among people.
9. Thinkers who believe in some natural rights forget that these rights are derived from society. In the words of T.H. Green, "There can be no right without a consciousness of common interest on the part of members of the society."
10. Criticising the social contract theory Bluntschli has pointed out, "It makes the state and its institutions the products of individual caprice."

The social contract theory, therefore, has been rejected by the modern thinkers. This theory has however, done the service of contradicting the theory of divine origin and force theory. Rousseau's principles have been very much helpful in the establishment of democracy. At least this theory lays emphasis upon the fact that the State can continue only if there is some explicit or implicit contract between the ruler and the ruled and among the ruled themselves.

EVOLUTIONARY THEORY

According to the followers of evolutionary theory, the State has not been born but is a result of evolution. In the words of Burgess, "The proposition that the State is a product of history means that it is gradual and continuous development of human society." Thus, the State has gradually evolved.

Elements in the Evolution of State

The following elements have made important contribution in the evolution of State:

1. Blood relationship: Blood relationship has been the most important source of unity among human beings. The families united to form the tribe and the tribal leader was the first king. Thus both in patriarchal and matriarchal societies, state has evolved out of families.

2. Religion: Pointing out the value of religion in the formation of State, Gettel has written, "In the earliest and the most difficult periods of political development religion alone could subordinate barbaric anarchy and teach reverence and obedience. Thousands of years were needed to create that discipline and submission of authority on which all successful governments must rest." Thus, religion had been the supporter of unity, obedience, discipline, sacrifice, self-submission etc. in the State.

3. Authority: Authority has been the most important element in the evolution of the State. States, first small and then big, were formed on the basis of authority.

4. Political consciousness: By the gradual evolution of political consciousness autocratic kingship gave place to limited kingship and finally to democracy. Thus, the State has changed form with the change of political consciousness.

5. Economic need: As the economic associations and institutions gradually became complex new types of state were evolved to solve their needs.

6. Social tendency: In the end, the social consciousness of men has been the most important factor in the evolution of the states. Thus, State is a growth and not a make.

The evolutionary theory of the origin of the state incorporates the important elements of divine origin theory, force theory, social contract theory etc. and includes various elements such as religion, social consciousness and political consciousness etc., in its explanation of the origin of the state. It is therefore, more convincing synthetic, multi-sided and dynamic than all other theories.

NATURE OF STATE AUTHORITY AND POWER

On the basis of the nature of state power and authority and claiming legitimacy, Weber classified three types of political systems. These three types of political systems are as follows:

1. National legal authority: Contemporary political systems are based on national legal authority. They are based on impersonal laws or contractually established notions of legal authority derived from a system of explicit rules of laws that determine the legitimate uses of power. Authority in such a political system is vested in offices or positions not in the people who temporarily occupy those posts. Power is diffused through a hierarchy. Responsibility is relative obedience not owed to anybody personally but to enacted rules and regulations which specify the terms of obedience. Selections to the highest echelons of power is made through a process of selection which is a test of popularity. Qualifications are ascribed to the office and the incumbent is supposed to adhere to it. Selection to the lower positions is made according to the qualification and competence of the incumbent. The law is the absolute leader. The person in command is typically the "superior" within a functionally defined competency. Dutiful obedience to the political authority is channeled through a hierarchy of offices. Technically, this operation rests on organisational discipline. Bureaucracy which is a concomitant of contemporary societies represents the pure type of legal authority. Modern structure of state and city governments represents national legal authority. Other types comprise rotating office holders or officers chosen by lots of popularly elected officers. Parliamentary and committee administration and all types of collegiate bodies are included in this type. Democracies nearly correspond to this type of authority.

2. Traditional authority: Monarchies, on the other hand, depend upon traditional authority. In traditional societies people tend to regard as sacred the way things have always been done. Kings, priests, chieftains and elders are part of the sacred order. They are ascribed of such a place to maintain the sanctity of traditions which inheres in particular persons so prescribed, who may either inherit it or be invested with it by a higher authority say God. Positions are hereditary and people have a sense of personal loyalty to the occupants of kings. The traditional authority rested both in the office and office holder. Principles of administration rested upon substantive considerations of ethical equity, justice or utilitarian expediency. It depended on personal allegiance. The scope of the legitimate prerogatives of a subordinate rested upon the will of his master. Such political systems are kingships.

3. *Charismatic* authority: Dictatorships, oligarchies and one party political system etc., tend to legitimatise their authority through the *charisma* of the leader or an ideology. *Charismatic authority* rests upon affectual and personal devotion of the follower to the lord and his gifts of grace or *charisma*. They comprise especially magical abilities, revelations of heroism, oratory etc. The emotional rapture is the source of devotion to the leader who is blindly followed. The purest types are the prophet, warrior hero and demagogue. In this type of authority obedience is given exclusively to the leader as a person for the sake of his extraordinary qualities, and rests only as long as people ascribe these qualities to him and he is able to prove their effectiveness. Irrational devotion and personal opinions dominate in *charismatic* authority. Thus, charismatic authority depends upon the ability of the leader to influence his followers as to his ideologies and policies. That is the sole factor which guides the existence and continuance of a political system. Rules and traditions are relegated to the background. Hitler and Mussolini ruled their state depending on their *charisma*. This type of authority has been alleged to Indira Gandhi in India particularly during the period of emergency.

All the major political systems of the world depend on some or other form of these three types of authority or an admixture of them. Thus, the American democracy claimed legitimacy first through the *charisma* of George Washington and the national legal bureaucracy of U.S.A. England rests upon both a constitutional monarchy and a democracy. The government of Indira Gandhi had these elements. The Janata leadership lacked *charisma*.

FORMS OF THE STATE

According to Spencer the source of the origin of the State is the fear among people. It may be pointed out here that according to Spencer the origin of religion is in the fear of the dead souls. The development of the authority of the State leads to a tyranny of strong men. The power and authority of these persons induces fear among people. The terrorised people are sapped of their moral strength and will power and the domination of strong on them becomes firm. According to Spencer there are three stages in the evolution of the state. These are : (1) Military State; (2) Industrial State, and (3) Ethical State, Now, we shall discuss in brief the characteristics of each state.

1. Military State: The primary form of state, according to Herbert Spencer, was a military state. In order to explain this form of the State, Spencer has used the principle of social evolution. In the beginning, the society was simple, indefinite and homogeneous. At this stage society was undeveloped and little organised. At times different communities used to indulge in war against each other. In the course of wars some persons happened to show great acts of bravery and heroism and they emerged as strong men and leaders of the group. In wars they acted the roles of commanders and their commands were acceptable to others. At this stage chances of war were rather few and therefore there used to be no permanent chief or Commander. With the passage of time society became more complex and in complex society the chances of war also increased. At this stage the need for a permanent chief arose. When the tradition of permanent chief came into force, the chieftainship became hereditary. Now, with the death of the chief the son of the chief used to replace him. Thus the post of chief became hereditary and this was under the framework of the patriarchal system. Gradually, a council of advisors to aid the chief himself came into being. The council of advisors was appointed by the chief himself. Some advisers were elected and they were supposed to represent the public interest. Thus, the authority of the State came into being.

The chief function of the military state was to engage in wars of self-defence and expansion. In this state the individual has little value.

2. Industrial State: After the fall of military states, the industrial state came into being. In the military state the aim and purpose of the State was to amass the military strength. But amassing of military might and waging war do not satisfy the aspiration of people. People want industrial prosperity. To this purpose public and the government pays attention to the development of industry and commerce. As the industrial development picks up the structure of the State also undergoes change. In an industrial state the development and growth of industry is the aim of the state. In the industrial state the tendency of attacking other states declines. Gradually, the industrial development gives rise to industrial state. In the industrial state the individual enjoys much more freedom than the military state. There is also less interference in the personal life and liberty of people. There is also some amount of attention to the welfare of people.

3. Ethical State: The idea of an ethical state is an imaginary conception of Spencer. The military and industrial state are in existence. But the rise of an ethical state is still in the womb of future. According to Spencer as industrial progress reaches its peak the prosperity would be universal and all the conflicts would disappear. In the state of extreme industrial development, the man's selfish interest would wane and give way to altruism. When this state will be reached man would automatically follow the moral law. There will be no need for external discipline. Man would automatically obey and observe the morality. All conflicts would cease.

Herbert Spencer was a firm believer in individualism. According to him it is the individual and not society which is primary, individual is not to be sacrificed at the altar of state; rather the utility of society is valid only in so far as it subserves the interests of the individual. According to him annihilation of state does not mean the destruction of the individual. Spencer was a firm votary of individual freedom. In order to preserve the freedom of the individual he formulated a law known as Law of Equal Freedom. According to this law an individual is entitled to same amount of freedom which he is prepared to accord to others. According to Spencer, indeed the real aim of both society and State is to secure freedom for the individual. Therefore, according to him, the functions of the State are quite limited. Spencer was of course not an anarchist, he did not want to dispense with the State altogether. Indeed the State had certain important functions to perform. Spencer has drawn up a clear cut list of functions which a State need to perform and those in which it should by no means interfere. Following is the list and brief discussion of the functions which a State need to perform and also those functions in which it may interfere.

THEORIES OF STATE RIGHTS

Before elucidating the rights of the State it is necessary to understand that there is considerable difference of opinion on this subject. Most of the theories and opinions on this subject can be divided into the following classes:

1. Individualism: Hobbes, Locke, Bentham, J.S. Mill and Herbert Spencer attached greater importance to the individual than to the State in the organisation of society. Hence, these philosophers are not in favour of State interference. Hobbes favours the policy of *Laissez Faire*, and suggests that the administration of education should be left to independent citizens. Bentham is of the opinion that the State exists only to increase the happiness and contentment of the citizens, and therefore, the State should interfere only to the extent to which it adds to an increase in the sum total of happiness. Spencer believes that social progress is based on the principle of struggle for survival, and from this he argues that it is the duty and responsibility of the State that it should assist the people in their struggle for survival. Yet, even in this assistance, the state must take care not to restrict the freedom of the individual. Raymont has summarised the opinions of the individual philosophers in these words: "In fine, there has been a strong tendency amongst English political thinkers from Locke to Spencer towards distrusting the intervention of the State beyond the absolutely necessary limits, though opinions have differed considerably as to how far those limits should extend." Putting it succinctly, individualist thinkers favour the adoption of the *Laissez Faire* policy by the State.

2. Collectivism: Collectivist thinkers oppose the views of the individualists. This school of thought has been subscribed to by such eminent thinkers as Matthew Arnold, Carlyle, Ruskin, Edmund Burke and others. Carlyle and Ruskin vigorously opposed the concept of *Laissez Faire*, and suggested in contrast a complete state monopoly of education. Thinkers of this school suggest that the state's responsibility does not end with protecting the people. It must also contribute to their growth and development in other spheres also, and for this it has the right to take complete control into its own hands. The State should be given comprehensive rights to protect the nation and its people from external aggression, to apply in practice the national policies, to punish the criminals, to increase and equitable distribution of national wealth, to tax the people, to provide means for protecting the health of the people, to emancipate culture by proper control, etc.

3. Totalitarianism: Collectivist thinking in its extreme form becomes totalitarianism, which theorises that the participation of the State is the most comprehensive form of human communities. In fact, the boundaries of the State and the society are identical. According to Hegel, complete development of the child is impossible in the absence of an education for citizenship, provided by the state Totalitarian thinkers are of the opinion that the child should not only be educated by the State, but also for the State.

4. Pluralism: Propounders of this philosophy want to delimit the powers of the State by a written Constitution, for they are in favour of the independence of citizens. It is suggested that the extent of the State's powers should be clearly defined, so that other institutions like the family, church, etc., can make important contributions to social life.

5. Anarchism: Thinkers belonging to this school are opposed to the existence of any kind of governmental or state authority in society, and for that reason the very question of state control of education does not arise. Anarchism argues, from the absence of any central authority, that the individual's development is best achieved in a condition of complete freedom. Such a condition naturally leads to mutual co-operation between individuals, and this is the precondition of proper development.

6. Welfare State: Most of the views expressed above are extremist in nature. The concept of the welfare state is an attempt at achieving some balance between the widely divergent views about the authority of the State expressed in these philosophies. In the present age, the State is believed to aim at welfare of the citizens. In view of this, it becomes the duty of the State to make provisions for the best possible kind of education. Wherever the people have failed to create educational institutions, the State should step in and fill the vacuum. In addition to this, it is desirable that the State should retain some control over education in order to achieve the welfare of the people. For example, it can compel parents to send their children to school, if the parents are not inclined to view this with favour. But state control should be accompanied by state assistance also. The state should arrange for universal and compulsory education.

LIMITS OF STATE RIGHTS

Actually even the legal viewpoints set some limits upon statutory rights. The factors which limit the rights of State are as follows:

1. Fundamental rights: The citizens of every state are accorded certain fundamental rights. These fundamental rights are immune to any state attack.

2. Rights of social organisations: There are many social organisations in a state which have their own rights and which are essential to social life. Normally, the State does not violate the rights of these social organisations.

3. Rights due to social traditions, customs and conventions: Normally, the State does not interfere with the social customs, traditions and conventions and the rights ensuing from them.

4. Constitution of the State: The Constitution of the State, too, limits the rights of the State. The rights in democracy, dictatorship and various other constitutions are different.

5. International conditions: In asserting its authority, the State has to pay due attention to other states and international bodies. Any overlooking to this aspect can even endanger its existence. Thus, when a State uses its rights it keeps in view not only its own citizens and their social institutions but other states as well.

In brief, the fundamental rights of citizens, social customs, traditions and conventions, rights of social organisations and nature of the State and international situations limit the rights of the State, otherwise the State is sovereign in its limited area. Thus, the rights of the State are not unlimited even from the legal or practical viewpoint.

FUNCTIONS OF THE STATE

From the totalitarian opinion it seems that the State can perform every act but such an idea is false. Actually, from the viewpoint of means, too, the State is incapable of working for all the necessities of individuals. Thus, the State cannot even be recognised the sole means let alone an end. According to MacIver and Page, some functions are within the province of the State only, other functions for which the State is comparatively more suitable, still other which would fare better if left alone by the State and there are finally those functions which the State is incapable of implementing. Having understood these four distinct kinds of functions, it will become obvious that the State cannot be treated as sovereign over the individual. The following are the functions of the State:

1. Functions peculiar to the State: There is a general difference of opinion in respect of this class of functions but generally only the State can organise justice, peace, education and order, determine the scales of measurements and arrange for currency etc. No other institution can perform these functions.

2. Functions for which the State is well-adapted: There are many functions which the State can carry out more efficiently than other institutions. Such functions include protection of forests, looking after the foodstuffs, protecting animals, arranging for education, constructing recreation grounds, installing public conveniences, etc. In the state, natural resources can be exploited by other organisations too but in order to maintain a standard of efficiency an authority is required which only the State is capable of supplying. Similarly, the State can conduct plans of social welfare and security better than other institutions, who will have to make larger pecuniary sacrifice and would yet not achieve the same standard as would the State at less monetary expense to itself.

3. Functions for which the State is ill-adapted: There are many cultural, religious and class addicted activities for welfare which the State is ills adapted to. These functions can be done better by other organisations.

4. Functions which the State is incapable of performing: There are many functions which cannot endure State control at all. For example, the State cannot control public opinion, formulate laws for the conduct of individuals or change and transform social customs, traditions and conventions. Public opinion is formed due to many social and other causes, people's conduct depends upon their individual characters while social customs, traditions and conventions are perpetually involved in a process of autonomous alterations.

The foregoing description of the functions of a State has made it obvious that the State cannot perform all functions. The State cannot be treated as the sovereign authority. An individual is the member of a family and society before he is the citizen of a State. And before he is a member of society he is a human being, a self-conscious being. In this way, the duties and responsibilities which he acquires by virtue of being a human being, a member of society and family, are outside the province of the State which cannot interfere with them on this account. Actually, when compared to the rights of the individual the rights of the State are ulterior. The State has been assigned its rights for their development, though it will have full authority to dissuade an individual from hindering the development of another fellow-being.

Functions of the State According to MacIver[1]

(*Internal Aspect*)

	I **Order**	II **Protection**	III **Conservation and Development**
A.	**Physical Basis**		
1.	Establishment of areas and frontiers of political authority — local, regional, national	Exercise of the police function, securing life and property	Promotion and regulation of the physical conditions — hygienic requirements, housing, occupational, recreational conditions — of HEALTH.
2.	Establishment and control of the forms of communication and transportation		Conservation and economic utilisation of NATURAL RESOURCES.
	Establishment of units and standards of computation, measurement, value etc.		Planning and general control of urban and rural development.

Cont.

1. R.M. MacIver, *The Modern State*, pp. 190-91.

	I **Order**	II **Protection**	III **Conservation and Development**
B.	**Social Structure**		
	Definition of political powers and spheres of authority:	Maintenance and protection of authorities politically determined	Establishment and development of facilities of EDUCATION
1.	territorial — local, regional, national		
2.	functional — division and co-ordination of political services		
	Definition of general rights and obligations of citizenship and territorial residence	Maintenance and enforcement of rights and obligations politically determined—JUSTICE AND LIBERTY	Promotion of the external conditions of OPPORTUNITY
	Formulation of specific rights and obligations of persons and associations, e.g.,	in their political significance; including protection of the community against the encroachments of specific associations, e.g.,	Establishment of national museums, assistance of scientific research and of non-controversial cultural aims.
1.	within the family association; regulation of the marriage contract etc.	against monopoly and 'unfair competition', against social disturbances and economic dislocation through economic disputes, against racial, religious, and partisan pressure	Promotion of industrial, agricultural, commercial and financial development in relation to general and not particular advantage.
2.	within the economic order; regulation of currency, economic contracts etc.		

Cont.

	I **Order**	II **Protection**	III **Conservation and Development**
3.	within other social relationships; definition of professional or occupational status, registration, incorporation etc.	Assurance for the whole community of minimum standards of decent living, e.g., in respect of wage rates, employment, upbringing of children, prevention of destitution	Provision of the means of inquiry into social problems of general significance.
	Service of social information, collection and arrangement of statistics etc., relating to population, trade and commerce and all kinds of social phenomena	Care for and preservation of 'social wreckage'	

FUNCTIONS OF STATE ACCORDING TO KARL MARX

In the *Communist Manifesto* (1848) Marx and Engels laid down following functions of a State:[2]

1. Abolition of property in land and application of all rents of land to public purposes;
2. A heavy progressive or graduated income tax;
3. Abolition of rights of inheritance;
4. Confiscation of the property of all emigrants and rebels;
5. Centralisation of credit in the hands of the State by means of a notional bank with state capital and an exclusive monopoly;
6. Centralisation of the means of communication and transport in the hands of the State;
7. Extension of factories and instruments of production owned by the state, the bringing into cultivation of waste lands, and the improvement of the soil generally in accordance with an economic plan;
8. Equal liability of all to labour. Establishment of industrial armies, especially for agriculture;
9. Combination of agriculture with manufacturing industries, gradual abolition of the distinction between town and country by a more equitable distribution of population of the country;

2. Marx-Engels, *Selected Works* (3 Volumes), Vol. I, p. 126.

10. Free education for all children in public schools, abolition of children's factory labour in its present form, combination of education with industrial production;

A learned Marxist writer on this subject enumerates the functions of a Communist State as under:[3]

1. One of the main domestic functions of the proletarian state in the transitional period is the function of suppressing the exploiting classes, the bourgeoisie in the first place. Deprived of its political domination the bourgeoisie cannot reconcile itself to its defeat and the loss of power and privileges, and therefore viciously resists the victorious proletariat. The dictatorship of the proletariat is necessary for overcoming the resistance of the bourgeoisie, for defeating it in fierce class battles. The suppression of the exploiters is a compulsory task of the proletarian state whatever its form, but this can be done in various forms depending on historical conditions. As Lenin says: "The dictatorship of the proletariat means a most determined and most ruthless war waged by the new class against a more powerful enemy the bourgeoisie whose resistance is increased ten-fold by its overthrow...."[4]

Functions of State

Constitutional Functions	Ministrant Functions
1. Keeping of order and providing for protection of person and property from violence and robbery,	1. Regulation of trade and industry including coinage of money, establishment of weights and standards, tariffs and even navigation laws,
2. Fixing of the legal relations between man his wife and parents and children,	2. Regulation of labour,
3. Regulation of holding, transmission and inter-change of property and the determination of its liabilities for debts or crimes,	3. Maintenance of thoroughfares including management of railways and other internal improvements,
4. Determination of contract rights between individuals,	4. Maintenance of postal and telegraph systems,
5. Definition and punishment of crime,	5. Manufacture and distribution of gas and maintenance of water works,

Cont.

3. Afanasyev, *op. cit.*, pp. 290-92.
4. Refer to his "Left-Wing Communism — An Infantile Disorder" in his *Collected Works*, Vol. 31, pp. 23-24.

Constitutional Functions	Ministrant Functions
6. Administration of justice in civil cases,	6. Sanitation, including medical relief and public health,
7. Dissemination of political duties, privileges, and relations of its citizens, and	7. Education,
8. Dealings of State with foreign powers, preservation of State from external danger or encroachment and the advancement of its international interests.	8. Care of the poor and the incapable,
	9. Care and cultivation of forests, and
	10. Prohibition laws.

Source: Wilson, *The State*, pp. 42-44.

2. The suppression of the bourgeoisie, however, is not an aim in itself for the proletariat. Its main aim is to build socialism, to create a new socialist economy. What makes this task so difficult is that the socialist revolution begins when there are no ready-made economic forms of socialism. It is the task of the dictatorship of the proletariat to organise the economic life of society, to build up a new type of economy superior to capitalism, the economy of socialism. As Lenin says: "The dictatorship of proletariat is not only the use of force against the exploiters and not even mainly the use of force.... The proletariat represents and creates a higher type of social organisation of labour compared with capitalism. This is what is important, this is the source of the strength and the guarantee that the final triumph of communism is inevitable."[5]
3. The activities of the State in building up socialist economy and guiding all economic affairs in the country is the main *economic* and *organisational* function of the State of the dictatorship of the proletariat. The task of the proletarian State in fulfilling this function is to secure socialism's economic victory over capitalism and attain a higher level of the social organisation of labour than under capitalism. Once it has nationalised the basic means of production, the proletarian state immediately takes over command positions in the economy and organises its planned, science-based management. Under the guidance of the Marxist party the State carries out the socialist industrialisation

5. Refer to his paper "A Great Beginning" in his *Collected Works*, Vol. 29, p. 419.

of the country and collectivisation of agriculture and on the basis of continuous development and improvement of production, raises the material well-being of the people. As socialism progresses, the economic and organisational function of the State gains in scope and with the victory of socialism embraces literally all branches of the national economy.

4. Yet socialist construction is not confined to the establishment of a socialist economy. It is inconceivable without a steadfast growth of the awareness and culture of the people, and the obliteration of the survivals of the past in their consciousness. It is only natural, therefore, that the education of the working people, particularly the semi-proletarian strata and peasantry, in the spirit of socialism, the promotion of their general education and professional and cultural level is one of the key tasks of the proletarian state. It is all the more important to solve the problem because the exploiters for centuries enslaved the working people and in every way suppressed their striving for culture and knowledge. The proletarian state guides the cultural revolution which is an important element of the socialist revolution. The role played by the State in promoting cultural development and the education of the working people finds its expression in its cultural and educational functions.
5. In the sphere of foreign policy the activity of the proletarian state is characterised by the function of the struggle for peace between the peoples, and the function of the country's defence against imperialist aggression. As it persistently works for peace, the state of the dictatorship of the proletariat constantly strengthens the country's defence and its armed forces.
6. But the most typical function of the Communist State is to prepare the way for its own withering away so that the classless society is converted into the stateless condition of life. All public affairs in economic and cultural spheres would be managed by the free and voluntary associations (Soviets of the people). Such bodies would merge with the society and become organs of the public government through which all members of society would participate in economic and cultural activities. As Lenin says: "The State will be able to wither away completely when society adopts the rule, 'From each according to his ability, to each according to his needs."[6]

6. Lenin, "State and Revolution" *in Collected Works*, Vol. 25, p. 474.

Weaknesses of Marxian Theory

1. The Marxian theory of state has its own weaknesses. It is altogether absurd to say that a bourgeois state has only one function — perpetuation of the system of exploitation of the working class at the hands of the capitalist class. If a capitalist state has only one function of this kind, then a Communist State may be accused of being a thoroughly dictatorial system of its own kind.
2. A Communist State does many public welfare services and it establishes new social order by and large free from social and economic evils, but it permits no room for dissent or freedom of thought and expression.
3. Marx's talk about final withering away of the State is a wishful thinking. Instead of doing the job of preparing its own eventual doom, such a state has converted itself into a highly bureaucratic and concentrated system of power. Keeping it in view, a critic says: "Although Marxism has developed as one of the most radical anti-statist conceptions, with suitable modifications, it was transformed into a statist ideology."[7]

STATE AS END OR MEANS

1. State as an end: Plato and Aristotle considered State as the highest moral association which alone could give us 'good life'. The State is a self-sufficing institution that embraces within it the whole complex of social cravings and needs of men. The State is prior to the individual not in terms of the process of history but in terms of its real nature. This is the idealistic or metaphysical view in which society and state are identified. In modern times, Rousseau of France and Hegel of Germany elaborated the same point to the extent that State was defined. In the words of Hegel, the State "is the highest expression of that social morality, at once precipitated in and enforced by social opinion, which lies behind the life of the family, behind the life of all other social groups, and behind the life of the political community itself."[8] As State is the highest institution, there can be nothing above it Bosanquet held that there could be no anti-thesis between State and individual. The Fascist Mussolini declared 'everything for the State'. The modern collectivists and socialists also take the State as an altar at whose altar the interest of the individual should be sacrificed. Such a view justifies the case of State absolutism. As Joad puts it: "Since the State is regarded as representing and containing within itself

7. S. Stojanovic, *Between Ideals and Reality*, p. 8.
8. Barker, *op. cit.*, pp. 27-28.

all the individuals' social aspirations and, at the same time, fulfilling all his social needs, whatever claims the State may make upon the individual are held to be based upon an absolute authority."[9]

2. State as a means: According to this view the individual is the end at whose altar the interest of the State should be sacrificed. Some political thinkers evolved the idea of 'natural rights.' To them the State has no right to deprive a man of his natural rights, while the individuals have a right to challenge the action of the State if it undermines their rights having their source in their very existence and rational nature. Locke sanctioned that the ruler was bound by the terms of social contract and if he failed in giving due and effective protection to the three natural rights of the individuals relating to their life, liberty and property he could be replaced. This idea was restressed with greater vigour by social theorists like Herbert Spencer and Adam Smith in the 19th century. Liberalism issuing forth in the form of exalting and glorifying the system of democracy stands on the premise that "State is merely an institution or a means by which certain objects are accomplished and it is an end in itself."[10]

Thus, the authority of the State should be taken as justified in terms of its accomplishments. The State is not an end. It is a means for the good of the individuals, though the extent of its powers and functions gives to it a value greater than that of any other group or association in society. As Laski says: "It is, in fact, the final depository of the social will. It sets the perspective of all other organisations. It brings within its powers all forms of human activity under its control as it deems desirable. It is, moreover, the implied logic of this supremacy that whatever remains free of its control does so by its permission. The State does not permit that men should marry their sisters; it is by its graciousness that they are allowed to marry their cousins. The State is the keystone of the social arch. It moulds the forms and substance of the myriad human lives with whose destinies it is charged."[11]

THE END OF THE STATE: DIFFERENT VIEWS

1. *Aristotle*: To Aristotle the true end of State is the realisation of 'good life'.
2. *Locke*: To Locke it is the 'common good'.
3. *Bentham*: To Bentham it is 'the greatest good of the greatest number'. While the word 'good' in the case of Aristotle has

9. C.E.M. Joad, *Guide to the Philosophy of Morals and Politics*, p. 585.
10. Garner, *op. cit*, p. 70.
11. Laski, *A Grammar of Politics*, p. 21.

distinctly ethical implications; in the case of Locke and Bentham it has material overtones.

4. *Holtzendorff*: Distinguishing between the ideal and the actual ends of the state this German writer lays down that its actual ends are three — development of national power, maintenance of justice and law, and promotion of social progress and civilisation of the people.
5. *Adam Smith*: This English economist talks about three great purposes of the state — protecting the people from foreign invasion or internal violence, protecting every individual from the injustice or oppression of every other member, and creating and maintaining certain works and institutions which no individual or body of individuals would like to erect and maintain.
6. *J. W. Burgess*: The leading American writer also presents a three-fold classification of the end of State as — *primary*: establishment and adjustment of the government and liberty, *secondary*: perfection of the principle of rationality and the development of national genius and final: perfection of humanity.
7. *F. W. Wilson*: He tells us about these ends of a modern welfare state — satisfaction of wills, attainment of moral progress, realisation of the greatest happiness of the greatest number, development of individual personality, maintenance of rights, balancing as well as protection of interests.[12]
8. *Pennock and Smith*: The major purposes of the modern state are security, justice, liberty and welfare.[13]
9. *Garner*: He puts his three-fold classification of the end of State thus :[14]
    1. The original, primary and immediate end of the State is the maintenance of peace, order, security and justice among the people who compose it. No State which fails to achieve these ends in a reasonable degree can justify its existence.
    2. The State must look beyond the needs of the individual as such to the larger collective needs of society — the welfare of the group. It must care for the common interests and promote the national progress by doing for society the things which the common interests require, but which cannot be done at all, or done efficiently, by individuals

12. F.G. Wilson, *The Elements of Modern Politics*, pp. 141-59.
13. Pennock and Smith, *Political Science*, p. 137.
14. Garner, *op. cit.*, p. 73.

acting singly or through voluntary associations. This may be called the secondary end of the State and refers to the development of the national capacities and perfection of national life.

3. The promotion of the civilisation of mankind at large may be considered the ultimate and highest end of the State. This is the mission-of-civilisation theory that was powerfully defended by the German writers.

Thus, the State has a triple end: first, its mission is the advancement of the good of the individual; then it should seek to promote the collective interests of individuals in their associational capacity; and, finally, it should aim at the furthering of civilisation and progress of the world.[15]

However, the time and circumstances as well as the stage of political development have greatly affected the relative emphasis placed in any particular state upon above mentioned ends.[16] Gettell rightly said that "much depends upon the degree of civilisation, the stage of political development, and the nature of the problems of the period."[17] The ultimate end of state is the maintenance of *order*. As MacIver points out, "It is imposed no less by democracy than by despotism, by empire and by federation. But the form of order is always determined by a dominant purpose. Just as there is one form of order in a menagerie, another in a prison, another in an army, another in a school, another within a family, another in a fraternal society — so there is one form of order in a slave-state, another among a free people; one form in a class state, another in a democracy. The conception of order changes as we pass from the idea of the state as exploitative to the idea of the State as ministrative. It ceases to be order as a condition of domination and becomes an order as a condition of the common welfare."[18] Charles Merriam says that "by itself order may be slavery, prison or concentration camp, exploitation of many by few, of the weak by strong, an apotheosis of might and shame of right. But it is respected and followed when it becomes the implement of common good."[19]

FUNCTIONS OF MODERN STATE

A. Compulsory Functions

1. Defence against foreign attack: The most urgent function of the State is defence of the country against foreign attack. It has to make adequate

15. *Ibid.*
16. Pennock and Smith, *op. cit.*, p. 138.
17. Gettell, *op. cit.*, p. 383.
18. MacIver, *op. cit.*, p. 184.
19. Charles Merriam, *Systematic Politics*, p. 45.

preparations in the form of weapons and land, sea and air forces. It has to take special notice of things which can create the danger of attack from other countries.

2. Internal peace and security: The policy of a State at home is quite as important as is its foreign policy. It is the prime duty of the State to maintain internal peace and security. An increase in communal riots, thefts, cases of dacoity and rebellion can endanger the existence of the State itself. The state maintains peace and order through police and army.

3. Protection of the rights of citizens: In every State the citizens possess certain rights like rights to life, property, freedom of thought etc. It is incumbent upon the State to protect these rights, for which it has to formulate essential laws, arrange for proper administration and organise justice.

4. Justice: In this way justice is a compulsory function of the State. This provides for obedience of laws in the State, maintains order and protects the rights of everyone.

B. Voluntary Functions of the State

Besides these compulsory functions of State the following are its voluntary functions:

1. Education: In the modern age, all states consider it their duty to make adequate arrangement for the education of their citizens. A State of uneducated citizens can never progress. Thus, the State makes arrangement for primary schools and colleges and universities so that higher education in sciences, agriculture and the humanities may become possible. Arrangements are made for adjoining research centres, libraries, zoos, store houses and art classes etc. Efforts are made to provide free primary education. Capable students are awarded scholarships by the State. But the state should avoid unnecessary interference in educational centres.

2. Health: Along with education, modern states try to provide for the protection of health. Provision is made for sanitation, hospitals, free medicine, vaccination and essential energising foods for the poor. Medical colleges are opened to end the dearth of capable doctors. Government research centres and training schools for nurses are opened.

3. Protection of the old, poor and invalid: Modern states have also begun making arrangement for the old, unemployed people who are given pension. The facility of insurance insures the security of everyone. Orphanages and homes for destitutes are created.

4. Arrangement of public welfare services: The State organises the railways, postal and telegraphic facilities, wireless etc. It is the duty of the State to make arrangements for means of transportation such as buses, railways, aeroplanes and ships etc.

5. Social and economic improvement: Another of the State's duties is affecting social and economic improvement. The state lays down laws against harmful customs and makes necessary arrangements for their enforcement.

6. Encouraging trade and industry: It is also the duty of the State to encourage trade and industry and to develop it as well. Almost everywhere in the world, it is the State which controls economic system and the mint. It is the State which standardises the scales of measurement and weighing. The country cannot benefit by international trade if it does not make the proper laws for import and export. The State should establish factories of the key industries in order to implement and initiate other industries in the country. The State should also encourage cottage industries.

7. Organisation of labour: The State should direct its efforts to the improvement of conditions of labourers and lay down rules to obviate the probability of their exploitation. It is the responsibility of the State to make efforts towards labour welfare.

8. Proper use of natural resources of the country: A country can become powerful by land, forests, rivers, minerals and agricultural products. Maximum benefit should be extracted from them, on this subject, the State should direct the necessary precautionary measures, research and search for new mineral products and lay down laws for the utilisation of forests, mines, land etc.

9. Arrangement of recreation: In order to maintain the novelty and excitement in the life of the public the State should provide means for recreation. For this film industry, dramatic societies, etc., ought to be encouraged.

Actually, the function of a modern State is not merely administration but an integral welfare and development of its subjects. Thus, its functions have been aggrandised. The turbulence of local situations does make an appreciable though slight alteration in them, while different political schools of thought have recognised different functions of the State. Thus, nothing final can be said upon this subject. The only theory which can be universally acceptable is that the State should function in a manner calculated to add to public welfare but the scholars differ in their opinions about that in which lies this public welfare. It is here that the guidance of the sociologist is needed. He has to determine the supreme and ultimate objective of the individuals. The State shall collect the means to the attainment of this ideal. As an example, the supreme ideal of an individual is self-realisation or an integral development. Thus, it is for the State to utilise the means to his physical, mental and spiritual development.

STATE AND COMMUNITY

Many people come to treat the State as a community. But the State is only a political association in the community. Defining community, G.D.H. Cole has written, "By community I mean a complex of social life, a complex including a number of human beings, living together under conditions of social relationships, bound together by a common however constantly changing stock of conventions, customs and traditions and conscious to some extent of common social objects and interests." The same scholar of political science has defined State as a means which organises particular human society, both in its internal and external relation, into a corporate body. Accordingly, the State is actually the means for the welfare of community. It can be described as a part of community. It is created for the fulfilment of certain objectives.

State is More Limited than Community

A State is more limited when compared to community. It is of course true that it does control a major part of social functions and relations but still many aspects of human life are excluded from it. A communal life is more comprehensive than the life of a citizen. In a community, the individual is a member of many other associations besides the State. The laws of the state exert their influence upon a very small part of the person's life. MacIver has truly written, "As social beings, we are more than merely citizens of a state. We enter into many relationships, we carry on many social activities, not as members of state but as social beings, as friends, or lovers, as members of families, of churches, of clubs or other groups." As a self-conscious being the individual thinks independently of others and attempts self-development. Moral life is even wider than the political and social life. An individual acts more as a social being than as a citizen and more as a self-conscious being than as a social being. And this moral nature of his is the most comprehensive of all.

State is an Association

Actually, the State is an association despite some differences which it professes from the other associations. The State is here referred to as an association in the sense that its establishment is motivated by particular objectives. It has some special functions. It can neither perform all functions and nor does it exercise sovereign authority over the individual. There are other associations besides the State in society which cannot be replaced by State, in the implementation of whose functions the State is neither appropriate nor capable. The State was made the sovereign in some countries like Italy or Germany but the experiment did not prove a success. MacIver has said quite correctly, "The State can effectively supervise only the external aspects of life. Beyond all else, it cannot under any conditions be a substitute for those cultural organisations which express the variant beliefs, opinion of modern interests and ideals of the diversified groups of society." Actually, the State is a political association whose objective is to maintain peace and order in the community and to raise the standard of living while creating circumstances conductive to the free integral development of every citizen. There are a number of activities like religious, moral, economic, social and psychological which the State cannot perform. Even the sovereign state of Germany could not take into its hands the functions of the Church.

State is a Means to the Welfare of Community

In this way, State is not itself an end. It is a means to which rights are assigned for governing over society and individual for their own benefit. When the State ceases to be of any use to the individual its need will also end. According to Engels, the State will dissolve of itself. Many thinkers like Marx, Engels, Gandhi, Kropotkin, Tolstoy, Sri Aurobindo etc., have recognised the disutility of State in an ideal order. The theories of the origin of society also support this view that it is a means, not an end. The end is the integral development of the individual and society. The State is accorded its rights by the society and individual. It governs because that is what it is meant for. It is created for the proper utilisation of natural resources, maintaining peace and order, defence of the country from external aggression, protection of health arrangement for means of transport and communication and other activities of a similar nature. It does not annihilate other associations but organises and encourages them. Even in sovereign states like the U.S.S.R. the State has not interfered in the activities of the family. The State in Germany never triumphed over the Church. F.L. Schuman has written, "in the Church and Church alone, the Nazi dictatorship has found an inseparable obstacle to its absolutistic pretentions." Actually, a good State is one which makes its objective the benefit of community and works for its attachment. It is useless in the event it fails to achieve the communal benefit and is changed by revolutionaries. In the words of MacIver, "It is best conceived of as an agency of the community with very broad and important functions, but nevertheless limited." From the moral viewpoint the State is a means to the integral development of society and the individual.

STATE AND EDUCATION

Before going on to a detailed analysis of the relationship between the State and education, one must see the extent to which the State can play a part in social life. In other words, one must see how far education is a subject of state control, guidance and assistance. In modern societies, one finds that education is provided in government controlled institutions as well as privately managed institutions. Many educational institutions are also controlled and managed by religious institutions. And even among the government or state controlled institutions, one finds that some are administered by the central authority and others by State or local self-governing bodies. Another aspect of the State control of education is to determine the spheres which the State should take under its own wings and the areas which can be safely left to the control of the people. In the present day, every government, be it totalitarian or democratic, must contribute to education. There is no doubt that in a democracy the government is elected by the people, but it cannot be denied that the people themselves cannot evolve an educational pattern which can look after the educational needs of every individual. And, at the same time, it is also realised that democracy cannot be successful in the absence of universal education. Hence, modern democratic states also play a large part in educational organisation.

Education in a Welfare State

The concept of the welfare state is an attempt at achieving some balance between the widely divergent views about the authority of the State expressed in these philosophies. In the present age, the State is believed to aim at welfare of the citizens. In view of this, it becomes the duty of the State to make provisions for the best possible kind of education. Wherever the people have failed to create educational institutions, the State should step in and fill the vacuum. In addition to this, it is desirable that the State should retain some control over education in order to achieve the welfare of the people. For example, it can compel parents to send their children to school, if the parents are not inclined to view this with favour. But state control should be accompanied by state assistance also. The State should arrange for universal and compulsory education, at least at the primary level. It must also provide suitable textbooks to the students, or encourage other people to produce such books. The State has the authority to impose taxes upon the people to collect funds for educational purposes. It is the duty of the State to determine the proper syllabi for State institutions as well as other institutions controlled by private groups of individuals. Some anarchist and individualist thinkers may oppose state control of education to this extent, but there is no denying the fact that the people cannot successfully put into effect a complete educational programme. Raymont presents a balanced view when he comments, "We observe that education, like the other beneficial influences at work in a civilised community, may be conducted by all or any of three means: first by voluntary effort with a view to profit; secondly by voluntary effort arising from philanthropic or religious motives; thirdly, by the agency of the State."

Limits to the Control of Education

Having accepted that the state must exercise control over the educational system, it becomes necessary to determine the extent to which this control should be exercised. Historically viewed, education has been carried on in every State through a variety of means and agencies. On the one hand, one finds colleges and schools run by individuals for profit while on the other one runs across institutions created by religious groups or philanthropists who have collected funds from private individuals for this purpose. In addition, one finds state aided institutions in every country. Even J.S. Mill, who objects to state control of education, has admitted that the State should establish some ideal educational institutions which should serve as models and which should inspire the people to create similar institutions. Mill objects to the State control of education on the ground that the State tries to educate the people along lines which support its own ideology and thus it controls the ideas of the people. This belief is not completely without logic and supporting evidence, because communist states do try to control the thinking of the younger generations by intellectually feeding them on communist literature. It amounts to slow brainwashing. Much the same tendency has been seen in the past in totalitarian state which also tries to control the thinking of the people by making educational institutions the centres of state propaganda. This is unfair and improper. In fact, state control in education is exercised with the sole purpose of preventing encroachment upon the political and social independence and freedom of the people, because this is essential for a proper development of personality. In the second place, the State has at its disposal unlimited means and resources which enable it to arrange for education on a large scale, something which is beyond the reach of private individuals and groups of individuals. Briefly speaking, it is desirable that State control of education should be guided by the principle of the least possible infringement of the liberties of the people. The welfare State provides for education precisely on this principle. With the establishment of democratic governments, the sphere of education is widening rapidly with the result that the responsibilities of the State are increasing. The State imposes taxes on the people in order to finance education and then compels people to send their children to schools and colleges. It also supervises educational arrangements in institutions not controlled by it to ensure uniform standards, and also provides financial aid to them.

Functions of State in Education

Explaining the functions of the State, MacIver and Page have pointed out that there are certain functions which the State alone can perform, others which can be performed by others but not so efficiently as by the State, and yet others which are best left to other agencies, apart from those which the State does not have the ability to perform. The provision of education falls into the first and second of the above four categories, because not only is the State the best equipped for this task, it is in fact the only agency capable of coping with the educational problems of populations of remarkable size. The State alone can provide universal education to such a large number of people. The functions of the State in the sphere of education can be summed up as follows:

1. Provision of proper schools: The State should establish different kinds of schools — primary, secondary, higher learning and professional colleges — so that the local requirements of the people can be fulfilled. In addition to this, the State must also correlate these various institutions in such a way that the effort at education is not wasted.

2. Making primary education compulsory: At least at the primary stage, the State should make all education compulsory, free and universal. This kind of education, at least the elementary education, is absolutely necessary for the mental development of people. Hence, the State should compel parents to send their children to schools.

3. Providing finances for education: The State must plan for and provide the finances required for education. Some people have advanced the argument that the provision of free and compulsory primary education will reduce its value in the eyes of the people. While this may be true, the State is faced with the necessity of doing so, because the private sector has failed to provide primary education for the masses. It is now accepted that every modern State must provide free and compulsory education to all children in the country. Apart from primary education, it has been experienced that private resources are never sufficient to provide proper secondary and higher education to adequate numbers of students. Even here institutions have to seek the assistance of the State. In addition to the creation of primary and secondary schools, and universities and professional colleges for higher learning the State helps the cause of education by providing scholarships and financial help in different forms to poor but brilliant students. In many Western countries the number of students receiving state aid in one form or the other frequently rises to fifty per cent of the total number enrolled in the university. In India, this stage has not been achieved, and consequently many brilliant students are deprived of the opportunity to study.

4. General control and guidance: One important aspect of state functioning in the sphere of education is control, inspection and guidance of individual institutions. The state government officials plan syllabi for various levels of education, with the help of educationists and other learned people. In. the same manner, the State does not take independent decisions about educational matters, but seeks the advice and guidance of experts. The State should normally not interfere in teaching methods, but leave it to experienced teachers, researchers and scholars. Besides, the State can also not profitably guide the techniques of evaluating educational ability. This, too, is the task of the teacher and the educationist. All that the State can lay down, in the way of guidance, is that some method of evaluating educational ability must be introduced at each level of education. The State may also require this method to be so accurate, dependable and valid that it may serve as a basis for evaluating the individual's fitness for various tasks.

5. Providing skilled educators: It is clear from the preceding paragraph that there is little the State can do in the absence of skilled educators. Hence, it is a major responsibility of the State to provide such educators. Even if the national educational policy has been formulated by brilliant thinkers and incalculable effort has gone into its creation, it will fail to achieve anything if there are no skilled educators to implement it. The responsibility of the State does not end with putting up building for schools, filling such schools with educands and making arrangements for the administration of the institution. As Raymont has pointed out, "Educational salvation lies, not in bricks and mortar, nor in sumptuous equipment, nor in paper curricula, nor in elaborate machinery of whatever kind, but in the subtle influence of informed men and women upon the pupils committed to their care. A good teacher, in sympathy with his work, and doing it under reasonably liberal condition of service will achieve better things in a barn than a bad or dissatisfied one will achieve under the best of external circumstances". Hence, it is desirable that the State should take upon itself the responsibility of providing trained and qualified teachers, and of seeing that their conditions of service create the satisfaction so necessary for the job. The educand's mental health depends very greatly upon the mental health of his educator. More often than not, in most non-governmental educational institutions one finds conditions of work which are not at all conductive to mental balance, for example, varying scales of pay, physical conditions of work, absence of opportunity to progress, etc. The State should investigate all such conditions and improve them, and also enact legislation which secures the rights of people working in private institutions.

6. Training in citizenship: In the sphere of education, one important function of the State is to train young men and women in citizenship. For this, the State must create institutions for training in science, industry, agriculture, etc. The cultural training and advancement of the people can be provided for by creating art galleries, cultural committees, means of recreation etc. Now-a-days, states send cultural delegations to other countries. Another way in which the State can help in improving cultural standards is by facilitating the international exchange of teachers and students. In a democratic society, it is necessary for the state to maintain a healthy level of social living, by creating conditions conductive to the physical and mental development of its people and by assisting all private agencies engaged in similar work. Political training is also essential in a democratic country, because political awareness must be created if proper leadership is to emerge. It is for the State to exploit all means of communications — newspapers, radio, television, cinema, etc., — in order to acquaint every individual with the latest in political, economic and social thinking, and also to inform him of all economic and industrial progress taking place within the country. In this way, it can be seen that the political education of people living in a democratic country depends entirely upon the co-operation of the State.

STATE AND RELIGION: SECULAR STATE

The idea of secular state is a novel concept developed in societies which include different religions. A secular state is one which allows for the existence of all religions and all sorts of religious beliefs and all shades of opinions. It prescribes religious tolerance and equal respect to all religions. There is no state religion in a secular state. Each person is free to profess and practice his religion without causing inconvenience to others and practice his fear of sanctions or punishment. In a secular state religious institutions like church, mosque, temples and gurudwaras are allowed to exist and maintain property and carry religious functions.

The idea of secular state is a fit concept for countries like India which inhere a composite culture with different religions and sects. Secular state is at once an attempt to separate politics from religion and also an attempt to effect effective state control over checking unnecessary religious classes and misunderstandings. It is an idea most suited to a democracy. Secularism allows for the broader understanding and contact between people in all the spheres of life without any inhibition by their respective religions. Hence, secularism broadens one's outlook and makes for better understanding of the values of democracy.

STATE AND GOVERNMENT

Louis XIV, the king of France, used to say, "I am the state." He did not distinguish between the State and the Government. The two, however, differ in the following respects:

1. While the State is abstract, the Government is a concrete organisation.
2. According to Rousseau, "Government is a living tool through which the will of the State is formulated, expressed and realised." Thus, while the State is the end, the Government is the instrument or means. About the Government Laski has said, "It exists to carry out the purpose of the State. It is not itself the supreme coercive power. It is simply the mechanism of administration which gives effect to the purpose of that power."
3. Defining the Government, Garner has written, "The Government is the collective name for the agency, magistracy, organisation through which will of the State is formulated, expressed and realised." Thus, while the Government only includes rulers, the State includes both the ruler and the ruled.
4. While the State requires a definite piece of land, the Government does not necessarily need it. It may be even without a country.
5. Government may come and go but the state continues. Thus while the State is permanent, the Government is changing. In the historical period, the Government are constantly changing while the State remains the same.

6. The authority of the State is fundamental. Its authority is supreme. The Government, on the other hand, derives its authority from the State. It has no fundamental authority of its own.

The above-mentioned distinctions between the State and the Government, however, should not lead us to forget the close relationship between the two. In fact the two have been only theoretically distinguished. One cannot be found without the other. State and Government go together. The State acts through the Government. In the words of Garner, "Government is the machinery through which common policies are determined and by which common affairs are regulated and common interests promoted... .without Government the population would be an incoherent, unorganised, anarchic mass with no means of collective action."

STATE AND MINORITIES

Who are Minorities?

We may define a minority as a group of people, who because of their physical or cultural characteristics, are singled out from the others in the society in which they live for differential and unequal treatment; and who therefore regard themselves as objects of collective discrimination. "Differential and unequal treatment" does not necessarily mean that one is at the bottom. If two well-trained and competent persons compete for a job of high prestige and income and one loses out on the grounds of his group membership alone, this does not indicate a low-class status, but rather a minority group status. A minority group is a group which, regardless of where it is on the class ladder, faces barriers to the pursuit of life's values that are larger or greater than the barriers faced by persons otherwise equally qualified. This is a distinction superimposed on the class system. A member of a minority group, then, is not necessarily a member of lower class, but he is lower on the stratification ladder than he would be were it not for his group membership. Wherever there are minority groups there is, by definition, discrimination. It implies the application of standards which are arbitrary and unfair by dominant standards. The central meaning of "minority group" of those who are thus identified is precisely that they are judged by standards which are in violation of major social values.

Distinctive Marks of Minorities

The symbols by which minorities are distinguished may be religion, language, national origin, race or some combination of these and other characteristics. All over world the minority-majority scale is prevalent in different degrees of discrimination. The Negroes are the popular minorities in the U.S.A. even today. In India the term minorities is often applied to Muslims, *Harijans* and backward classes on account of their general disabilities accorded by the dominant groups. In India the caste system with the ritual sanction is responsible for the creation of a minority of people, who are afforded discriminatory treatment by the bulk of the society. The untouchables and other depressed castes, the scheduled tribes etc., have been the oppressed in our society down through the ages.

STATE AND SOCIETY

The following distinctions between the State and society clarify the differences in their nature:

1. Extension: As compared to society the State is less extended. While the society includes social, economic, religious, cultural, political, all types of human relationships, the State includes only political relationships. The society is more extensive than State and the State is a more limited concept.

2. Basis of organisation: In the words of Barker, "'The area of society is voluntary co-operation, its energy that of goodwill, its method that of elasticity while the area of the State is that of mechanical action, the energy force, its method rigidity.' Thus, the basis of organisation of the society and State is different.

3. Rules or norms: The laws of the State are different from the social norms. At their back is the sanction of political authority and system of punishment. They are therefore, obligatory. The social norms, on the other hand, are made by customs and traditions. This disobedience does not involve any punishment except social censor. Most of the people therefore, while they are afraid of state laws, have not much regard for social norms.

4. Authority: Public opinion rules in society, which is not very effective. The state, on the other hand, has political authority which compels the citizens to obey the dictates of the State.

5. Land: Society is not confined to a particular land. It may be scattered in the whole world. The State, on the other hand, is limited in a particular piece of land, big or small.

6. Area: While the area of society includes the whole man, the State is not so extensive. Man may live without state but not without society.

7. Period: Historically the society preceded the State. In the words of Maclver, "In the earliest phases, among hunters, fishermans, root diggers and fruit gatherers, there have been social groups which knew nothing or almost nothing of the State. Today there remain simple people, such as certain groups of Eskimos, which have no recognidable political organisation."

8. Meaning: While the word society has been used in several meanings such as general society or a society or association etc., the word state conveys a definite meaning. Its connotation and denotation is more clear.

9. Aims: The aims of society are more comprehensive than that of the state. Its aims are economic, political, social, biological etc., while the aims of the State are only political.

10. Membership: The membership of a society is natural but voluntary while the membership of a state is acquired but obligatory. Society is a voluntary and state compulsory organisation.

In spite of the above distinctions, both society and State aim at human welfare, are organisation of human beings, are natural, ancient and results of gradual evolution to reach the present forms.

QUESTIONS FOR EXERCISE

1. Define State and discuss the elements which go to make a State.
2. Define State. What are its essential attributes?
3. Define State and discuss its changing notions.
4. What do you understand by the following notions of the State:
   (a) Ethical notion and legal notion,
   (b) Power notion and notion of class structure.
5. Distinguish State from society, community, association and the Government.

8

The Rise and Growth of the Modern Nation States

The origin of State is veiled in the midst of obscurity. No one can say definitely when the State might be said to have come into existence. Its growth was a slow and steady evolution extending over a long period of time. Its starting point was the family, and its discipline was the crude form of the Government. The first distinctively unit was perhaps the tribe. It was a great transition when man entered the stage of Statehood from the tribal stage. It took place when the small tribes grew up and were divided into groups like nobles, free men and slaves. There were conflicts between the groups in the tribe. To resolve the conflict there was felt the need of regulating the activities of men in groups. In various parts of the world most of the tribes reached the stature of State. The modern States are known as the Nation States. They are the result of long historical process.

STAGES IN THE GROWTH OF MODERN NATION STATE

1. The oriental empires: According to Gettell, "The tribal States were usually small in size and were governed by the Chiefs often assisted by advisory councils. Some were nomadic, others were permanently settled in definite areas. The stronger tribes often attacked the weaker ones and acquired their territory. The members of the tribe obeyed their leader. After some times, these tribal chiefs or leaders became the ruler. Thus, empires like Egypt, Babylon etc., came into existence." It is said, "War begot Kings". These empires were not very stable. There was centralisation of power. The units were given autonomy on local affairs. The early empires were the results of wars and victories. The rulers were despots. The slavery was prevalent. The rulers were backed by the religious priests. The empires were big but the administration was weak and inefficient.

The revolts were frequent. Due to frequent warfare the empires were divided into pieces. The early States had humble beginnings in the warm and fertile planes, watered by great rivers. There were rich valleys where production was plentiful with the least amount of exertion. The rapid growth of population led to the division of soçiety. Those who possessed surplus wealth, leisure and power easily dominated over the weaker classes. Some very great empires arose as the Sumerians, Assyrian, the Persian, the Egyptian and the Chinese. Their authority rested on fear and despotism. Thus the first type of States which rose in the historical times were the imperial states in the orient. The oriental empires were inland or continental powers. The early empires were subject to revolts and aggressions. They were soon divided into pieces.

2. The Greek city states: The second important stage in the development of Sate was reached in Greece.

Features of the Greek City States

1. They were independent and self-governed. It was a great experiment in the art of self-government.
2. They were the development of the local patriotism and self-sufficiency.
3. The natural environment of Greece was congenial for the development of local patriotism and self-sufficiency.
4. The city states of Greece were the typical examples of direct democracy.
5. The Greeks were passionately devoted to their city states.
6. Citizenship implied a direct and active participation in all the functions of civil and military life.
7. In spite of high degree of excellence achieved by the Greek city states they suffered from certain drawbacks. The intense love of independence verging on separation ultimately resulted in their collapse.

3. Roman empire: While the Greeks gave' quality, idealism and genius through their small city states, the Romans achieved much through their empire and distinguished themselves as great political organisers, conquerors, law givers and creator of peace and uniformity in institution over their far flung empire.

Roman Republic was an aristocratic republic. The whole authority was into the hands of two annually elected consults. Rome became the centre of civilisation. The population was divided between Patricians and Plebians. The Patricians were the working class. They were exploited by the Plebians but not like Greek slaves. By the close of the first century B.C. almost whole of the civilised Western world was united in a single political system. The rise of Augustus as Emperor announced the fall of the Roman Republic.

An effective system of centralised administration developed to hold the empire together. The whole empire was divided into provinces and each province was put under the charge of a Roman official. The Senate had an important position but the emperor exerted control over it. The aristocrats, the Church and the emperor joined hands to exploit and crush the liberties of the people. The institution of democracy was suppressed. As such an empire could not last long, it disintegrated and the feudal chiefs took over the administration in their hands.

4. The feudal state: When the Roman Empire disintegrated there was a period of confusion. The vast Roman Empire was broken into pieces. Vast territories fell into the hands of powerful nobles or feudal lords. A feudal community developed around the personality of the noble. Feudalism is a form of Society and Government which prevailed in Europe from 476 A.D. — 1500 A.D. This type of society came to be established on the fruits of the Roman Empire. According to the feudal theory, the Kings were the vassals of the emperor who in his turn was the vassal of God. They received their dominion as fiefs to be held on condition of loyalty to their Lord. Each King divided his dominions into large parts and granted each part to a noble called the tenant in chief. He continued to hold the land as long as he fulfilled his obligations. After his death the rights and duties of vassal age passed on to his heirs of the lord. The tenant in chief divided their lands into smaller units and gave them to their vassals on similar conditions. The process of division and transference continued to many stages. The feudal system was marked by an absence of the idea of a sovereign power.

5. The Christian church and the state: When the forces of feudalism were promoting separatist tendencies, the Church and Holy Roman Empire proved themselves to be strong unifying factors. The idea of a universal Christian society prevailed in the middle of medieval period. Thus society was to be governed by the spiritual authority of the Church. Out of the confusion of the feudal system emerged the superior authority of the Church. It was able to provide a centralised authority and order. The Pope claimed his superiority over all the princes. A separate system of law and courts developed for the clergy. The Church was well organised. It functioned like a State.

The Renaissance and the Reformation did much to undermine the authority of the Church. The reformists exposed the weakness, corruption, immorality and false teachings of the Church. They supported the idea of individual liberty. The Reformation movement gave a rude shock to the ideas of the universal Church and the Holy Roman Empire.

6. The national government of the modern times: In the 16th and the 17th centuries a capitalist class was formed. They amassed wealth and became very powerful to influence the society. Renaissance and Reformation added to their wealth. The Feudal Lords could not compete with the capital and industrial economy. The feudal order declined and capitalism came to dominate the economy. It demanded nationalism. This gave birth to liberalism which demanded liberty for the individual. The geographical exploration, the discovery of gun powder and the ideas of liberal thinkers had a favourable effect on the institution of absolute monarchy. There appeared strong national monarchies on the ruins of feudalism. But monarchical absolutism did not remain unchallenged very long. The common people began to question the duty of passive obedience to governmental authorities. There was a prolonged contest for political authority between the King and the people. The Glorious Revolution of England, the American War of Independence and the French Revolution played a very important role in the transition from royal absolutism to democracy. The common man realised that the Government existed not for its own sake but for the good of the governed.

In the 19th century great movements of national unification took place first in Germany and Italy. Nationalism became a passion everywhere and people were in favour of establishing national states. In the 20th century people opposed colonial rule and despotic rule. Russia established Communist rule and removed despotic rule of Czar in 1917. After Second World War, many countries got themselves relieved from colonial rule in Asia, Africa and Latin America. India, Burma, Egypt, Indonesia, Ghana, Nigeria, Algeria, Vietnam etc., were the new countries which gained freedom from colonial rale. These countries that found their economies completely shattered by the colonialists are now busy in rebuilding their economy. They are called developing countries or third world countries. They follow the policy of non-alignment to safeguard their hard earned independence.

MEANING OF NATION

One of the most satisfactory definition of nation was advanced by Ernest Barker more than forty years ago: A nation is a body of men, inhabiting a definite territory, who normally are drawn from different races, but possess a common stock of thoughts and feelings acquired and transmitted during the course of a common history; who on the whole and in the main, though more in the past than in the present, include in that common stock a common religious belief; who generally and as a rule use a common language as the vehicle of their thoughts and feelings; and who, besides common thoughts and feelings, also cherish a common will, and accordingly form, or tend to form, a separate state for the expression and realisation of that will.[1]

What Constitutes a Nation?

In his famous lecture at the Sorbonne in 1882, Ernest Renan said, "What constitutes a nation, is not speaking the same tongue or belonging to the same ethnic group, but having accomplished great things in common in the past and the wish to accomplish them in the future."

A nation is not necessarily the human and physical incarnation of a State. A State may composed of several nations. We often speak of the multinational state. But as in modern parlance the terms *nation* and *state* are used almost interchangeably, the major political units which exist today may appropriately be called *nation-states*. As Hans Morgenthau suggests, "the nation needs a state. 'One nation — one state' is thus the political postulate of nationalism; the nation-state is its idea."[2]

Meaning of Nationality

Nationality may be defined as the distinctive quality of a group which has a common origin and tradition. It may imply both national character and the spirit of belongingness to a nation or a group of people possessed of such a spirit. The sociologist Louis Wirth defines a nationality as "a people who, because of the belief in this common descent and their mission in the world, by virtue of their common cultural heritage and historical career aspire to sovereignty over a territory or seek to maintain or enlarge their political or cultural influence in the face of opposition."[3] Frederick Hertz defined it as "a community formed by the will to be a nation."[4] It is "nothing material or mechanical," observed Arnold J. Toynbee, "but a subjective psychological feeling in a living people."[5]

1. *National Character and the Factors in Its Formation* (London, 1927), p. 17.
2. Morgenthau, p. 160.
3. Louis Wirth, "*Types of Nationalism,*" *American Journal of Sociology*, XLI (May, 1936), 723.
4. Frederick Hertz, *Nationality in History and Politics*, 3rd ed. (London, 1951), p. 12.
5. Arnold J. Toynbee, *Nationality and War* (London, 1915), p. 13.

Meaning of National Self-determination

According to Hayes, *National self-determination* means "the right of individuals to determine the sovereign state to which they would belong and the form of government under which they would live."[6] It is the principle by which nationalities justify their efforts to acquire "nationhood" in the form of "statehood".

Meaning of Patriotism

Patriotism may be defined as love of country. It is not necessarily associated with the nation-state. The addresses of Pericles to the Athenians, of Hannibal to the Carthaginians, of Cicero to the Romans are among the greatest examples of patriotic oratory. Today, however, patriotism, like nationalism, is associated with loyalty to the nation-state. Though it inspires some of the finest of human sentiments, it can become intense narrow and infinitely dangerous. In its exaggerated form it is known as *chauvinism*.

MEANING OF NATIONALISM

1. Hayes: Nationalism consists of "a modern emotional fusion and exaggeration of two very old phenomena — nationality and patriotism".[7]

2. Hans Kohn: "Nationalism is first and foremost a state of mind, an act of consciousness."[8]

3. Professor Louis L. Snyder: "...Nationalism a product of political, economic, social, and intellectual factors at a certain stage in history, is a condition of mind, feeling, or sentiment of a group of people living in a well-defined geographical area, speaking a common language, possessing a literature in which the aspirations of the nation have been expressed, attached to common traditions and common customs, venerating its own heroes, and, in some cases, having a common religion."[9]

CRITICISM OF NATIONALISM

In 20th century nationalism became "the common form of political life all over the earth," but "everywhere nationalism differs in character according to the specific historic conditions and the peculiar social structure of each country." Due to the "stress upon national sovereignty and cultural distinctiveness" it has become "a deeply divisive force." When it "spread to Eastern Europe and later to Asia...nationalism tended

---

6. Hayes, p. 10.
7. Carlton J.H. Hayes, *Essays on Nationalism* (New York: The Macmillan Company, 1926), p. 6.
8. Hans Kohn, *The Idea of Nationalism* (New York: The Macmillan Company, 1944), p. 10.
9. Snyder, pp. 196-97.

toward the closed society, in which the individual counted for less than the strength and authority of the national whole."[10]

"Nationalism," said Snyder, "is neither wholly logical nor rational. Its roots lie in the illogical, irrational, and fantastic world of the unconscious." It is "in part a psychological response to grave threats of insecurity." Since it "is not innate instinct, but rather a socially conditioned, synthetic sentiment," it cannot be understood without reference to the findings of psychology and psychoanalysis.[11]

The Dangers of Nationalism

Modern nationalism was associated with democracy and liberty. But today far from promoting democracy and liberty nationalism often places these blessings in jeopardy. It has often proved to be wholly compatible with autocracy and totalitarianism. Unless carefully watched it tends to restrict the area of human freedom. Nationalism and liberty are not coterminous, while the former may prove to be an ephemeral phenomenon in history, the latter will long endure.

Nationalism is generally condemned as an evil force because it tends to degenerate into ever more intolerant forms which have been a major cause of war. In the final chapter of his *Essays on Nationalism*, Hayes distinguished between nationalism as a historical fact and nationalism as a belief. As a belief, nationalism has been "a curse and nothing but a curse." Rabindranath Tagore held that nationalism was a great menace because it called for a "strenuous effort after strength and efficiency" and thereby "drains man's energy from his higher nature where he is self-sacrificing and creative."[12] Arnold Toynbee's *A Study of History* contains many references to crimes committed in the name of the nation-state and of nationalism during the last three or four hundred years. As Vladimir Solovyev wrote about nationalism: "In its extreme form it destroys a nation, for it makes it the enemy of mankind."[13]

INSTRUMENTS OF NATIONALISM

The schools, the press, and the radio are the most powerful instruments for the propagation of nationalism. These instruments are deliberately used to serve the State. Nationalistic propaganda is widespread even in the free world. In America nationalistic propaganda is found in textbooks in use in all schools, from the primary to the most advanced levels. Texts

10. *Prophets and Peoples: Studies in Nineteenth Century Nationalism* (New York: The Macmillan Company, 1946), p. 4.
11. Snyder, pp. 89-110.
12. Rabindranath Tagore, *Nationalism* (London, 1917), p. 110.
13. Kohn, *Prophets and People*, p. 205.

have been criticised as "un-American" because they gave too favourable treatment to unicameralism, social security, and the United Nations. In Los Angeles, local pressures were generated to prevent instruction in the public schools on the work of UNESCO.

SYMBOLS OF NATIONALISM

Nationalism is propagated by the use of symbols and "social myths." Among the most commonly used symbols are patriotic slogans and songs, flags, uniforms, shrines and monuments, public spectacles, pageantry, and ritualism. These symbols may encourage love of country. Beliefs in them are among the finest of human sentiments. However, these same symbols may and do serve dangerous masters when they are used to instill hatred of other peoples and a false sense of the nation's "glory" and "destiny." As Hayes said, "Integral nationalism has surpassed all its predecessors in rites and ceremonies, in mysticism and devotion, and likewise in intolerance."[14] This has been observed in Fascist Italy, Nazi Germany, Communist Russia, and Communist China.

FORMS OF NATIONALISM

Nationalism defined, it does has diverse forms which can be analysed in different ways. It has been described as "good" and "bad," constructive and destructive, material and spiritual, conscious and sub-conscious. Hans Kohn has drawn a most useful distinction between (1) nationalism in the Western world, and (2) nationalism outside the Western world. It helps to explain "the process of cultural influence and resistance in non-European areas."[15] The most complete analysis of the origins of nationalism of Kohn's *The Idea of Nationalism*. Among the best summaries of the historical evolution of *Nationalism* are Hayes, *The Historical Evolution of Modern Nationalism*; Shafer, *Nationalism*: *Myth and Reality*; Kohn, *Nationalism*: *Its Meaning and History*.

Stages of Nationalism

1. Views of Hayes: Hayes described five principal successive types of stages of Nationalism — humanitarian, Jacobin, traditional, liberal, and integral. The first four types originated in the 18th century and took distinctive form in the period of the French Revolution and Napoleon and during the 19th century. Integral nationalism was a growth of the 20th century, characterised by the policies of totalitarian states.

14. Hayes, *Historical Evolution*, p. 299.
15. Snyder, p. 121.

2. Views of Wright: A similar classification of the stages in the development of nationalism is presented in Quincy Wright's monumental work, *A Study of War*[16] Wright discussed in succession medieval, monarchical, revolutionary, liberal, and totalitarian nationalism.

3. Views of Snyder: Professor Snyder discerned four stages in the Chronology of Nationalism. Integrative Nationalism (1815-71), Disruptive Nationalism (1871-90), Aggressive Nationalism (1890-1945), and Contemporary Nationalism (since 1945). During the first stage nationalism was a unifying force, expressed in the unification of Italy and of Germany. During the second, subject nationalities of Austria-Hungary and other multinational states clamoured for independence. During the third, "Nationalism became virtually identical with aggressive imperialism," and the "collision of opposing national interests", led to two world wars. During the early years of the contemporary stage "political nationalism asserted itself in the form of widespread revolts against European masters," and communism "in its Stalinist form took on the trappings of nationalism in the Soviet Union."[17]

NATIONALISM IN THE 20TH CENTURY

Before the outbreak of World War I, many people believed that while the 19th century had been an age of nationalism, the 20th century would be an age of internationalism. However, in the 20th century nationalism assumed everywhere virulent forms. It continued to shape the international politics of the Western World. It became a worldwide phenomenon, attaining new heights of emotionalism. In the newly emergent states of Asia and Africa; it achieved a curious kind of linkage with international communism. It was one of the underlying causes of the First World War. Professor Hayes said, "Nationalism paved the way of statesmen and prepared the mind of peoples for the World War.... Its immediate cause was the murderous activity of a secret nationalistic society of Jugoslavs. Its fighting was done by "nations in arms," whose morale was sustained by nationalist propaganda.... Its most obvious immediate result was the triumph of the principle of national self-determination in central and eastern Europe. The last of the non-national empires on the continent were shattered — the Austrian, the Russian and the Ottoman and from their ruins were constructed new or enlarged nation states.... The World War not only issued from nationalism but led to a more intense nationalism. In Europe the newest nation states almost

16. See the section on the evolution of nationalism in the chapter entitled "Nationalism and War" II, 1004-1009.
17. Snyder, pp. 116-17.

instantly passed from liberal pronouncements to illiberal conduct and speedily vied with older nation states in establishing nationalist tariffs, armies, schools, and other agencies of propaganda and in discriminating socially if not legally against dissident minorities."[18]

KINDS OF 20TH CENTURY NATIONALISM

1. Totalitarian Nationalism

(A) *Fascism*: Fascism gained power in Italy only three years after Versailles, in Germany and Japan in the early thirties, and in Spain in 1936. It was the first lush flowering of modern totalitarianism. It was a form of Nationalism more powerful, more encompassing, more brutal, and more dangerous than any previous variety. To quote Kohn "Though, this fascist nationalism took various forms in different countries, according to their national traditions and social structures, it represented in all its forms a total repudiation of the liberal ideas of the 17th and the 18th century revolutions, of the rights of the individual and of the desirability of a rational international order based upon the equality of men and nations.... Nationalism in its fascist period...assumed for beyond anything known in the period before 1914, an absolutist and extremist self-assertiveness, glorifying war between nations or races as the supreme and final meaning of life and history."[19] It was this type of Nationalism which culminated in World War II.

(B) *Communism*: Unlike fascism communism is an international and not a national gospel. In practice, however, both within and outside the Communist world, communism has become increasingly nationalistic. The Soviet rulers posed as champions of nationalism in Asia and as enemies of colonialism and imperialism. Native Communist leaders identifying themselves with nationalist movements, scored notable successes in Indo-China, Korea, and China. The Chinese Communists succeeded in taking over the nationalist revolution that had been underway ever since it had overthrown the Manchu dynasty in 1911-12.

During World War II, when German armies were occupying the western part of Russia, the Russian people were exhorted to rise up in defence of "Mother Russia", In the post-war years, the Soviet government encouraged the nationalism of Russia's many minorities, permitting their cultural, political, and economic institutions to be "national" in form as long as they are "proletarian" in spirit and substance.

18 Hayes, *Nationalism*, p. 247.

19. I. Kohn, *Nationalism and Internationalism in the 19th and the 20th centuries*, p. 210.

Since his open break with the rest of the Communist world, Tito has relied primarily on Yugloslav nationalism. Elsewhere in the Communist world communism has gone national.

2. Integral Nationalism

Charles Maurras and Maurice Barres, have called "integral nationalism," the characteristic form of the 20th century. Maurras himself once described integral nationalism as "the exclusive pursuit of national policies, the absolute maintenance of national integrity, and the steady increase of national power — for a nation declines when it loses military might." Hans Morgenthau has insisted that there is a basic difference between the nationalism of the 19th century and the "nationalistic universalism" of today:

"To call by the same name what inspired the oppressed and competing nationalities of the 19th century and what drives the superpowers of the mid-twentieth century into deadly combat, is to obscure the fundamental change which separates our age from the preceding one. The nationalism of today, which is really a nationalistic universalism, has only one thing in commons with the nationalism of the 19th century — the nation as the ultimate point of reference for political loyalties and actions. But here the similarity ends. For the Nationalism of the 19th century the nation is the ultimate goal of political action, the endpoint of the political development beyond which there are other nationalisms with similar and equally justifiable goals. For the nationalistic universalism of the mid-twentieth century the nation is but the starting point of a universal mission whose ultimate goal reaches to the confines of the political world. While nationalism wants one nation in a State and nothing else, the nationalistic universalism of our age claims for one nation and one state the right to impose its own valuations and standards of action upon all the other nations."[20] Morgenthau's "nationalistic universalism" is not nationalism but a peculiar interpretation of the foreign policy objectives of the superpowers.

Thus the 20th century has proved to be another age of nationalism. Nationalism expanded to the emerging countries of Asia and Africa. It survived in the 'Western World where it made devil's efforts to formulate common defence.

CONSTITUENT ELEMENTS OF NATION

What are the constituent elements of a nation? The answers given by scholars to this question are not identical. Some have emphasised the

20. Morgenthau, p. 337.

objective basis of nation. Barker has treated topography as a fundamental element in the development of a nation. Arthur Keith has made no distinction between nation and race. But some other scholars have stressed the subjective basis of nation. Among them are Earnest Renan, J.S. Mill, Ramsey Muir, and William McDougall.

Objective Elements

Prominent among the objective constituent elements of nation are the following:

1. Geographical unity: Hertz and Barker have placed much emphasis upon geographical unity as one of the constituent elements of a nation. Barker has written that if he were asked to evolve a formula for the creation of nation he would suggest that one should start by taking a part of land. In order to keep the residents together there must be some kind of organisation or government. If there was no language previously, then let a language circulate for its own influence. Let some beliefs and worships unify the sentiments of the people of the community, and through the influence of centuries a nation would be ready after some time. There is no doubt that the presence of a common homeland helps much in the development of national sentiment but there are other examples in which the nation has existed even without any geographical area. For example, the Jews retained their nationality and continued as a nation over a period of 2000 years even without any geographical area, simply on the basis of religion. Their communal sentiments were centred in Palestine and after the Second World War they established a new nation Israel. The example of the Jews does not prove that a definite geographical area or geographical unity is not an essential element in the evolution of a nation. It merely proves that a nation can continue to exist even without a geographical area.

2. Unity of language: Language is the medium for the expression of emotions and thoughts and hence it can do much towards the evolution of a national sentiment. This leads to the development of a literature and a culture which in its turn promotes national unity. There is a close affinity between nation and language, because thought and sentiment have intimate relation with speech. Language is not mere words. Each word is charged with association that touch feelings and evoke thoughts. One cannot share these thoughts and feelings unless one can unlock their association by having the key of language. Ramsay Muir attributes more importance to language than to race as a constituent element of nation. Undoubtedly, unity of language is very much important for the nation. Today, the conflict ranging over the language question in India has seriously endangered national unity. Due to this reason Hindi has been accepted as the national and state language in the Indian Constitution and efforts are being made for its development. This will influence profoundly the development of sentiment of nationality and the organisation of the country.

But this does not prove that in the event of there being more than one language the existence of a nation is impossible. India itself is a precise example of this. In Switzerland three languages are spoken, French, German and Italian. Two languages are spoken in Belgium. The Scottish dialect varies considerably from that of England. This does not create any difficulty in the national unity of these countries. The same language is spoken in Great Britain and U.S.A. and yet they are two distinct nations. These examples do not prove that language has no importance in the development of a nation. All that they do indicate is that under certain circumstances, the national unity of a country can be maintained intact in spite of multiplicity in language.

3. Community of race: Some thinkers, of which Arthur Keith is one example, have disdained from distinguishing between race and nation. Zimmerman has observed that an element of a particular kind of community sentiment is embedded in nationality. In this the element of common racial descent is probably the most important. It has also been emphasised by Lord Bryce, Leacock and Burgess. And yet it is manifestly impractical to look upon similarity of race as essential, since in no country can one find purity of a race. Pillsbury has written that generally race no longer has any importance in the development of nationality. Today, there is no pure nation. In England there has been a mixture of the Celt, Roman, Angle, Briton, Saxon and Norman races. In India many races, among them Dravid, Shak, Arya, Hun, Moghul, and Turk, have congregated and mixed. And this is the history of all countries.

4. Community of religion: The Jewish example indicates the importance of community of religion as the constituent element of nation. The main basis of the nationality of Poland, Japan and Ireland was religion. It was the power of a unified religion which helped to maintain the unity of Greeks in the face of the injustice of the Khalifas of Turkey. The main base of the newly born nation Pakistan is religion. But even than a community of religion cannot be regarded as an essential element of nation. In most modern nations the State is secular and the followers of different religions are to be found in the same country. But of course there can be little doubt that a common unity of religion strengthens the sentiment of nationality.

5. Political unity and independence: According to some scholars, political unity and independence are necessary prerequisites for the development of the sentiment of nationality. In the Middle Ages when India was divided into numerous small states, the sentiment of nationality was not as much developed as it is now due to political unity in the country. During the reign of the British the sentiment of nationality was in a dormant state. This is true, and further, it is also true that the injustices heaped upon the people encouraged and were instrumental in the development of nationality in India. Thus, independence cannot be considered to be an essential element of nation. Similarly, a nation can continue to exist even in the absence of political unity. Barnes and Becker have written that during 1772-1794 when Germany, Austria and Russia divided Poland into pieces and Polish government had vanished, even then the Polish national group continued to exist to develop and to exhibit firmness in its function. In this way, political unity and independence are not essential elements for a nation though nevertheless, they do assist in the development and growth of nationality, and in strengthening the nation.

Subjective Elements

In addition to the above mentioned objective elements some subjective elements also make important contributions to the growth of a nation. Some scholars attach greater importance to these elements rather than the other elements. Renan and Mill write, "There must be a consciousness of a heroic past, true glory, common experience and sacrifices, feelings of pride and shame, joy and grief, connected with the past." Of the many subjective elements some are the following:

1. Community of interests and traditions: The subjective elements of a nation consist in the awareness of the traditions of present interests and ideals towards which all are similarly disposed. In this way, in the growth of nation a community of interests and traditions is of considerable importance. In India, the Hindus and Muslims were engaged in a very prolonged conflict and in the end the Muslim League rested only when it had formed a Muslim nation in the form of Pakistan, In the background of this development was the reality of a fundamental disagreement and incongruity in the traditions of the Hindus and Muslims. While Hindus pay respect and homage to all the ancient history, culture, philosophy, religion and traditions, etc., of India, many Muslims have faith only in the history, saints, divinities, traditions, etc., of Arab and Iran. Due to this reason, in spite of the indefatigable efforts of such leaders as Mahatma Gandhi, Hindus and Muslims could not find any common ground on which to create a nation. The traditions and beliefs of many Muslims who live in India even today differ from those of Hindus and many among them fail to recognise any identity in the interests of the Hindus and their own interests. In this way there does not appear to be a sufficient growth of the national sentiment in them and they are often caught indulging in anti-national activities. Hence, a community of interests and traditions is essential for the unity of the nation.

2. Community of political aspirations: A community of political aspirations is of great importance for the growth of a nation. Take India as an example. Here, when people aspired to make an independent nation by ousting the British rule, extremely powerful national sentiments were generated and people united, forgetting their differences. The demand for an autonomous government has generated national unity in many countries. This is the history of Poland, Czechoslovakia, Hungary, and Yugoslavia, etc.

3. Community sentiment: Community sentiment is so much important as one of the constitutive elements of nation, that MacIver and other sociologists have deemed it fit to define nationality on its basis. According to this view nationality is a type of community sentiment created by historical circumstances and supported by a strong common psychological factor due to which the members of the nation aspire to have a common government exclusively their own. It is this consciousness of nationality which makes the nation. In modern times the modern nationalities have been constituted by the power of an idea and not by the call of the blood. Toynbee has dubbed this community sentiment as popular will and has recognised it as the main element of nationality.

From the foregoing description of the constituent element of nation it would have become apparent that among them the more important are the subjective rather than the objective elements, Hertz has enumerated the following elements which are essential to a nation:

1. People should have desire to be one nation.
2. They should particularly endeavour for unity and strength, and this may be realised only when there is political, economic, religious and social equality among them.
3. They should be free from foreign rule and domination.
4. They should have a definite desire for distinctiveness and originality.
5. In particular, they should strive for honour, prestige, renown and moral as well as military superiority or ascendancy.

IS THERE A NATIONAL CHARACTER?

The definition of national character may be best given as the sum total of interests, aspirations, ideals and traditions, widespread and influential enough to mould and present the nation's image to others. The national character of a country has been described in a number of ways. The first to contemplate upon this problem were the Greek writers, who cogitated upon the national character of the various City States. The citizens of Sparta were considered to be more active and strong, and the Athenians more talkative. De Tocqueville studied the national character of America a century ago. Among more modern studies the names of A. Siegfried's *America Comes of Age* and D.W. Brogan's *The American Character* may be suggested. The Chinese national character finds representation in Lin Yutang's *My Country* and *My People*. The national characters of various countries or nations have been expressed symbolically, for example the American is represented by Uncle Sam, the English by John Bull and the Russian by Bear. In Europe, different qualities are treated as characteristics of different individual nations. Generally, the English are believed to be reserved, the Germans disciplined and the French volatile. In India, Bengalis are considered art lovers, the Punjabis materialists and the Rajputs brave.

Many scholars have pondered over the question whether there is any national character. Montesque has maintained that the character of a nation is expressed in its peculiar traits and these are influenced by climate, culture, forms of law and government, customs and religion, etc. As a consequence of the inter-action of these factors one finds unique kinds of sentiments, aspirations, thoughts and activities, etc., in the people of every nation. Of the other thinkers who have contemplated upon this problem, those that can be mentioned are McDougall, Hertz, Morris Ginsberg and Blackburn.

McDougall has expressed his views on the question of national character in his book *Group Mind*. In his opinion each national group has its own genius and its character is conditioned by it. This national character is profoundly influenced by geographical peculiarities, purity of the race and freedom of movement. According to McDougall, different races have innate or inherent mental differences which are permanent and influence the national character. For example, the Negroes are carefree, fatalistic and exhibit unrestrained emotional violence. The Irish are poetical, the English empiricists and the French of a deductive bent of mind, Asians are fatalists, The Indians are intensely intellectual and moral.

McDougall's thinking appears to indicate that national character is static but experience does not bear this out. There is no doubt that differences in individuals can be found even when in communal form and that there is a national character, but it is not permanent and static and neither is it to be found equally in all individuals. As a general rule, it may be true that Bengalis are comparatively more art loving than the Punjabis and that Rajputs are more brave but this can hardly be interpreted as meaning that all Bengalis are art lovers and all Rajputs are brave. Broadly speaking, the Indians may be more religious than the Americans but one may nevertheless find religious people in America and irreligious atheists in India. Besides, even the common character of the same nation or people is continually changing. For example, one will not find that bravery in the present day Rajput which one is wont to expect of him. Looking at it from this viewpoint one is apt to realise the correctness of the proposition that "National character is always in the making, it is not something given once for all." The development and growth of national character is influenced by geography, economic conditions, culture, political organisation, class structure, religion and language, to select only some of the factors. In this way, national character is unstable and flexible.

WHAT IS NATIONALITY?

Nationality is a cultural and ethnic concept. Its characteristic trait is spiritual. It is a group of people who speak the same language and cherish common historical traditions thus constituting distinct cultural society.[21] By acquiring political unity and sovereign independence nationality becomes nation-state.[22] It generates a sense of unity among the people. Sentiment of nationality is the community sentiment to be found in the members of a nation, which keeps their organisation. It is the feeling of a people who have a common history, common language, common culture, and who live in a common geographical area. It is a mental state, a spiritual condition based upon common traditions, common customs, common reminiscences of the past and common future aspirations.

Nationality and Statehood

In distinguishing between nationality and statehood it may be said that while nationality is a way of living, thinking, feeling, statehood

21. "Nationality is a group of people who speak either the same language or closely related dialects, who cherish common historical traditions and thus constitute a distinct cultural society,...a nationality by acquiring political unity and sovereign independence becomes nation state."

— Hayes, *Essay on Nationalism*, (1962), p. 5.

22. "Nationality is a people which has not yet become organised politically." In ideal sense, "it is an inspiration towards united national existence." — Rose

is inseparable from civilised way of living. Like religion, nationality is subjective, the statehood, on the other hand, is objective. While nationality is a psychological condition of mind statehood is a political condition of law.[23]

In this way sentiment of nationality differs from sentiment of nation or state. Political organisation as well as political independence and domination are not essential for it. It is a mental state, a spiritual condition based upon the memories of common traditions, common customs, a common past and the aspiration of a common future. It is psychological. It is in the minds of the nation's members. The nation rests on it. The existence of a nation cannot even be contemplated in its absence.

SENTIMENT OF NATIONALITY AND WORLD PEACE

Examining the sentiment of nationality as actually found in different nations, one comes across two of its forms — a healthy and a distorted form. In the first form it had its origin in the Western Europe in the 18th century. At that time not only was it one which was to form a nation but also one which demanded supreme loyalty of the individual.

Now-a-days this form of nationality is being communicated to the Eastern world. In its original and healthy form it threaded together various human groups and gave them strength and organisation, made them independent states by freeing them from foreign domination, ousted the old feudal states and in their place created the present state governments. It established modern democracies, ended the rule of the privileged classes in old states and reinstated them on the democratic basis of the common public. In this way, the sentiment took a large share in making the base of the state more comprehensive.

Having performed such useful function, nationality became progressively exclusive like the other sentiments of social solidarity. Its distorted form was manifested in the shape of chauvinism and imperialism. The sentiment of chauvinism pays attention to only its own nation, wants to do everything for it solely and does not keep in view similar interests of other nations. This sentiment limits man's mental horizon to his own nation exclusively and makes him the blind supporter and follower of his own nation even though it may be in the wrong and may be harming others. The sole ideal of the states which are engrossed in sentiments of a similar kind is to augment their own power and status. When these states desire to carry out the economic exploitation of

23. "Nationality like religion is subjective, statehood is objective; nationality is psychological, statehood is political; nationality is a condition of mind, statehood is a condition of law; nationality is a spiritual possession, statehood is an enforceable obligation; nationality is a way of thinking, feeling and living, statehood is a condition inseparable from all civilised ways of living." — Zimmerin

weaker states by depriving them of their political independence in order to gain authority over areas producing raw materials and over markets of manufactured goods with a view to their own economic progress one finds the second distorted form of nationality.

It is evident from this lengthy exposition that in its distorted form, nationality is a curse to international peace. It is this distorted sentiment of a nationality which led many European countries, in the last century, to include many areas of Africa and Asia in their sovereignty. Germany and Italy became envious of the British and French colonies in Asia and Africa. It injured their sense of national prestige to be left behind any other nation in the race of imperialism. Hence in Italy and Germany, preparations were made for war and military training was imparted on a large scale. In the leadership of Nazi party under Hitler, Germany gained so much in military strength that it endangered the freedom of all the other nations of the world. The sense of nationality was deeply ingrained in Hitler's Germany. A majority of citizens were anxious to sacrifice their all for the nation. These sentiments of sacrifice and hard work have been a cause for pride in any nation, but in their exclusive form Germans dreamt of spreading their sovereignty over the entire world. In their own elated condition they had no thought for the national prestige of other nations. Italy was in much the same condition. In this way, twice did chauvinism plunge the world into world wars. The First World War which lasted from 1914 to 1918 and the Second World War which lasted from 1939 to 1945 were both the results of this chauvinism.

After the First World War, the League of Nations was formed to solve international problems. But due to chauvinism the League of Nations became the ground for intrigues and manifestly failed to attain its objectives. Following the Second World War, the United Nations Organisation was established to solve international problems and to establish world peace. It has undoubtedly had a better measure of success than the previous international organisation but this is not sufficient in any way. Many nations have no regard for it whatsoever. The South African policy of apartheid is continuing in spite of repeated cautions to the contrary from the U.N.O. The major nations like Russia, America, Britain and France are engaged in gaining their own objectives through political intrigues. Today, the most difficult obstacle in the path of U.N.O. is a strong and one-sided nationality. International peace is impossible as long as this continues to exist.

But it is only the one-sided and distorted form of nationality which is a curse to international peace. The healthy form of nationality is a blessing for it. It is the pure and healthy form which is causing the gradual degeneration of imperialism. It is due to this that imperialist powers were ignominiously crushed in Egypt. It is the support given by it that is allowing small nations to raise their proud heads and to make valuable contribution to the solution of international problems having been freed from foreign domination. Actually, the sentiment of nationality is a strong force. Its use or misuse depends on man. If he has learnt any lesson from the two world wars he will have to keep a check upon Chauvinism. Internationalism and Chauvinism are mutually contradictory sentiments but healthy nationalism and internationalism are mutually complementary. Internationalism will lose its power if it excludes the sentiment of nationality. What is needed to strengthen the sentiment of internationalism is to make the sentiment of nationality more pure, healthy and comprehensive and not to exclude it. Only then can international peace be established. It is this pure and singular world peace for which India is endeavouring today.

Thus an international order requires that the progress of any country should not be such as to hinder the progress of other nations. In addition to this, the powerful nations should assist the weaker nations. In this way, an international order requires peaceful coexistence, mutual help and international brotherhood. International law is insufficient to make an adjustment between a sentiment of nationality and these requirements. For this, what is needed is the development of a sentiment of internationalism, and this can be achieved by the extension of a healthy nationality. United Nations Organisation is an important step in this direction and its various branches do afford numerous nations to co-operate with each other on various projects but in order that these efforts may be blessed with success, there must be intense propaganda for the promotion of the sentiment of nationality.

INTERNATIONALISM

The 20th century is also an era of increasing interdependence and internationalism. In the words of Kohn, "The Nationalism of the post-1945 era is in many ways, different from that of 1900. It regards itself as compatible with international or supernational organisations; it knows of the interdependence brought about by recent technological changes.... Nationalism has assumed again in most countries, and not only in the 'new' countries, the populist and revolutionary character which it had before 1848."[24]

24. Kohn, *Nationalism and Internationalism in the 19th and the 20th centuries*, pp. 219-20.

Today, as Professor Kohn has observed, "we are living in the age of pan-nationalism on all continents." It is not surprising that Nationalism has assumed so many different forms ranging from Communist patterns and ultra nationalistic forms to constructive associations of national and international trends and movements.

Future Role of Nationalism

"Undoubtedly, it is a divisive force in a world growing more and more interdependent, a force capable of producing bitter tensions and one-sided, self-righteous judgements that threaten the rational solution of international conflicts." But "today the possibility is growing that ...the age of nationalism and of warring nation-states" may be transformed "into an age of an uneasy but on the whole peaceful coexistence of nationalism with their various civilisations, traditions, and ideologies, which, like everything in history, are subject to change and transformation."[25]

The doctrine of nationalism has given strength and cohesion to the prevailing pattern of international society. It has been a flexible doctrine, evolving through the years as conditions have changed and giving rise to many schools of interpreters. It has been used in the interests of democracy and liberalism, as well as in those of absolutism and totalitarianism. Actually, there is nothing inherently evil about it. D.W. Brogan called nationalism "this great destructive, constructive force." If uncontrolled or misused, it can lead to tyranny and war; but if directed to constructive purposes it can evoke some of the finest of human sentiments for the service of worthy ends.

NATIONAL INTEREST

What is the National Interest?

The foreign policy of every country is at all times designed to promote the national interest. A volume published by The Brookings Institution makes a helpful distinction among national interests, objectives, policies, and comments: "Stated broadly, *interests* are what a nation feels to be necessary to its security and well-being; *objectives* are interests sharpened to meet particular international situations; *policies* are thought-out ways of attaining *objectives*; and *commitments* are specific undertakings in support of policy." Again: "*National interests* reflects the general and continuing ends for which a nation acts."[26]

25. *Ibid.*, pp. 239-40.
26. *Major Problems*, 1950-1951, pp. 243, 383.

Definition of National Interest

1. Objectivist and subjectivist definitions: Joseph Frankel has divided the various approaches adopted to define the concept of national interests into two broad categories — objectivist and subjectivist. In the first category are included all those approaches which view national interest as a concept which can be defined or examined with the help of some definable criteria. In the second one are included those definitions which seek to interpret national interest as a "constantly changing pluralistic set of subjective references."

2. Broad and single interest definition: Differences regarding the meaning of the concept of national interest are found between those who view it in broad sense and those who conceive it in terms of a number of concrete single interest. Generally the decisions at the operational level are conceived in a narrow context and only few dimensions are taken into account. At this level the process of reasoning is inductive while at other levels it becomes more deductive. Again, the people with theoretical inclination take greater interest in the aggregate, while those with scientific bias lay more emphasis on the single dimension of the concept.

3. Brooking's institute: National interest is "the general and continuing ends for which a nation acts."

4. Charles Lerche and Abul Said: National interest is "the general long-term and continuing purpose which the state, the nation, and the government all see themselves as serving."

5. Dyke. National interest is an interest which the states seek to protect or achieve in relation to each other. While the above two definitions interpret national interest in terms of permanent guide to the action of the state, the definition of Dyke mainly refers to national interest as an action. Obviously, the first two definitions seem to be more logical.

Development of the Concept

In the ancient and the medieval times the states pursued certain substantial interests on the basis of which their relations were conducted. In the early middle ages the laws of Christianity formed the basis of these relations and the states were expected to ensure that their laws conformed to these principles. However, with the emergence of the secular power the Church was looked upon as the enemy of national interest. The national interest meant the interest of a particular monarch in holding fast to his territories due in extending his domains and in aggrandizement of his empire. In course of time the popular bodies challenged the authority of the monarchs and asserted themselves. This resulted in the growth of democracy. Now the 'honour of the prince was replaced by the honour of the nation'. Thus, the concept of national interest passed from the feudal and monarchical system to the republic and democratic system. It soon gained a common usage in the political and diplomatic literature. Thus, the term 'national interest' gained currency only after the emergence of the national state system, increase in popular political control and the great expansion of economic relations.

Types of National Interest

Thomas W. Robinson has broadly classified the national interest into six categories, viz., primary interest, secondary interest, permanent interest, variable interest, general interest and specific interest. These are as follows:

1. Primary interests: These include the preservation of physical, political, and cultural identity of the State against possible encroachments from outside powers. These interests are permanent and the State must defend them at all costs. No compromise of these interests is possible.

2. Secondary interests: These are less important than the primary interests though quite vital to the existence of the State. These include the protection of the citizens abroad and ensuring of diplomatic immunities for the diplomatic staff.

3. Permanent interests: These refer to the relatively constant and long-term interests of the State. The change in the permanent interests is rather slow. An example of this type of national interest is provided by the determination of Britain to maintain freedom of navigation during the past few centuries for the protection of her overseas colonies and growing trade.

4. Variable interests: These refer to those interests of a nation, which are considered vital for national good in a given set of circumstances. Thus, the variable interests can diverge from both primary and permanent interests. These are largely determined by "the cross currents of personalities, public opinion, sectional interests, partisan politics, and political and moral folkways."

5. General interests: These refer to those positive conditions which apply to a large number of nations or in several specified fields such as economics, trade, diplomatic intercourse etc. For example, it was the general national interests of Britain to maintain balance of power on the European continent.

6. Specific interests: Through the logical outgrowth of the general interests, specific interests are defined in terms of time or space. For example, Britain considered it a specific national interest to maintain the independence of the Low countries for the sake of preservation of balance of power in Europe.

7. Identical interests: In addition to the above six types of national interest, Prof Robinson refers to three other interests which he calls "international interests". These include the identical interests, complementary interests and conflicting interests. The Identical interests refer to interests which are held in common by a number of states. For example, both U.S.A. and Britain have been interested that Europe should not be dominated by any single power.

8. Complementary interests: These refer to those interests, which though not identical, can form the basis of agreement on some specific issues. For example Britain was interested in the independence of Portugal against Spain because it wanted to control to reign of the Atlantic Ocean. Similarly, Portugal was interested in the British maritime hegemony because this was a safe means of defence against Spain.

9. Conflicting Interests: These are interests other than the identical and the complementary interests. These are not fixed. These undergo a change due to the force of events and diplomacy. Thus, the present time conflicting interests may become complementary interests in future. Likewise, the complementary and identical interests may also get transformed into conflicting interests.

Methods for Promotion of National Interest

Broadly speaking three methods are used for the promotion of national interests:

1. Coercive measures,
2. Alliances, and
3. Diplomatic negotiations

1. Coercive measures: The coercive measures adopted by the states for the enforcement of national interest broadly fall into two categories according to Beard (i) the measures taken within the State which do not infringe directly upon the State against whom they are taken and (ii) measures directly operating against the State which are the object of enforcement procedure. The acts falling in this category are of negative character, even though they may produce positive effect. Some of the important measures which fall in this category include acts of non-intercourse, embargoes, boycotts, retaliation and reprisal, severance of diplomatic relations etc. Any one or all of these measures can be employed by the State for the advancement and enforcement of its national interest.

Even though these measures are considered coercive they are non-violent in character and do not produce any international crisis. These involve the use of physical force. These are of quite a wide range and include actual display of force. History is replete with numerous examples when different states resorted to the display of force to enforce their national interest. The State can also take certain measures on its own soil to advance its national interests which ultimately operate against the enemy State. These include action like seizure and confiscation of the property of the offending State or its subjects by way of compensation in value for the wrong, suspension of operation of treaties, embargo of ships belonging to the offending states lying within its ports, seizure of ships at sea etc. All these methods are *prima facie* act of war. The State against whom they are directed has to determine whether it wants to engage in war or not. In extreme form these measures can take the shape of actual bombardment of coastal areas or military occupation of an inland centre.

2. Alliances: Alliances are concluded by two or more nations for the protection and promotion of common interests. As a result of the alliance the protection of these common interests becomes a legal obligation which the member states are duty bound to discharge. These alliances may be concluded for the protection of a large variety of national interests. Their nature and the duration depends on the nature of the interest sought to be protected. According to Prof Robinson, 'The advantage of pursuing the national interests through alliances, of course, lies in the translation of inchoate, common or complementary interest into common policy and in bringing the nation's power directly to bear on questions of national interest."

Relations of Alliance to National Interests

Prof Morgenthau has advanced the following propositions regarding the relations of alliance to national interests.

(i) *Duration*: The degree of generality of common interests expressed in alliance are related to the duration of the alliance. Thus, the general alliances will be of short duration while the limited alliance shall be long lasting.

(ii) *Primacy*: The relative degree of primacy of national interests expressed in an alliance is inversely proportional to the power of the nation. Thus, a weak and a strong nation will enter into alliance to defend the primary and secondary interests respectively.

(iii) *Strength*: The weaker partner of alliance is dependent on the stronger one and is tolerated as long as there is complete identity of interests between the two.

(iv) *Interest*: Even if an alliance is based on equality it will not succeed unless there is identity of interests.

(v) *Balance*: A one-sided alliance, in which one party receives the benefits and the other party carries most of the burden, can be concluded only if there are complementary interests.

(vi) *Cohesion*: The degree of cohesion of an alliance depends on the community of interests felt by the participants.

(vii) *Legal ties:* It is not essential that every community of interests should be given the shape of an alliance because the legal ties between two nations cannot overbalance the national interests of the nation.

(viii) *Ideology*: Ideology can help in strengthening the bonds of an alliance provided the alliance is based on common or complementary interests. If there is no community of interests in the alliance, the alliance based on ideology alone cannot be effective.

(ix) *Common enemy*: Finally, the alliance built by the nations against a third country or common enemy are generally vague and lack concrete objectives.

3. Diplomatic negotiations: Diplomatic negotiations are used to reconcile the divergent interests of the State through the process of "mutual give and take." These prove fruitful only if the interests of concerned states are complementary or compatible. In such cases an agreement can be reached through mutual bargaining. In the case of incompatible or conflicting interests negotiations are virtually impossible.

In the larger interests of the international community the states must try to protect certain common interest, for example, they must avoid use of nuclear weapons. They should not resort to war in view of the highly destructive nature of these weapons. They must realise that the outbreak of a war will not only mean the possibility of their defeat but also destruction of the domestic society and civilisation. They must prefer diplomacy over war.

NATIONAL INTERESTS AND FOREIGN POLICY

Foreign Policy is Based on National Interests

The national interests influence the formulation of foreign policy of a country. The states generally do not publicly admit that their foreign policies are based on their self-interest. However, responsible people have admitted this fact. For example American Secretary of State Hughes admitted in the 1920's that "Foreign policies are not abstractions but the results of practical concepts of national interest." In his article "Another Great Debate: The National Interest of United States" Morgenthau asserts that the foreign policy "seeks the defence of the national interest by peaceful means" and to defend the national interest restrictively and rationally defined "against the national interests of other nations which may or may not be thus defined." I.D. Duchacek has observed "National leaders as a rule never pursue national policies that are in the interest of any nation other than their own." He further asserts "In planning, formulating, adopting and executing foreign policy, national leaders and their aids are confronted with a variable spider's web of conflicting claims and values. Yet priorities, that is, the practical not ideal, contents of the national interest must finally be established in terms of preferred goals and in relation to the power of one's own nation and that of other nations. Both national goals and national means must simultaneously be related to dangers or opportunities on the international scene; not only other nation's power but also their intentions must be properly evaluated." In short, the national interest is the predominant factor in the formulation of a country's foreign policy.

Foreign Policy is not Based on National Interests Alone

Prof Reynolds holds that it is not always possible to base the foreign policy of a State on its national interests alone. He argues that the foreign policy of a State can be based on national interest only if the interests of the various nations are homogeneous. It shall indeed be a costly proposition to pursue a policy based on national Interests, when the interests of the various nations are of a heterogeneous character. This is likely to lead to a war. As Reynolds puts it, "Since self-extending heterogeneous values of unlimited range must almost certainly lead to major armed conflict, national interests must require their limitations. National interests cannot, therefore, always in all circumstances be identified with the values of the community; and when to this is added disagreement about the basic general purposes for which humans exist the difficulty of giving any generally applicable empirical content to the nations of national interest becomes apparent."

Promotion of Self-interest

The leaders of a State do not necessarily always try to promote the national interest alone. Sometimes they use foreign policy as a tool to strengthen their internal position. For example, Sukarno of Indonesia diverted the people from the acute economic and social problems by adopting the policy of confrontation towards Malaysia.

Maintenance of *Status Quo*

Sometimes the national interest comes to be equated with the maintenance of the existing political institutions even at the cost of the interests of the general people. The statesmen normally assume that the survival of the State, over which they preside, is the supreme national interest though it may not always be so. For example, it attempts to preserve the State lead to the destruction of its people, then these attempts could not be in the national interest. In other words, the national interest of the people could be served by the demise of the State. But such an action is not likely to be approved by the political leaders, to whatever political party they may belong. Thus, the decisions of the political leaders are not always taken in the larger national interest.

Limitation of the Concept

Prof Reynolds asserts that "the concept of national interest is, therefore, an unfortunate and on the whole unhelpful one. It is normally attached to the notion of the estate and so sacrifices state goals. It directs attention to a particular human group into which human ought to be organised and the preservation and advancement of which accordingly ought to be the criteria for judgement of action. But if individuals are the proper referent, a distinction needs to be drawn between strictly state goals and the goals that national interest prescribes." He further argues that in essence of national interest "should relate to the real interests of the people, and this interest is not to be seen as being necessarily contained within the State context. This notion of a 'real interest' is difficult to conceive.... But even if it can be seen as a theoretical norm, it cannot in practice be identified and will not serve as a means of judging particular decision or particular actions. State decision makers, who claim to be acting in the national interest misuse the notion, cannot have the perfect information necessary to validate their claims and so are pulling the wool over other people's eyes; and possibly over their own."

CONSTRAINTS ON NATIONAL INTEREST

Foreign policy claiming to operate in the national interest must have some reference to the physical, political and cultural entity called the nation. Morgenthau maintained that it must be determined in the light of possible usurpation by sub-national, other national and supernational interests. These are serious constraints on the national interest.

1. Sub-national interests: At the sub-national level there is group interest particularly represented by ethnic and economic groups. These tend to identify themselves with the national interest. Thus, they confuse the issue.

2. Other national interests: The other national interests may usurp the national interest of a State in two ways, *viz.*, through treason and criminology.

(i) *Treason*: An individual may commit treason on behalf of a foreign government either out of conviction or out of monetary gains.

(ii) *Criminology*: This may prompt a person to promote the interests of a foreign government. There is every possibility of an ethnic minority of a country identifying itself with a foreign government and promote its interests under the guise of the national interests of its own country.

3. Supernational interests: The national interests of a country may be usurped by the super-national interests in two ways — through religious bodies and international environment.

(i) *International organisation*: Though religious bodies have ceased to be effective instruments of supra-national interests at present, the international organisations certainly operate against the national interests of the states by compelling them to pursue only such policies which do not operate against the interests of other member-states.

(ii) *International environment*: These exercise a profound influence on the decision makers in the formulation of a country's foreign policy. The State as a unit of the international community, is bound by certain regulations conventional, customary, ethical, legal or institutional and the framers of the foreign policy have to operate within these limitations. They have not only to keep the national interests in mind but also give due weightage to the interests of other states who are equally determined to fight for their national interests. They must keep a watchful eye on the policies and actions of other states. They must have a trace of various international developments. This implies that a State which seeks to play an active international role must take decisions according to the conditions prevailing around. It should be willing to overhaul its foreign policy according to

> the exigencies of time. In case it fails to do so it will be cut off from the main currents of the world affairs. This will prove that its leadership is not far-sighted. It is clear that "the major influence on foreign policy making thus derives from the fact that it is made with reference to other similarly acting bodies over which the policy-makers of the State in question have no authority or jurisdiction, and that the international arena within which policies are made is in high degree anarchical."

Asserting the need of compromising the national interests with the interests of other nations, Prof Morgenthau says "the national interest of a nation which is conscious not only of its own interests, but also of that of other nations must be defined in terms compatible with the latter. In a multi-national world this is a requirement of political morality; in an age of total war it is also one of the conditions for survival." Thus, while formulating the foreign policy of the political leaders must keep in sight the domestic factors like geography, natural resources, industrial capacity, demography, impacts of various groups and interests in the society, strategic position of the country etc. The resources available for the pursuit of the national interest are necessarily limited in quantity and kind. All the states cannot promote their objectives with equal vigour. Therefore, the states should allocate their scarce resources as rationally as possible.

QUESTIONS FOR EXERCISE

1. Define and distinguish nation, nationality and nationalism.
2. Define national interest and discuss its kinds.
3. Explain the methods adopted for the promotion of national interests.
4. Explain the relationship between national interests and foreign policy. What are the constraints of national interest?

9

The Political System

Political science makes a deep and systematic study of political system. Political system determines political power, political culture, nature of the State, political mobility and so on. Its chief characteristic is political allocation which has been defined by Marion Levy, "As the distribution of power over and responsibility for the action of the various members of the concrete structure concerned, involving on the one hand coercive sanctions, of which force is the extreme form in one direction, and on the other, accountability to the members and in terms of the structure concerned, or to the members of other concrete structures."[1] The political system is sanctioned by the State and the political power. David M. Wood has defined political system by saying, "Political system thus becomes a set of interrelated variables conceived to be politically relevant and treated as if they could be separated from other variables conceived to be politically relevant not immediately relevant to politics."[2]

S.H. Beer and A.B. Ulam has shown that, "Political system has emerged as a part of the broad way of looking at all social behaviour. From that perspective, the political system is a structure that performs a certain function for a society. In the fewest possible words, that function is to make legitimate policy decisions."[3] In the words of Almond and Powell, "It directs attention to the entire scope of political activities within a society, regardless of where in the society such activities may be located."[4] Further explaining the concept Almond and Powell say, "When we speak of the political system we include all the interactions which

1. Levy, *The Structure of Society*, Princeton, Princeton University, 1952, p. 469.
2. Stephen L. Wasby, David M. Wood, *Political Science: The Discipline and its Dimensions*, Calcutta: Scientific Book Agency, 1970, p. 492.
3. S.H. Beer and A.B. Ulam, *Patterns of Government* (New York: Random House, 1968), 8th ptg., p. 21.
4. Almond and Powell, *Comparative Politics: A Developmental Approach* (Boston: Little Brown, 1966), p. 17.

affect the use or threat of use of legitimate physical coercion. The political system includes not only governmental institutions such as legislatures, courts and administrative agencies, but all structures in their political aspects. Among these are traditional structures such as kinship ties and caste groupings; and anomie phenomena such as assassinations, riots and demonstrations; as well as formal organisations like parties, interest groups, and media of communications."[5]

Political system, obviously, must include the salient characteristics of system. The term 'system' is rigorously defined "to single out from all classes, aggregates, or phenomena" those which can satisfy the following criteria:

1. One can specify a set of elements.
2. Among at least some of the elements, one can specify identifiable relations.
3. Certain relations imply others.... Dynamics is added (to this definition) by including a time dimension.
4. A certain complex of relations at a given time implies a certain complex (or one of several possible complexes) at a later time.... A dynamic theory of system is, therefore, one which enables us to deduce certain future states from a given present State."[6]

According to Almond, a system "implies the interdependence of parts and a boundary of some kind between it and its environment."[7] The criterion of 'comprehensiveness' means that when we speak of the political system, we include all the interactions — inputs as well as outputs — which affect the use or the threat of the use of physical coercion."[8] Then by 'interdependence' we mean that a change in one subset of interactions "produces changes in all the other subsets."[9] Finally, by the existence of a 'boundary' in a political system., we mean that there are points where other systems "end and the political system begins."[10] The result is that while the word 'political' signifies an attempt to separate out a certain set of interactions in a society in order to relate it to other sets, by 'system' is meant "attribution to a particular set of properties of these interactions."[11]

5. *Ibid.*, p. 18.
6. Anatol Rapoport, "Some System Approaches to Political Theory," in David Easton (ed.), *Varieties of Political Theory*, pp. 129-30.
7. *Op. cit.* p. 19.
8. *Ibid.*, p. 7-8.
9. *Ibid.*, p. 8.
10. *Ibid.*,
11. *Ibid.*, p. 7.

INFLUENCE OF POLITICAL SYSTEM

Explaining the influence of political system Almond and Powell point out, "In the end it may be remembered that the political system produces a certain output for the society: legitimate policy decisions. The goals at which these decisions aim may be precise and programmatic, or only vague and general. They may be accepted readily or reluctantly, by many or by few. But to call them policy decisions is to stress that they do have consequences for the society, and to note their legitimacy is to draw attention to the main characteristics that make them political. Through the political system goals for the society are defined and carried out by legitimate policy decisions."[12]

PROPERTIES OF POLITICAL SYSTEM

According to Almond and Powell the political system is known by the following properties:

1. Comprehensiveness: A political system is comprehensive. It includes inputs as well as outputs. It includes all the interactions which affect the use of physical coercion. It is more concerned with the political aspect of kinship and lineage, status and caste groups, religious and cultural bodies as well as anomic phenomena such as violent riots and street demonstrations.

2. Interdependence: A significant property of political system is the interdependence of its various parts. A subset of interactions produces changes in all other subsets. It is so because the functioning of the subsets is inter-dependent. For example, changes in the technology of communication transform the electoral process, the political parties, the legislature and the executive.

3. Boundaries: Every political system draws boundaries between society and polity. According to Almond, "When we talk about good and bad boundary maintenance, we must use criteria appropriate to the system. In one case diffuseness and intermittency may be appropriate boundary maintenance; in another specialised secular structures are appropriate."[13]

CHARACTERISTICS OF POLITICAL SYSTEM

Besides the above-mentioned three properties, Almond points out the following five characteristics of a political system:

12. *Ibid.*
13. *Ibid.*, pp. 8-9.

1. Universality: Political systems are universal. They may be primitive or modern, developing or developed but they are known by a legitimate pattern of interaction which maintains internal or external order. This internal structure makes political system fundamentally the same, known by the following four characteristics:

(i) That all political systems have political structure.

(ii) The same functions are performed in all political systems, even though these functions may be performed with different frequencies in different kinds of structures.

(iii) All political structures, no matter now specialised, are multifunctional.

(iv) All political systems are 'mixed[5] in the cultural sense.[14] It may be noted here that in spite of this four-fold similarity, political systems differ in the relative dominance of one part over the other and also in the pattern of mixture of the composite components.

2. Political structure: Each political system is characterised by some political structures. These are the bases of its articulative, aggregative and communicative functions. Different political systems differ in specialised structures.

3. Political functions: Each political system is characterised by certain political functions. These are known by functional analyses of the political system, the models of which will be given in sequence. Lasswell advises seven categories of functional analysis as (i) Intelligence — information, prediction, planning, (ii) Recommendation — promoting policy alternatives, (iii) Prescription — enactment of general rules, (iv) Invocation — provisional characterisations of conduct according to prescriptions, (v) Application — final characterisation of conduct according to prescriptions, (iv) Appraisal — The assessment of the success or failure of the policy, and (vii) Termination — the ending of prescriptions and of arrangements entered into within their framework.[15] According to Almond the input categories, include: (i) Political socialisation, and recruitment, (ii) interest articulation, (iii) interest aggregation, and (iv) political communication; and the output category includes: (i) rule-making, (ii) rule-application, and (iii) rule-adjudication functions."[16] The model of political system presented by Almond is given on page 139.

14. *Ibid.*, p. 11.
15. *Ibid.*, p, 15.
16. *Ibid.*, p. 17.

Almond's Model of Political System

Political System

Characteristics	Properties	Functions
1. Comprehensiveness 2. Interdependence 3. Boundaries	1. Universality of Political systems 2. Universality of Political structure 3. Universality of Political functions 4. Multifunctionality of Political functions 5. Culturally mixed character of Political systems	

Functions

Input	Output
1. Political socialisation and recruitment	1. Rule-making
2. Interest articulation organised interest groups	(a) Prescription
	(b) Termination
(a) Institutional	2. Rule-application
(b) Non-associational	(a) Invocation
(c) Anomic	(b) Application
(d) Associational	
3. Interest aggregation	3. Rule-adjudication
(a) Party Systems	(a) Rule-application
(i) Authoritarian	
(ii) Dominant-authoritarian	
(iii) Competitive	
(iv) Competitive multi-party	
(b) Performance of aggregative functions	(b) Rule-appraisal
(i) Secular or pragmatic bargaining	
(ii) Absolute value-oriented	
(iii) Particularistic or traditional	
4. Political communication	
Variables of comparison	
(i) Capabilities	
(ii) Conversion functions	
(iii) Maintenance and adaptation functions	
(iv) Inter-relation among these three kinds	

4. Multifunctionality: A political structure is multifunctional. The Western models of political system have a tendency of limiting political structure. What is peculiar to modern political system, is a relatively high degree of structural differentiation. This may be seen in different parts of political structure such as the legislative, the executive bureaucracy, the courts, the election system, the political parties and organised interest group. Secondly, political system regulates and controls intermittency and traditionality. In the words of Almond, it "can penetrate it, regulate it, translate its particularistic and diffuse impacts into the modern political language of interest articulation, public policy and regulation."[17]

5. Culturally mixed character: Culturally speaking, political systems are mixed in character. It is due to this characteristic that one finds some features of modern political system derived from primitive political system. That Eastern or Western, ancient or modern political systems are not pure but mixed. In the words of Almond, "What is useful in these concepts of multifunctionalist cultural dualism, and political acculturation is that they set aside once and for all the geographic, cultural and analytical polarisations which have plagued our efforts at social and political comparison. We have been talking of 'modern' and 'pre-modern', 'developed' and 'under-developed', 'industrial' and 'agrarian', 'western' and 'non-western', or the Parsonian syndromes of universalism-specificity-achievement-affective neutrality, versus particularism-diffuseness ascriptive-affectivity. The universe of political systems is less tractable to simple contrasts than we have supposed. We need dualistic models rather than monistic ones, and developmental as well as equilibrium models, if we are to understand differences precisely and grapple effectively with the processes of political change."[18]

VARIABLES OF POLITICAL SYSTEM

According to S.H. Beer and A.B. Ulam, the following are the variables working in a political system:

1. Pattern of political culture: Pattern of political culture includes the beliefs, conviction, and the attitudes of the people towards the political system. The attitudes condition the interest and goals to be persuaded the means to reach the goals and the acceptance or rejection of decisions. Pointing out the importance of the pattern of political culture Beer and Ulam write, "As cultural background they will have great bearing upon the fortunes of the political system: whether it is stable or unstable; whether it is capable of orderly and gradual development or is caught in paralysing stalemate; whether the struggle for power is kept within bounds or burst forth in self-destroying excess."[19]

2. Pattern of power: Pattern of power refers to means by which the process and action of decision-making may be influenced. Each group in a political system, has authority or power which influence the process of decision-making. Different political parties enjoy this pattern of power.

17. *Ibid.*, p. 19.
18. *Ibid.*, p. 25.
19. S.H. Beer and A.B. Ulam, *Patterns of Government*, p. 30.

For example, the Supreme Soviet is in fact controlled not by the members but by the Communist party. Similarly, the pressure groups influence decision-making in American Congress.

3. Pattern of interest: The pattern of interest means the set of goals pursued by the individuals or groups for protecting and promoting their specific interests. This is realised by achieving power. Therefore, different political parties try to be powerful in a political system. The interests may be positive or negative, special or general but they do influence the policy of the government.

4. Pattern of policy: Policy consists of decision. It shows through a series of decisions with a binding character. Pointing out the result of political culture, pattern of power and the pattern of interest in pattern of policy, Beer and Ulam write, "The final outcome is the pattern of policy. The decision as a product is not an inert thing. It is part of a further stage of political or social process. So from asking what was decided, we go on to ask what are the consequences of this decision in those further stages. While the patterns of power and interest focus attention on the origins and emergence of decisions, the pattern of policy focusses attention on its content and consequences."[20]

THEORY OF CAPABILITY

According to Almond the structure and culture of a political system is determined by its capability. While the structure is the system of status and roles, the political culture, "consists of the attitudes, beliefs, values and skills which are current in an entire population, as well as those special propensities and patterns which may be found within separate parts of that population."[21] From the point of view of political culture, Englishmen are conservative and French violent. The capability of a political system means the way it performs as a unit in its environment. In the words of Almond, "When we speak of the capabilities of a political system, we are looking for an orderly way to describe its over-all performance in its environment."[22] The capabilities of a political system may be regulative, expective, distributive or responsive. While totalitarian political system is regulative and expective, socialism is distributive and democratic system is responsive. A scientific study of different political systems may be made on the basis of capabilities. This may provide an

20. *Ibid.*, p. 59.
21. Almond and Powell, *Comparative Politics: A Developmental Approach*, p. 23.
22. *Ibid.*, p. 28.

occasion for comparative studies. The study of a political system from interdisciplinary point of view may provide a broad framework for understanding.

However, some political scientists and sociologists have objected to the categorisation of modern governments from the point of view of political systems. As O.R. Young has pointed out, a study of modern governments from the viewpoint of systems theory, "may be helpful in organising material on human relationship into systemic patterns in such a way that questions concerning pattern maintenance, stability, regulation, and so forth can be posed fruitfully, it does not have as much to offer for studies dealing with the political aspects of such matters as perception, expectation, formation, or cognition."[23] However, the value of political system approach cannot be minimised. It has been rightly said by Wasby, "Until the systems approach was developed, political scientists studying one area of politics or government had no way in which to place in context the phenomena they were studying or to relate institutions to each other systematically. Not only does the political systems framework encourage political scientists to check for such inter-relationship, but also it provides a large-scale map of the political worlds so that researcher can see which areas remain unexplored."[24]

QUESTIONS FOR EXERCISE

1. What is political system? How did its concept develop?
2. Describe the properties and characteristics of political system.
3. Give Almond's model of political system. What are the variables of political system?

23 Young, O.R., *Systems of Political Science*, New Jersey: Englewood Cliffs, 1968, p. 24.

24 Stephen L. Wasby, *Political Science: The Discipline and Its Dimensions*, Calcutta: Scientific Book Agency, 1970, p. 109.

10

Sovereignty

Sovereignty is the most important constituent element of a Modern State. It is this element which distinguishes the State from all other associations we cannot think of any State without sovereignty. It is the supreme power over citizens and associations. The concept of sovereignty has been called the very basis of Modern Political Science. It is this concept which distinguishes State from other institutions and places a State over and above every other institution or association. But it has given rise to a lot of controversy and confusion. It is a term about which there exists confusion and contradiction of thought. In fact, the concept has been changing with the transformation of social, economic and intellectual forces. Sovereignty denotes the supreme power of the State. This rests with the person or persons and exercises the power and is called Sovereign. It is the essential element of a State. Any State which is internally and externally free is called a Sovereign state. Sovereignty is absolute, exclusive, universal, permanent, unalienable and indivisible.

Two Views on Nature of Sovereignty

Sovereignty is an essential element of State. It is an attribute that makes State the pre-eminent association of society. As C.L. Oyseau says, "Were the State deprived of it, it would no longer be a State and whoever had it would have the State inasmuch as he would have the sovereign authority (supreme power). For sovereignty is the form which causes the State to exist; indeed, the State and sovereignty in the concrete are synonymous. Sovereignty is the summit of authority, by means of which the State is created and maintained."[1] It manifests itself in the form of a law binding on all concerned individuals and their groups.

1. Cited in Bertrand de Jouvenel, *Sovereignty*, p. 180.

NATURE OF SOVEREIGNTY

1. The traditional view: It holds that the State is an absolute and morally supreme organisation endowed with a coercive power for assuring the realisation of the ideal of peace and security. This is the very *raison d'etre* of a political organisation. Hence, the State can legitimately claim total allegiance of man to its authority issuing in the forms of law. It may punish those who violate its commands being its 'will' in the concrete form. The traditional view is called 'monism', because it regards sovereignty as absolute, unlimited and indivisible.

2. Pluralist view: Opposed to monism the 'pluralists' seek to justify the limited and divisible nature of sovereignty. They attack the doctrine of an absolute State. They contend that there "are other essential associations on a parity with the State. Man's social nature, as they maintain, finds expression in numerous groupings, pursuing various ends — religious, social, economic, professional, political; no one of the groups is superior, morally or practically, to the others."[2]

Thus, sovereignty is an essential attribute of State. It is the only element that distinguishes State from any other association like a family or a school, or from a whole set of associations and relations like a society or a nation. According to Prof C.H. Mcllwain, sovereignty "is the central formula under which we may try to rationalise the complicated facts of our modern political life."[3] It finds its place in the supremacy of the will and power of the State. As Garner points out "in every fully independent State there is some person, assembly or group (e.g., the electorate) who or which has the supreme power of formulating in terms of law, and of executing the collective will; that is, the final power to command and enforce obedience to its authority. Other associations have collective wills, and may formulate opinions, but it is the peculiar characteristic of the State that its will alone dominates and over-rides in the event of conflict all other wills, whether of persons or of associations. To it all other wills are potentially subject. The will of the State, once declared, represents the last word regarding the matter upon which it has made a decision."[4]

THE MEANING OF SOVEREIGNTY

The 16th century French political thinker, Jean Bodin (1530- 96) was the father of the modern theory of sovereignty. Published in Paris in 1576

2. F.W. Coker, *Recent Political Thought*, p. 497.
3. C.H. Mcllwain, *Constitutionalism and the Changing World*, p. 47.
4. Garner, *Political Science and Government*, p. 156.

his *De la Republique*, contained the first systematic presentation of his theory. Sovereignty, defined Bodin, is "the supreme power of the State over citizens and subjects, unrestrained by law."[5] Thus sovereignty was identified with royal absolutism. The power of the sovereign monarch was absolute and unlimited, unrestrained by any human authority. It was equipped to resist the universalist claims of the papacy and the Empire.

The earlier writers — Bodin, Hobbes, Locke, Rousseau and modern political scientists — Jellinek, Duguit, Kelsen, and Laski interpreted sovereignty in varying terms. During the modern period, it has frequently changed its content, its laws, and even its functions.[6] It has given rise to the concept of "popular sovereignty." It has been regarded as a major stumbling block to hopes and plans for supernational organisation and co-operation.

"Few political conceptions," observed Professor Mcllwain, "have been the subject of so much discussion amongst us in the last hundred years."[7] "No word in political science," declared Professor Coker, "is used with a greater variety and meanings."[8] Some political scientists contend that the concept is obsolete, or even dangerous.

Sovereignty is a concept of modern political theory. The Greeks had no idea of this term. We may take note of the fact that Aristotle used their term 'supreme power' of the state in different sense. During middle ages the jurists, the theologians and other writers used terms like *summa potestas* (highest power of the State) or *plenitudo potestatis* (supreme authority of the State) in a sense different from what we mean now by the term sovereignty.

DEFINITIONS OF SOVEREIGNTY

1. *Grotius*: Sovereignty is the supreme political power vested in him whose acts are not subject to any other and whose will cannot be over-ridden.
2. *Blackstone*: Sovereignty is the supreme, irresistible, absolute, uncontrolled authority in which the highest legal power of the State resides.
3. *Jellinek*: Sovereignty is that characteristic of the State by virtue of which it cannot be legally bound except by its own will or

5. *Ibid.*, p. 157.
6. Quincy Wright, *A Study of War* (Chicago: University of Chicago Press, 1942), II, 898-99.
7. Mcllwain, p. 47.
8. Francis Coker, "Sovereignty," *Encyclopaedia of the Social Sciences* (New York: The Macmillan Company, 1937), XIV, p. 268.

limited by any other power than itself.

4. *Pollock:* Sovereignty is that power which is neither temporary not delegated, not subject to particular rules, which it cannot alter, nor answerable to any other power on earth.
5. *Wilson*: Sovereignty is the daily operative power of framing and giving efficacy to the laws.
6. *Willoughby*: Sovereignty is the supreme will of the State.
7. *Duguit*: Sovereignty is the commanding power of the State, it is the will of the nation organised in State; it is the right to give unconditional order to all individuals in the territory of the State.
8. *Burgess*: Sovereignty is the original, absolute and unlimited power over individual subjects and associations of subjects.
9. *Laski*: The sovereignty of the State issues orders to all men and all associations within its area; it receives order from none of them. Its will is subject to no legal limitations of any kind. What it proposes is rightly by mere announcement of intention.
10. *Jenks*: Sovereignty is an authority which, in the last resort, controls absolutely and beyond appeal the actions of every individual member of the community.
11. *Carre de Malberg*: Sovereignty is not power but rather a quality; it is the supreme characteristic of a power — supreme in the sense that this power admits no other above it and no other compete with it.
12. *Donald F. Russell*: Sovereignty is the strongest power and supreme authority within a State, which is unlimited by law or anything else, since otherwise it would neither be strongest nor supreme.
13. *Oppenheim*: Sovereignty is supreme authority, an authority which is independent of any earthly authority.
14. *Kelsen*. In its original and only specific meaning, sovereignty means supreme authority.

DIMENSIONS OF SOVEREIGNTY

1. Internal dimensions: In the internal sphere the idea of sovereignty means that the State has highest authority within the area under its control. All people and their associations are under the control of the State. The State has the power to make and enforce a law throughout its territory. State is the final power to command and enforce obedience. State is subject to no legal limitations. As Gettell says: "Sovereignty, properly speaking, deals with the internal relations of a State to its inhabitants; it is a term of constitutional law rather than of international law. It is a legal concept and deals with positive law only. It would be conducive to clearness of thought and would avert much controversy if the term 'sovereignty' were applied only to what is usually called *internal sovereignty* and the term 'independence' were used for what is sometimes called *external sovereignty*"[9].

2. External dimensions: In external sphere the idea of sovereignty implies freedom of state from any alien subjection. A dependent people cannot be called a State. They live and have to act according to the will of another State. However, if in pursuance of some international treaty or agreement a State accepts limitations on its freedom of action, it does not amount to the loss or destruction of its sovereignty, it is a self-imposed limitation. For example, the association of a sovereign State with the Commonwealth of Nations or with the United Nations. In fact, the external aspect of sovereignty is an extension of its internal aspect in the international sphere. In the words of Le Fur "it is only an abbreviated expression for designating the totality of rights by which internal sovereignty manifests itself *vis-a-vis* foreign states."

The above-mentioned two aspects of sovereignty should not be distinguished too much. Both these are two sides of the same attribute. Sovereignty has its expression in the form of a 'command' given by the State that is binding on all concerned with it. According to Giddings, "In all the dictionaries there is no other word that has more disastrously been conjured with by the metaphysical juggler.... Jurists and political theorists, losing sight of concrete fact, gave their minds to abstractions. And sovereignty became for political science a thing that never was on sea or land."[10] It issues forth in the form of the law of the state. Thus, from the legal standpoint, "the State is a total order, and the only total order precisely because the State and the law are identified."[11]

ESSENTIAL CHARACTERISTICS OF SOVEREIGNTY

1. Universality: The power of the state is all-comprehensive. It covers all people and their associations living under the area of its control. It is co-extensive in its operation with the jurisdiction of the State. It comprehends within its scope all powers and things within its territory,

9. Gettell, *Political Science*, p. 123.
10. Giddings, *The Responsible State*.
11. Benn and Peters, *Social Principles and Democratic State*, p. 63.

except the embassies, consulates and legations where the law of the foreign country is applied. Even that takes place according to the will of the State. The State accepts some principles of international law for manifesting its commitment to the behaviour of the civilised nations of the world. It shows the quality of *exclusiveness*. It implies the quality by virtue of which there "can be one but supreme power in the State, legally entitled to the obedience of the inhabitants. To hold otherwise would be to deny the principle of the unity of the State and to admit the possibility of an *imperium in imperio* (State within a State)."[12]

2. Absoluteness: The authority of the State is supreme as well as absolute. It knows no limits on the formulation, expression and realisation of its will. The State may make and enforce any law and it is binding on all concerned. There can be no other authority to revoke or rescind the law of the State. However, a State may deny to itself some area of action by the logic of self-imposed limitations as specified in its Constitution or in the text of some international treaty or convention. Sir Henry Maine refers to social customs and traditions as important limiting factors on the power of the sovereign. Laski says that in purely juristic terms this implies that, in practice, legally unlimited power "turns out to be power exercised under condition fairly well-known to each generation."[13]

3. Permanence: Sovereignty is the permanent quality of the State. The holder of sovereignty may die, but the power of the State survives. It is passed on to his successor. A State may lose its sovereignty only when it is conquered by some other State and converted into a colony or a dependency. In the national anthem of English people 'God save the King', the word 'king' signifies both the head of the State and the immortal authority as supreme power of the state. The phrase, 'King is dead, long live the King', implies that "sovereignty does not cease with the death or temporary dispossession of a particular bearer on the reorganisation of the State, but shifts immediately to a new bearer, as the centre of gravity shifts from one part of a physical body to another when it undergoes external change."[14]

4. Inalienability: Sovereignty cannot be alienated. It is the very essence of the personality of the State. When a sovereign dies his office is given to his successor. It is change in the government and not an abdication or surrender of sovereignty. However, a State may cede away a part of its territory to another State by some voluntary or involuntary agreement.

12. Garner, *op. cit.*, p. 170.
13. Laski, *A Grammar of Politics*, p. 52.
14. Garner, *op. cit.*, p. 170.

This is not the surrender of its whole sovereignty, Lieber points out that sovereignty can no more be alienated than a tree can alienate its right to sprout, or a man can transfer his life or personality to another without self-destruction,[15] Thus, by the quality of inalienability is meant that attribute of the State by virtue of which it cannot cede away any of its essential elements without self-destruction."[16]

5. Indivisibility: Then, the sovereign power of the State is indivisible. The will the State cannot be divided into many wills. Maintaining this view Hobbes, Rousseau, Hegel and Austin are called monists. As Calhoun says that "sovereignty is a whole thing, to divide it is to destroy it. It is the supreme power in a state, and we might just as well speak of half a square, or half a triangle, as of half a sovereignty."[17] A federal system is not based on the division of sovereignty. In it the powers of the government are divided between a central (national or federal) government on the one hand and provincial (regional or constituent) governments on the other. Thus, a federal system stands on the principle of the distribution of governmental powers and not that of sovereignty of the State. As Gettell says: "What is divided in a federal system is not sovereignty which resides as a unit in the State as a whole, but the exercise of its various powers, which are distributed in accordance with a constitutional system among various governmental organs."[18]

To sum up, sovereignty is the exclusive, all-comprehensive or universal, inalienable, permanent and indivisible power of the state.

KINDS OF SOVEREIGNTY

1. Nominal and real sovereignty: These may be distinguished as follows: A nominal or titular sovereign is one whose authority is in name only; a real sovereign is one who actually uses his powers. The English monarch is the best example of a titular sovereign who reigns but does not govern. The real exercise of powers is vested in the ministers under the Prime Minister who are collectively responsible to the Parliament. Hence, it is said that 'king can do no wrong'. The President of India also belongs to this category. But the Presidents of the United States and France belong to the category of a real sovereign. They exercise the power of the state according to their best judgement. They may be held accountable for any wrong entailing from an act of their commission or omission.

2. Legal and political sovereignty: A legal sovereign has the highest

15. Letber, *Political Ethics*, Vol. I, p. 219.
16. Garner, *op. cit.*, p. 171.
17. Calhoun, *Works*, Vol. I, p. 146.
18. Gettell, *op. cit.*, p. 125.

power of making and enforcing a law. A law made by him is binding on all concerned people and parties. It may be changed or repealed by the same authority. The British Parliament may make any law as per its best judgement. It is omnipotent in that it "can adjudge an infant of full age; it may attain a man of treason after death; it may legitimise an illegitimate child, or, if it sees fit, make a man judge in his own case."[19] But, the voters can make and unmake a Parliament. The members of the Parliament cannot make a law that is not acceptable to the voters. If it happens, the voters may rise in revolt and thereby change their Parliament. Thus political sovereignty lies behind legal sovereignty. According to Gilchrist, "political sovereignty is the sum-total of influences in a State which lie behind the law."[20] However, the idea of political sovereignty is a fiction and a matter of confusion and controversy. While the will of the legislators may be manifest through their resolution in the form of a law, the will of the electorate cannot be so ascertainable. So Gettell remarks that "any attempt to find a political sovereign at the back of a legal sovereign destroys the value of the entire concept and reduces sovereignty to a mere catalogue of influences."[21]

3. *De jure* and *de facto* sovereignty: A *de jure* (legal) sovereign is one who occupies his office according to the well-established laws and practices of his State. By virtue of these he has the authority to issue commands and secure their obedience by the persons concerned. His occupation of the office and exercise of all power rests on the authority of the law of the land. But a *de facto* (factual) sovereign occupies the highest office of the State in an illegal or unconstitutional manner and makes use of force his will. As Bryce says: "The persons or body of persons who can make his or their will prevail whether with the law or against the law, he (or they) is (or are) the *de facto* ruler (or rulers), the person to whom obedience is actually paid".[22] In England Cromwell became the *de facto* ruler after the execution of King Charles I and dissolution of the Long Parliament in 1649. In France Napoleon became the *de facto* ruler after overthrowing the Directory in 1796. In 1958 Ayub Khan became the *de facto* sovereign of Pakistan after wresting power from President Iskander Mirza. However, the distinction of *de jure* and *de facto* disappears when the deposed sovereign gets back his power. For example, in 1945 the Emperor Haile Selaisse of Ethiopia who had taken asylum in England in 1936, returned to his country and once again became the Emperor

19. A.V. Dicey, *An Introduction to the Study of the Law of Constitution*, p. 66.
20. Gilchrist, *Principles of Political Science*, p. 94.
21. Gettell, *op. cit.*, p. 98.
22. James Bryce, *Studies in History and Jurisprudence*, Vol II, pp. 513-16.

after the defeat of Italy. The distinction also disappears when the *de facto* ruler legitimises his authority by changing the constitutional law of the land as was done by President Daoud in Afghanistan and by Khomeini in Iran after overthrowing the system of monarchy in their respective countries. Garner well says: "On account of the manifest advantages which flow from the exercise of power resting on strict legal right rather than upon physical force, the new sovereign sometimes has his *de facto* claim converted into a legal right by election or ratification.[23]

4. Popular sovereignty: Implying the highest power of the people it constitutes the foundation of a democratic order. In ancient times the Romans believed that the authority of the Commonwealth was derived from the corporate power of the people. Later, in medieval period it was reiterated by the precursors of the conciliar movement like William of Ockam and Marsiglio of Padua. Rousseau of France idealised the theory of social contract by holding that the authority of the state was based on the 'general will' of the people. Thomas Jefferson harped on the theme of the highest authority of the people. Today, this ideas has become an integral part of democratic theory, though in actual practice it assumes the shape of political sovereignty. As Garner says, "Unorganised public opinion, however powerful, is not sovereignty unless it is clothed in legal form, no more so than the informal or unofficial resolutions of the members of a legislative body in law. The sovereignty of the people, therefore, can mean nothing more than the power of the majority of the electorate, in a country where a system of approximate universal suffrage prevails, acting through legally established channels, to express their will and to make it prevail."[24]

AUSTIN'S INTERPRETATION OF SOVEREIGNTY

The best exposition of the idea of sovereignty is informed in its legal or juristic form. The will of the State has its best manifestation in the law of the State that has a binding character. Hence, the study of sovereignty from a strictly legal point of view, as given by Hobbes and Bentham, is important. However, the best exposition of this term is furnished by an English jurist John Austin (1790-1859). In his work *The Province of Jurisprudence Determined* (1832) Austin defined this term in these words: "If a determinate human superior, not in the habit of obedience to a like superior, receives habitual obedience from the bulk of a given society, that determinate human superior is the sovereign in that society and that society (including the superior) is a society political and independent."

23. *Op. cit.*, p. 168.
24. *Ibid.*, p. 165.

Stating Austin's view Henry Sidgwick wrote, "Positive law of any State is a general command to do or abstain from certain acts which is issued directly or indirectly by the sovereign of the State to a person or persons subject to his authority; the sovereign being that determinate person, or body of persons combined in a certain manner that the bulk of the members of the State habitually obey, provided that he or it does not habitually obey anyone else. It is implied in the conception of sovereign that the community, that has a sovereign, is *independent* in the sense that its government does not habitually obey a foreign power, and *orderly* in the sense that the bulk of the community habitually obeys the laws."

"From this definition together with the assumption that facts exist corresponding to the definition, two important consequences are inferred:

(a) The power of the sovereign cannot be legally limited — for, obviously, the sovereign cannot be coerced to act in a certain way by any command of his own;

(b) Sovereignty cannot, strictly speaking, be legally divided between two. or more persons, or bodies of persons acting separately, because any such persons or bodies of persons must have *ex hypothesis* powers legally limited in certain directions — these are certain things which each of them is by law prevented from doing; but if so, they are in habitual obedience to the authority that laid down the law, and it is this latter that is the real sovereign. For example, in a federal state, such as the USA, sovereignty, strictly speaking, does not belong to the Central Government nor to the separate governments of the federated states, but to the body,, whatever it may be, that is recognised as having authority to alter the conditions of federation."[25]

Nature of Sovereignty

1. Supreme and absolute power: In every independent political community or State, there is a supreme and absolute power in the hands of some person or persons (institution) whose will is the law of the State and, as such, is binding on all concerned persons and their associations.

2. The sovereign is a determinate person: The highest authority of the State is vested in the hands of some person or persons who may be identified and who may exercise it as per their best judgement. They may formulate, express and realise their will. Thus, sovereignty can lie only in

25. Sidgwick, *Elements of Politics*, pp. 651 -52. It may be seen in the statement of Stephen Leacock, "The moment one passes from the dry certainty of the Austinian conception of legality, all is confusion," *Elements of Political Science*, p. 61.

the legal form. Political sovereignty (supreme power of the electorate), or popular sovereignty (supreme power of the electorate) is a fiction. The vast electorate or the vast multitude of people cannot be identified with the sovereign of a State. They cannot formulate and express their resolve in the form of a law. Not natural or divine law but human laws may be the proper subject of study.

3. Indivisibility: The sovereignty is indivisible, because sovereign does not obey any other authority. The will of the sovereign is supreme over all persons and their associations living in the State. He is under nobody's control or subjection. The laws emanating from the authority of the state are like commands that must be obeyed so as to avoid the agony of suitable punishment:

4. Habitual obedience: The sovereign receives habitual obedience from the bulk of a given community. This obedience must be a matter of habit and not merely of an occasional ritual. It must be regular, undisturbed and continuous. However, society as a whole may not render such an obedience. In every society there may be a small section of the dissenters. It is enough that obedience comes from the bulk or the major part of the community.

5. Command is the essence of law: Whatever the sovereign wills is law. Failure to do so invites punishment. While the law of the State has a mandatory character, a usage and a custom is volitional. While obedience to law is not a matter of volition, the people may or may not observe their customs.

Juristic Sovereignty

The argument of Austin has a juristic complexion. It expressed sovereignty in a juristic form. The sovereign power of a State manifests itself in the form of a law that is a command to be obeyed by the persons and groups concerned. As Austin says: "Every positive law, or every law, simply and strictly so-called, is set by a sovereign person or a sovereign body of persons to a member or members of the independent political society wherein that person or body of persons is sovereign or supreme." He further says: "To that determinate superior the other members of the society are dependent. The position of its other members towards that determinate superior is a State of subjection or a State of dependence. The mutual relation which subsists between that superior and them may be styled the relation of sovereign and subject, or the relation of sovereignty and subjectivity." In short, the law is the regulator of the behaviour of the people and sovereign is the maker and enforcer of this law. There can be no political society without a sovereign power which "is the centre of gravity in a mass of matter."[26]

Austin's interpretation of sovereignty assimilates all the five characteristics of sovereignty — absoluteness, all-comprehensiveness, inalienability, indivisibility, and permanence. It is regarded as the best exposition of the idea of sovereignty in juristic terms.

Limitations of Austin's View

1. No real sovereign: So far there has been no sovereign in the world that may be truly identified with the model of the Austinian sovereign. Sir Henry Maine contends that even the great Tartars of China and the Mughals of India could not be taken as the concrete examples of the Austinian sovereign, because even the most power-drunk rulers of the world bowed their heads before the might of some natural or supernatural agency. The power of the sovereign has certain limits. These may be in the form of some religious or social customs having their sustenance in the deep-rooted convictions of the people. Only a despot with a "disturbed brain' may be the sole conceivable example of Austin's sovereign. There exists a vast mass of moral influences that perpetually shapes, limits, or forbids the actual direction of the forces by its sovereign.[27] Figgis makes a convincing observation: "But the truth is that this state in the sense of an absolute super-entity has never existed, and that it cannot exist. In theory it represents a despot ruling over slaves; in practice, even a despot is limited by the fact that slaves are after all, human; deny their personality as you like, then comes a point at which it asserts itself, and they will kill either the despot or themselves.... Attempts are made to get out of this difficulty by saying that the sovereign power, though theoretically illimitable, is limited in practice very materially; psychologically by its own nature, and externally by the fact that there are certain things which no government can do without resistance."[28]

2. Negligence of the power of usages and customs: The Austinian view of sovereignty ignores the importance of social usages and customs that have a binding character. People obey their established practices in the same way they obey the laws of the State. Hence, Machiavelli cautioned ' the ruler against playing with the customs of the people. It is also said that the law is nothing but a custom translated into the form of a written command of the State. A wise sovereign would never commit the mistake of playing with the customs of the people and imposing upon them a

26. Sir Henry Maine, *The Early History of Institutions*, p. 339.
27. *Ibid.*, p. 359.
28. Figgis, J.N., *Churches in the Modern State*, pp. 86-87.

law that is opposed to the well-established practices and sentiments of the people. Custom is the outcome of ages. Even an autocrat, like Peter the Great, is expected to be the guardian and servant of the customs of the people. As R.M. MacIver says all customary laws are in their origin spontaneous, not created by any deliberate will to organise, not created by the will of the State. "The State has little power to make custom and perhaps less to destroy it."[29] - Again: "For custom, when attacked, attacks law in turn, attacks not only the particular law which opposes it, but, what is more vital, the spirit of law-abidingness."[30] A French sociologist Leon Duguit goes so far as to say that it is not the state which creates laws, but it is laws which create the State. According to him, laws are merely 'the expression of social necessity'. Austin says that law is a 'command' of the sovereign and a command is a 'signification of desire' that is distinguished from other significations of desire by this peculiarity that the party to whom it is directed is liable to evil from the other, in case he does not comply with the desire. "But all laws of the State do not fit comfortably into the 'command pattern' of Austin. Many administrative orders do not fall into the category of a 'command' because of their quality of 'incomplete obligation'. One may ask what about judicial decision given by a court invalidating a law made by the legislature of the country. For instance, the American Supreme Court being the final interpreter of the Constitution can make the Congress and the President mean whatever it chooses. But it is not very convincing to treat a body whose primary function is to elucidate, interpret and apply known and established rules of law, as if it were the sovereign will, on whose pleasure their existence depended."[31]

3. No single absolute sovereignty: Austin's argument that the sovereign obeys none and receives habitual obedience from the bulk of a given society is disputed. In every political community there is a division of functions, though not of will. No government can be conducted effectively without such division. There is not one sovereign but three sovereigns like the executive, the legislature and the judiciary. These three ultimate authorities are independent of each other. The executive sovereign alone continues without intermission, whilst the legislature may be dissolved temporarily and the supreme judiciary is not always in session.[32] Sidgwick says that "in a modern constitutional state, political power that is not merely exercised at the discretion of a political superior

29. R.M. MacIver, *The Modern State*, p. 160.
30. *Ibid.*, p. 161.
31. Benn and Peters, *op. cit.*, pp. 75-77.
32. A.R. Lord, *Principles of Politics*, p. 89.

— and that must, therefore, be regarded as supreme or ultimate — is usually distributed in a rather complex way among different bodies and individuals; though it is also important to bear in mind that from the many forms of government in any State we can only conjecture very incompletely the actual distribution of the power of producing political effects."[33]

4. Covers only legal sovereignty: The interpretation of Austin covers the case of legal sovereignty alone. It rejects the cases of political and popular sovereignty. According to Austin, sovereignty cannot be vested in the people as a whole or even in the body of the voters, because both have an indeterminate character. The vast body of the voters or of the people of a country cannot have a will of their own which may be translated into the law of the land. Such a view is not acceptable today. The scholars of political theory laud democratic system as one based on the 'will of the people'. It is reflected in the saying 'voice of the people is the voice of God'. Even the autocratic legislators have had to bow their heads before the voters of their country. Even the so-called sovereign British Parliament cannot make a law that is taken as 'uncivilised' or 'barbarian' by the voters (people) of the country. However, the people in general may not recognise their real force that is visible to them in the times of a popular uprising. As John Chipman Gray insisted, "the real rulers of a society are *undiscoverable.*"[34] So Laski says that it "is impossible to make the legal theory of sovereignty valid for political philosophy.... A realistic analysis would probably content itself with saying that the will of the State is, for practical purposes, the will which determines the boundaries within which other wills must live. The will of the State, in fact, is the will of government as that will is accepted by the citizens over whom it rules."[35]

5. Not applicable to federal system: In a federal system the powers are divided between the central and the provincial governments and each is taken as autonomous in the sphere allotted to it. It looks like the division of sovereignty. The provincial governments have the status of co-ordinate governments *vis-a-vis* central government. Neither the central nor the provincial governments have an authority that may be termed absolute, exclusive and indivisible — essential qualities of sovereignty as given earlier. There may be centre-state controversies and confrontations in which victory may rest with either side. Either the interpretation of Austin applies to a country with a unitary system, or it should be revised

33. Sidgwick, *op. cit.*, p. 638.
34 See Laski, *op. cit.*, p. 55.
35 *Ibid.* pp. 55-56.

so as to be also applicable to a federal system. Austinian theory cannot be reconciled with a federal polity in which neither the central nor the regional governments can be termed 'sovereign'. Therefore, Laski says: "It has been pointed out that the discovery of sovereignty in a federal state is, practically, an impossible adventure."[36]

6. Pluralist: The pluralists desire to pluralise the concept of sovereignty. A very large number of social thinkers like Duguit, Durkheim, Figgis, Lindsay, Barker and Laski contend that the sovereign state has no right to discard the real significance of numerous social groups and associations that have a 'personality' of their own and also play a quite important part in satisfying needs of the people. If some portion of sovereignty is shared by these social groups and associations of the people it will be in the interest of individual liberty. As Laski says: "Men are members of the state; but they are members also of innumerable other associations which not only exercise power over their adherents, but seek also to influence the conduct of government itself.... But not less important as a limitation upon its power to determine itself is the control exercised over their own sphere of activity by different associations."[37]

7. Need of control on state's power: *Attack of the internationalists.* Like Hobbes and Rousseau, Austin denies the existence of any authority outside and above the State. The State knows no authority above it. It is the master of its own will Every State has the right to produce weapons of mass destruction, or to settle its disputes by means of force, or to do anything in violation of the principles of international law and international morality. However, the disasters of the two World Wars show that Austin's view of the sovereignty must be discarded. The power of the State must be regulated, even controlled, by some international authority so as to save mankind from the scourge of another great war that would bring untold sufferings. The whole idea of sovereignty should be restated in the light of the canons of internationalism. As Laski forcefully argues : "In such an aspect the notion of an independent sovereign State is, on the international side, fatal to the well-being of humanity. The way in which a State should live its life in relation to other States is clearly not a matter in which that State is entitled to be the sole judge.... International government is, therefore, axiomatic in any plan for international well-being. But international government implies that organised subordination of states to an authority in which each may have a voice, but in which also, that voice is never the self-determined source of decision."[38]

36 *Ibid.*, p. 53.
37. *Ibid.*, p. 59.
38. *Ibid.*, p. 65.

To sum up, Austinian interpretation of sovereignty is purely juristic. To quote Garner, "as a conception of strict legal nature, Austin's theory is, on the whole, clear and logical, and much of the criticism directed against it has been founded on misapprehension and misconception."[39]

VARYING IMPLICATIONS OF SOVEREIGNTY

Prof McIlwain observes that "few political conceptions have been the subject of so much discussion amongst us in the last hundred years."[40] Prof F.W. Coker holds: "No word in political science is used with a greater variety of meanings."[41] The origin and history of the concept of sovereignty and closely linked with the nature, the origin, and the history of the State. In the last two hundred years, particularly in advanced countries, the growth of the idea of sovereignty has overshadowed all other associations and sometimes gone far towards absorbing all the functions of society. The students of pluralism and internationalism have sharply reacted to it. They have desired to make the concept of sovereignty compatible with democracy and international co-operation. Thus, the real meaning of sovereignty now ranges from its absolute to its limited character.

1. The case of absolute sovereignty: Sovereignty is the highest and unlimited power of the State. All social associations are under the complete and unassailable control of the State. The distinction between the society and the State has been obliterated, Hegel advocates that the predestined end of political evolution is that the nation should be absorbed into the State. The irresistible growth in the field of State activity is justified by reference to sovereignty. It was interpreted as justifying the use of political power or symbolising the actual possession of it. As F.H. Hinsley puts it "Even in federal countries what was once not true of earlier times has become true in the past hundred years; the federal form of state is always a unitary state in the process of formation or dissolution."[42]

2. The case of 'limited sovereignty': The sovereign power of the State cannot be absolute. It should be restricted by anything like a religion or by its position as a 'satellite state'. Religion has an overriding authority over State matters in a theocratic system. Alternatively a sovereign State may become a member of some superpower's military alliance. In such a situation the sovereignty of the satellite state is truncated and the superpower has the political right to control its foreign and domestic policies and it may go to the extent of intervening in its internal affairs

39. Garner, *op. cit.*, p. 181.
40. McIlwain, *op. cit.*, p. 47.
41. Coker, "Sovereignty" in E.A.R. Seligman (ed.), *Encyclopaedia of the Social Sciences*, Macmillan, New York, 1968, Vol. XIV, p. 268.
42. F.H, Hinsley, *Sovereignty*, London: Cambridge Univ. Press, 1985, II Ed., p. 219.

as the USSR did in Hungary in 1957, in Czechoslovakia in 1968, and in Poland in 1984. As Hinsley remarks somewhat different circumstances "conspire with the doctrines of Marxism-Leninism to account for the fact that Soviet Russian state still seeks to uphold through die Brezhnev doctrine — the notion that the Communist states of eastern Europe are semi-sovereign protected states."[43]

3. The growth of internationalism: In international relations where sophisticated and less sophisticated states coexist, the concept of sovereignty might appear to have been confounded. Following the first World War the states perceived that these efforts required them to relinquish their sovereignty in at least that crucial area of relations between states which involves the decision to resort to war. As Hinsley says, "The evidence which undermines the analogy between the international system and primitive *body politik* is a positive evidence that the international system is a political system *sue generis*. And it is to be found in the fact that the states are not only moving towards the centralisation of the functions involved in applying international law which should be incompatible with their sovereignty but are advancing however slowly, in a different direction — one in which they are exercising their sovereignty to bring about an agreed redefinition of their rights and duties within the international system.'[44]

4. Demarcation of internal and external sovereignty: Some scholars of international law and international relations hold that the internal and external aspects of sovereignty should be demarcated. The concept of absoluteness and indivisibility of sovereignty should be confined to internal aspect. Quincy Wright suggests that the power of self-judgement in international controversies, the power to prepare and use armed force in international relations, and the power to impose arbitrary barriers to international trade are the three aspects of national sovereignty that are in most need of limitations.[45] Act 14 of the Draft Declaration of the Rights and Duties of States prepared by the International Law Commission of the United Nations says: "Every state has the *duty* to conduct its relation with other States in accordance with international law and with the principle that the sovereignty of each state is subject to the supremacy of international law." Palmer and Perkins contend: "Sovereignty, in its literal sense, means supreme authority, yet it must be limited under present conditions. It is absolute and indivisible, yet it must be qualified and divided. It is incompatible with international law, yet it must be reconciled with international law."[46]

43. Hinsley, *op. cit.*, p. 224.
44. *Ibid.*, p. 229.
45. Wright, "Fundamental Problems of International Organisation" in *International Conciliation* (April 1941), pp. 469-72.
46. Palmer and Perkins, *International Relations*, p. 29.

5. Divided and joint sovereignty: The traditional view of sovereignty does not accord with the growing idea of internationalism. According to new developments in the discipline of international law, the case of 'divided sovereignty' or 'joint sovereignty' has been taken into admission in the name of international co-operation.[47] Clyde Eagleton states: "Sovereignty cannot be an absolute term. It is as just foolish to say that sovereignty must be surrendered or eliminated as to say that sovereignty must be absolute and unrestrained.... The problem is not one of asking whether we should throw off a thing called sovereignty; it is rather one of asking with regard to what matters would we gain by having an international control, and in which matters would we gain more by reserving control to ourselves."[48] Today, the civilised states have put self-imposed restraints on their behaviour to play their part in the field of international peace and co-operation. When the Security Council passes a resolution of cease-fire states involved in a war stop.

To conclude, the traditional concept of sovereignty is outdated. The new idea of making sovereignty of the State compatible with the disciplines of international law and international relations is growing. To quote Carr, the concept of sovereignty "is likely to become in the fixture even more blurred and indistinct than it is at present."[49]

QUESTIONS FOR EXERCISE

1. Define sovereignty and discuss its characteristics.
2. What do you understand by sovereignty? Discuss the characteristics of the sovereignty of the State.
3. Critically examine Austin's theory of sovereignty. Does it adequately explain real conditions?
4. Examine Austin's theory of sovereignty and also its criticism by the pluralists.
5. Discuss the development of the idea of sovereignty with special reference to Austin's theory of sovereignty.
6. Write short notes on the following:
   (i) Legal Sovereignty, (ii) Political Sovereignty, (iii) *De-jure* and *De-facto* Sovereignty.
7. Analyse the legal concept of sovereignty. How would you differentiate it from political and popular sovereignty?

47. H.E. Cohen, *Recent Theories of Sovereignty*, p. 85.
48. Eagleton, *The Forces That Shape Our Future*, p. 176.
49. Carr, *The Twenty Years Crisis*, 1919-39, p. 230.

11

Monist and Pluralist View of Sovereignty

MONIST SCHOOL OF SOVEREIGNTY

According to the monists the State "is the supreme social institution; who recognise other forms of associations as essential to the existence of men but regard the position of the State as unique."[1]

Jean Bodin

The school of monism was first propounded in Jean Bodin of France of the 16th century in whose view sovereignty is the supreme and perpetual power of the state. The emperor is the supreme law-maker (*legibus solutus*) whose authority is unrestrained by any civil law. But Bodin refers to the law of nature and law of nations that bind the authority of the State.

Thomas Hobbes

Thomas Hobbes of England who maintained that laws are nothing but the commands of a political sovereign and there can be no legal limits to his highest legal authority. The Leviathan of Hobbes is the sole legislator, principal executive and chief judicial officer. He hears and decides all controversies and makes determination of facts and laws. He controls defence and levies taxes to support to administration. He chooses his own ministers and counsellors who are like his agents and responsible to him alone. As Hobbes says: "By the authority given to him by every particular man in the Commonwealth, he has used of so much power and strength conferred on him that by terror thereof, he is enabled to

1. F.W. Coker, *Recent Political Thought*, p. 498.

form the wills of them all, to peace at home, and mutual aid against their enemies abroad. And in him consists the essence of the Commonwealth (state)."[2]

J.J. Rousseau

Rousseau of France of the 18th century maintained that sovereignty that resides in the 'body politik' or 'general will, has no legal limitations, because the sovereign is formed wholly of the individuals who compose it. He has, and can have, no interest contrary to theirs. He is the sole judge of what is important for subjection to the general will. He errs only when he legislates for particular interests and when partial associations are formed at the expense of the great associations.[3] Thus, Rousseau, does the same what is done by Hobbes so far as the doctrine of monism is concerned. But while Hobbes talks of the legal sovereignty of a despot, Rousseau upholds the case of sovereignty of the true will of the people. G.D.H. Cole rightly observed: "Rousseau, as a matter of fact, unites the absolute sovereign of Hobbes and popular consent of Locke in the philosophical doctrine of popular sovereignty which has since then been the established form of political theory."[4]

Hegel

German philosopher Hegel maintains that the State is the highest stage of social development. It is an objectification of the real self of the individual. It is the externalisation of individual's freedom. It provides social life. It protects the norms of social morality. The will of the individual is merged with the will of the society. It then manifests itself in the form of a law or 'command' of the State that must be obeyed unflinchingly. The state can do no wrong. The law of the State is a concrete form of the will of the society in which the will of the individual is naturally implicit. State can claim total allegiance of an individual. As Wayper says, State "is the school master which brings him knowledge of the Spirit, of Absolute Reason. His real will impels him to identify himself with the Spirit. The Spirit is embodied in the State. Therefore, it is the real will to obey the dictates of the State."[5]

Austin

Austin vests all authority in the hands of a 'determinate human superior' who is not in the habit of obedience to a like superior. He rather receives

2. Hobbes, *Leviathan*, Ch. 18.
3. Rousseau, *Social Contract*, Book I, Ch. VII.
4. G.D.H. Cole, "Introduction" to *Social Contract* (Eng. Translation), p. xxiv.
5. Wayper, C.L., *Political Thought*, p. 168.

habitual obedience from the bulk of a given society. Such a sovereign authority makes the society political as well as independent. He discards the case of moral, metaphysical and customary laws. He gives all importance to the positive laws of the State that are in the nature of 'commands'. It is for that reason binding on all concerned persons and their associations. According to Coker, the whole statement of Austin "implies that in the structure of every independent political community it is possible to find a definite sovereign whose function it is to establish the law and whose position is above law; in every State there is some person or group of persons, some organ or collection of organs — the Tsar of Russia (before 1917), the British King-in-Parliament, the American Congress and Commonwealth legislatures in co-operatively amending the Constitution of the United States — that has legally unlimited authority."[6]

To conclude the theory of monism holds that State alone is competent to make and enforce law that is binding on all living under its control whether individuals or groups. This power cannot be shared by any other association. In any form of government, the supreme power of legislation, administration and adjudication rests with the departments of the State. To sum up in the words of Coker, "The so-called monistic doctrine has no preference as to the structure of government, as between centralisation or decentralisation, and contains no presupposition as to the desirable or expedient scope of State activity. Nor does the doctrine in any way imply that to criticise, disobey, or resist State authority is irrational, unethical, anti-social, or even impractical. The analytical jurist holds merely that the State exists to enact and apply law; therefore, the State cannot be subjected to limitations of the same character and authority as those which it is established to formulate and execute. He does not represent the State as irresponsible; he maintains only that it cannot be responsible to any authority of like character to itself. In brief, the State, as an organisation for law within a given territory, is legally superior to all groups within that territory."[7]

PLURALIST THEORY OF SOVEREIGNTY

The Pluralist Theory of Sovereignty is the result of social development in the 19th century such as democracy and industrialisation. It emerged as a democratic challenge to Austin's theory of absolute sovereignty. The Pluralists denied the absolutism of state on the ground that society is federal. Groups and associations perform as essential functions as State

6. Coker, *op. cit.*, p. 502.
7. *Ibid.*, p. 503.

performs. These groups and associations should be given as much sovereignty as is given to the State. This way the individual liberty will be protected. Unlike anarchist, pluralists were not against the State but they demanded division of sovereignty on some principles. They wanted State to serve as an arbiter over conflicting claims of different associations. The State should compete with other associations to establish its claims of superior authority.

Pluralist Meaning of Sovereignty

The pluralists consider monism as 'a pernicious or futile doctrine.'[8] They distinguish between State and society. They try to bring down the State from a place of supremacy to that of servitude. The State is just one of the social associations. It cannot claim total allegiance of man. Its authority should be shared by other social groups that satisfy man's needs and play an important part in the working of social mechanism. Thus, pluralists advocate a new kind of State that is neither omnicompetent nor omnipresent: It is just a little superior from other social groups and organisations. There is no unified system of law established by the exclusive authority of the State. There is no centralised system of administration. There is no generalisation of political will as so powerfully advocated by the champions of analytical jurisprudence. "On the contrary, the State is a multiplicity in its essence and manifestation, it is divisible into parts and should be divided." Thus, pluralism "undertakes to transform the State. It criticises and discredits the State as it is, and seeks to reduce it from a place of honour to a place of servitude."[9]

Negative and Positive Pluralism

Political pluralism has two sides — negative and positive.

(i) *Negative sense*: It does not appreciate the contention of the monists that State is an omnicompetent association in dealing with all affairs of the society.

(ii) *Positive sense*: It contends that the authority of the State must be shared by social groups and associations for two reasons:

 (a) These associations have a personality of their own; some of them are even older than the State.

 (b) They play an important part in meeting requirements of the individuals which the State alone cannot do. Thus, pluralists distinguish between State and society.

8. *Ibid.*
9. K.C. Hsiao, *Political Pluralism*, p. 8.

The Pluralistic Doctrine

Hsiao marks out these points of pluralistic doctrine[10]:

1. It emphasises individual freedom.
2. It introduces the group into political thought and shows the importance of social organisations.
3. It gives a more truly comprehensive view of the political process, which is to include not only government and law, but all social relations between men as many-sided moral beings.
4. It manifests a wholesome reaction to the paternalism and absolutism of the political state.
5. It has helped Western political thought to develop from abstract monism, through abstract pluralism to concrete monism.
6. It compels monists to restrict the State to its narrow political sphere.

Essential Features of Pluralism

1. The doctrine of political pluralism is a stern reaction against the traditional theory of sovereignty.
2. Pluralism rejects the contention that all authority should be vested in the State to the extent that social groups and associations become insignificant like stars by the brilliance of the sun.
3. Pluralists contend that the subject of the sovereignty of State should be restudied in the light of new facts telling us about the real worth and utility of numerous social groups and associations. As A.D. Lindsay says: "If we look at the facts, it is clear enough that the theory of sovereign state has broken down."[11] According to J.N. Figgis, the idea of sovereignty is like 'a venerable superstition' and it would go like the dogma of divine rights of kings.[12] E. Barker says: "We see the state-less as an association of individuals in a common life; we see it more as an association of individuals already united in various groups for a further and more embracing common purpose."[13] Laski says that it "would be of lasting benefit to political science if the whole concept of sovereignty were surrendered."[14]
4. According to pluralists, the social groups and associations have a 'personality' of their own. They also meet the requirements

10. *Ibid*, pp. 248-49.
11. Lindsay, "The State in Recent Political Theory" in *Political Quarterly* (1914), Vol. I, p. 136.
12. Figgis, *Churches in the Modern State*, pp. 45-49.
13. Barker, *Political Thought in England*, pp. 175-83.
14. Laski, *op. cit.*, p. 55.

of their members. The State must compete with them while maintaining the federal structure of the society. It must compete with churches, trade unions, employers' associations, friendly societies, political parties, and the like. But in case of conflicting demands, the pre-eminence of the State over other associations depends upon the superiority of its moral appeal. According to Figgis the State is like 'an association of associations of the society". Laski says, 'we give to it no peculiar merit.' The pluralists harp on the theme of the value of numerous social groups and associations that should entitle them for a share of sovereignty of the State. According to Coker the common feature of all discussions about the essential function of smaller groups "is the idea that the State is confronted not merely by unassociated individuals but also by other associations evolving independently, eliciting individual loyalties, better adapted than the State — because of their select membership, their special forms of organisation and action — for serving various social needs."[15]

5. Miss M.P. Follett sums up essential features (merits) of the doctrine of pluralism as[16]:
   (i) The pluralists prick the bubble of the present state's right to supremacy.
   (ii) They recognise the value of the group and see that the variety of our group life today has a significance which must be immediately reckoned with in a political way.
   (iii) They plead for a revivification of local life.
   (iv) They see that the interest of the State is not always identical with the interest of its parts.
   (v) Pluralism is the beginning of the disappearance of its crowd.
   (vi) Pluralism has seized upon the problem of identity, of association, and of federalism.

LEADING PLURALIST THINKERS

Originators of Pluralism

In the last quarter of the 19th century German sociologist Otto V. Gierke and an English historian F.W. Maitland may be regarded as the originators of the doctrine of political pluralism.

15. Coker, *op. cit.*, p. 508.
16. Follett, *The New State.*

1. *Gierke*: In his *Political Theories of the Middle Ages* Gierke discovered the medieval social life when guild system prevailed. In the unsettled conditions of those times, merchants, traders, craftsmen and others had their associations (called guilds) which had the character of autonomous corporations. As the medieval state was not a sovereign organisation, these social groups enjoyed autonomy. Gierke presented his research on the subject of social system of the middle ages. He also lauded it as a bulwark against absolutism of the State.
2. *Maitland*: He translated the work of Gierke into English. He also subscribed to the way of appreciating the medieval guild system. Both Gierke and Maitland looked upon social groups as having a will and consciousness of their own as distinct from those of the individual members. In their view, the purpose of the State was nothing more than co-ordinating and adjusting the working of various autonomous social groups. Thus, a new idea developed.
3. *J.N. Figgis*: He applied the pluralist idea in relation to the church. In his view, church had a personality of its own. The corporate personality of the church did not exist by any grace on the part of the State. The State should recognise that the church had powers of self-development like a person. Figgis said, 'Human society is not a sand heap of individuals related only through the state but an ascending hierarchy of groups.'
4. *Paul Boncour and Emile Durkheim*: They defended the case of the autonomy of numerous professional groups in a society. They contended that there should be particular sovereigns to decide matters where the special interest of some group was more important than the remoter interest of the majority besides there being a national sovereign deciding questions in cases affecting the common interest of the nation. They argued for the restoration of the ancient occupational association as a recognised public institution. As economic life was too specialised to be reached by the state they desired professional groups to be the basis of political representation as well as the source of economic regulation.
5. *Duguit and Krabbe*: Leon Duguit of France and Hugo Krabbe of Holland studied the case of pluralism from a legal point of view. Duguit contended that law was not a command of the sovereign. It "is independent of, superior and anterior to

political organisation, and is objective not subjective." Krabbe says : "The State is nothing but a legal community...a portion of mankind having its own independent body of legal relations. Hence, the State performs no function whatever except to impute legal value to certain interests." Thus, both Duguit and Krabbe suggested the course of decentralisation implying plurality of legal authorities. But Krabbe passes on from the plane of state as a national organisation to its adjustment with an international order. He maintained that the sense of right should extend to international affairs as well. International community must pass through the phase of the idea of sovereignty before the stage of state in the supernatural society is reached.

6. *Leading Thinkers of 20th Century*: Some leading English thinkers of the 20th century have contributed to the theory of pluralism. These include Lindsay, Barker, Cole, and Laski.
   (i) *Lindsay*: He declares that the corporate personalities in society are numerous. Many of-them attract deeper loyalties than the State because they are more homogeneous and represent a closer community of interest. If permitted, they prove themselves to be more effective agencies of social organisation.
   (ii) *Ernest Barker*: He rejects the Gierke-Maitland conception of the 'Real personality' of groups. But he accepts the main part of their doctrine — that these groups exist prior to any act of the State, each as a juristic person created by a common conviction among its members or its corporate character and function.
   (iii) *G.D.H. Cole*: He seeks to incorporate pluralist idea into the framework of his theory of guild socialism. All social affairs must be managed by the guilds of the consumers and the producers with interlinking communes and with a guild Parliament at the top making laws for the regulation of entire guild system.
   (iv) *Harold Laski*: His ideas about pluralism may be seen in his *A Grammar of Politics,* published in 1925 and also in some other writings that appeared earlier. His main arguments are the following:
      (i) *The state is only one of the social associations*: It meets our requirements, but other social groups also do the same in varying measures. Thus, the State cannot

exhaust the associative impulses of man and it cannot lay its claim for man's total allegiance to itself.

(ii) *If society is federal, authority should also be federal*: It implies that society is a network of numerous groups and associations and each group has its autonomous and corporate character, the state should have its own area of activity without destroying the areas of other social groups and associations.

(iii) *The areas of state authority*: These must also be determined in the light of moral adequacy and free conscience of the individual The claim of authority upon the individual is legitimate proportionately to the moral urgency of its appeal. The only State to which a man owes allegiance is one in which he discovers moral adequacy. Man's first duty is to be true to his conscience.

(iv) *State's competition with other social groups and associations*: In serving man and winning his allegiance the State should compete with other social groups and associations. It has no right to destroy or encroach upon the autonomy of other social groups and associations. We live not in a universe but in a multiverse. As Rousseau's general will is an impossibility, no association's will can be given the credit of finality.

(v) *The monistic view of sovereignty is inimical to the liberty of the individual*: Monistic view supports the case of an all-powerful State. An omnipotent State is the offspring of the religious struggles of the early modern age. But facts show that never in history has sovereignty existed as an absolute power and there have always been limitations on the scope and exercise of the authority of the State.

(vi) *The real function of the State*: It is to set conditions within which other associations move. Its mission is to enable the people, through these associations, to be the best selves which they are capable of. It co-ordinates the activities of the groups with a view to that end.

(vii) *State is not coextensive with society*: The State may set the keynote of social life, but it is not coextensive with it. It is a *communitas communitatum*. It is not the crowning point of a hierarchical structure. The State may be the regulator of a community. It is not the co-ordinator of all that a community includes.

(viii) *Fabian socialism*: After 1930 Laski discards the case of pluralism. Once a diehard pluralist, then a modified pluralist, then a Marxist, he ends as a Fabian socialist. He supports the case of increasing state activity in the public interest. In the fourth edition of his *A Grammar of Politics* (1934), he added a preliminary chapter titled 'Crisis in the Theory of State'. Here he frankly said: "The weakness, as I now see it, of pluralism is clear enough. It did not sufficiently realise the nature of the State as an expression of class-relations. It did not sufficiently emphasise the fact that it was bound to claim an indivisible and irresponsible sovereignty, because there was no other way in which it could define and control the legal postulates of society."[17] As G.N. Sharma points out while Laski "expressed himself enthusiastically in favour of the group particularly in his earlier writings under the influence of James, he became more and more critical of the pluralist attitude in his later' writings. The attempt to dethrone the State or to expunge sovereign authority from the community was abandoned and the necessity of state regulation of individual and group life came to be increasingly recognised."[18]

7. *R.M. MacIver*: In his book *The Modern State* the leading American sociologist MacIver contributes to the doctrine of pluralism with following arguments:

   (i) *The state exists within society*: State is not even the form of society. We see it best in what it does. Its achievement is a system of order and control. It regulates outstanding external relationships of men in society.

17. Laski, *op. cit.*, pp, xi-xii.
18. G.N. Sarma, *Political Thought of Laski*, p. 67.

(ii) *Society is prior to the State*: There have been social groups which knew nothing of the State. In earliest phases among hunters, fisherman's, fruit diggers, and fruit gatherers State originated at a certain stage of social development.

(iii) *Independent social forms*: There are social forms as family, church, club etc., which owe neither their origin nor their inspiration to the State. State protects social customs, it does not create them. The social motives like friendship of jealousy, establish too intimate and personal relationships to be controlled by the great machinery of the State.

(iv) *Distinction in laws*: Every association makes laws. In a demarcated or advanced society the law of the State alone is coercive. The laws of other associations bind their members only in so far as they prefer to accept them rather than lose the benefit of their membership.

(v) *Society is independent of state*: The State and society may not only be distinguished from each other, but it should be noted that society is independent of and above the State. Moreover, society is an open organisation, State is a closed hierarchical structure. Thus, the state cannot fully control an open organisation like the society. The concern of the state is limited to political affairs; hence 'things which are Caesar's.'

(vi) *Constitutional law above State*: The State is both the parent and the child of law. It makes ordinary law and is above it. But the constitutional law of the State is above the State which it cannot transgress. The view of Austin and other analytical jurists is wrong that law is a command that is given by the sovereign authority but it does not bind the sovereign himself.

(vii) *Not coercion but social utility*: The laws of the State are obeyed not because of the element of fear as conceived by the monists but because of the consideration of social utility. The root of obedience to law is not coercion but the social will of man to obey.

(viii) *Dimension of sovereignty*: If the state is merely an association among other associations, it cannot be the repository of all powers. Sovereignty should be divided between the State and other associations. Power is given to the State to perform some essential functions like those of protection, conservation and development.

(ix) *Sovereign power not required*: The State is required to maintain national unity, territorial integrity and civil law and order. But the state does not need sovereign power in order to do all this. These goals can be achieved even without applying the coercive apparatus of the State.

(x) *Authority and control in other associations*: Every association of any magnitude has grades of authority and control analogous to those of the State.

MacIver makes it very clear that his entire endeavour "is not to belittle the State that we have drawn these distinctions, but to define it. Its true sphere is so vast, its task is so endless, that no rightful limitations can detract from its worth. On the contrary, they reveal the conditions under which alone it can achieve its greatest measure of success. They show us not only what the State *is*, but they teach us what the State can be."[19]

Conclusion

The doctrine of political pluralism is an attack on the classical theory of monists. It is also a rejoinder as it offers an alternative picture of the state as 'an association of associations' with limited area of activity. As Coker points out, pluralism "is, in part, a rationalisation of recent practical movements that look in various ways towards a more decentralised application of social control. There are, for example, the plans to give greater recognition to vocational groups with the government service, by enlarging the powers and responsibilities of associations of public employees; the projects for reinvigorating local governing units by enlarging their functions and increasing their administrative autonomy and the suggestions that the State, in reorganising the control of industry so as to bring about a fairer distribution of wealth and broader opportunities of self-expression, under State auspices, rather than establish a direct governmental administration or regulation of industrial enterprises."[20]

CRITICISM OF PLURALISTIC THEORY OF SOVEREIGNTY

1. No unanimity about sovereignty: To' say that sovereignty should be shared by important social groups and associations is understandable, but there is no unanimity of thought on this point. What functions should be given to the State and what to other social associations? In what way and

19. MacIver, *op. cit.*, p. 22.
20. Coker, *op. cit.*, pp. 508-09.

to what extent the division of sovereignty should take place? These are some important questions which the pluralists fail to answer. As Coker rightly holds: "Perhaps the defects of the pluralists' analysis lie in part in their failure to make clear which of the specific functions assigned to the State by the monists they would deny to it, and in part in their underlying assumption that, if only an individual or a group be released from state control, then we shall have a condition in which spontaneous action, self-expression, and initiative will enjoy free play. Experience hardly bears out this assumption. Many who raise the loudest outcry against state encroachment upon individual or group freedom are the most ardent supporters, or the most complacently tolerant, of other forms of social coercion."[21] Alfred E. Zimmern has rightly warned that those "who talk of State absolutism are ignoring the simple truth that there is no tyranny like the tyranny of near neighbours. The smaller the group the tighter the strangle-hold over your life and activities."[22]

2. Impossible programme: The pluralists desire to do what is impossible. Sovereignty is a whole thing, which cannot be divided. As Calhoun points out the division of sovereignty would mean its destruction. The anarchists frankly condemn the State as an unnecessary evil and an instrument of exploitation and oppression and contend that it must be abolished root and branch. But the pluralists want to keep their cake and eat it too. They pretend to be non-anarchists, but what they really want to achieve would take them very close to stern anti-statists. They live in a world of paradox. Asirvatham rightly commented: "The pluralists do not want to abolish the State as the Anarchists and the Syndicalists wish to do, although the logical outcome of their theory may well be the same — abolition of the State."[23]

3. Reactionary approach: Pluralists draw inspiration from the social system of the middle ages when guilds, burghers and other corporate entities managed affairs of the people. But medieval times were full of anarchic conditions that could be done away with when a sovereign state came into being. The pluralists run backwards to take inspiration from the discredited system of the past instead of moving onwards and offering an alternative suitable for modern times. Barker's statement about guild socialism applies to the theory of pluralism that autonomous social, groups like guilds and corporations "may have their own diseases, in the middle ages they certainly had;" and today also a system of this kind "might mean a spirit of exclusive monopoly, a spirit of jealousy between

21. *Ibid.*, p. 517.
22. Zimmern, "Political Thought" in R.W. Livingstone (ed.), *Legacy of Greece*, pp. 321-52.
23. Asirvatham, *Political Theory*, VIII ed., p. 294.

guild and guild, a spirit of pettiness which preferred the small association to the great society in which it lives."[24] As Gilchrist points out, "pluralism, driven to its logical end, would disintegrate society replacing order and conditions of progress by chaotic mass of bodies or groups all contending for supremacy."[25]

Merits of Pluralism

1. Emphasis on liberty of the individual: Liberty of the individual is a very precious thing. It must be saved from the onslaught of an all-powerful state. The monists have made the State an all-powerful organisation which may justifiably encroach upon the freedom of the people. It has happened in countries under a totalitarian system expressed in the way some states behaved during the times of the two world wars.

2. Reconciliation of State and individual: The pluralists have sought to reconcile the authority of the state with the liberty of the individual. The State should recognise the importance of social groups and associations. It should thereby cut its power to a proper size.

3. Liberal-democratic system: Thus, pluralism is more close to the domain of a liberal-democratic system. It "has rendered a great service to modern political theory by inviting the political attention of the states to the reality of group life."[26]

QUESTIONS FOR EXERCISE

1. Discuss the Pluralist Theory of Sovereignty.
2. Critically examine the Pluralistic Conception of Sovereignty.
3. Examine the Pluralistic attack on Austin's Theory of Sovereignty.
4. Examine critically the Pluralist theory of sovereignty with particular reference to the views of Laski and MacIver.

24. Barker, *op. cit.*, p. 205.
25. Gilchrist, *op. cit.*, p. 108.
26. Asirvatham, *op. cit.*, p. 313.

12

The Theory of Rights

The study of rights occupies a very important place in the discussion of political theory. Rights are regarded as a bedrock of a democratic system. Their ideological development, their political, social and economic contents and implications and their legal status in the present day world is of paramount importance to political theorists. Rights define the position of the individual in a State. They offer a positive purpose to the State. Through them alone, the State promotes the general welfare of the society as a whole. The presence of rights is a proof that the State exists for the individual not the individual for the State. Rights virtually determine the status of a political civilisation achieved by the State. A right is the claim by an individual or by a group or association which is allowed and confirmed by other individuals and other groups. Rights enrich an individual's life. If there is an all round development of individual life, the social life will automatically be enriched.

According to Harold J. Laski, "Any system of rights, therefore, has three essential aspects from which it must be regarded. There is the interest of the individual, always, at least, ultimately, finally isolated from his fellow men. There is the interest of various groups in and through which his personality finds channels of expression. There is the interest of the community which is the total result of the whole pressure of social forces."[1]

Rights, liberty and equality are the three inter-related themes. Possession and enjoyment of certain rights requires liberty. Possession and enjoyment of such rights by all without any distinction on some artificial ground require equality. To talk of liberty means to talk of rights; to talk of liberty for all means to talk of equality. As Laski said

1. Laski, *A Grammar of Politics*, p. 141.

"without' rights there can be no liberty,"[2] and "every State is known by the rights it maintains."[3]

Definition of Right

1. *Laski*: Rights are "those conditions of social life without which no man can seek in general, to be himself at his best". They are the sum total of opportunities which ensure an adequate development and expression of an individual's personality.
2. *Bosanquet*: "A right is a claim recognised by society and enforced by the State".
3. *Barker*: "Any particular right which I have in a capacity of enjoying some particular status or employing some particular power of action which has been secured and guaranteed to me by law."

Thus, a right is a claim of an individual recognised by the community and the State. Thus, a proper definition of the term 'right' has three aspects.

1. A claim of the individuals: Though every claim cannot be a right. in order to be a right a claim should be like a disinterested desire, or something which is capable of universal application. What an individual wills should be of common interest. In asserting a claim one should feel like rendering a public service. The motivating force should be a rational consideration and not a personal caprice of the individual. As Barker says the will that issues in the form of a claim to something not only wills the good of itself, it wills the goodness of itself in relations to others. To quote his words, "It wills the goodness of society which is constituted by such relations. The goodness of the relations which constitute society means a system of rights."[4]

2. Social recognition: As individual's claim is backed by a disinterested desire, it receives social recognition. For example, an individual's claim that none should take his life, receives social recognition as every individual will in the same direction. The right to life is created by a recognition of the claim of this type. An individual's desire that none should take away his property creates in him a sense that he should not take away the property of others. It becomes right to property when it gets social recognition. In the words of Barker, "Claims thus recognised are translated into rights, and it is such recognition that constitutes them rights. Thus, if we care to make the distinction, we may say that rights have a double aspect. On the one hand, a right is a claim of an individual

2. *Ibid.*, p. 142.
3. *Ibid.*, p. 89.
4. E. Barker, *Political Thought in England* (1848-1914), p. 25.

arising from the nature of self-consciousness for permission to will his own ideal objects; on the other hand, it is the recognition of that claim by society and, therein and thereby, the addition of new power to pursue these objects."[5]

3. Political recognition: Until they are protected by the state rights are like moral declarations. When they think in terms of patterning their conduct according to the rules of 'common behaviour' individuals are guided by their real wills. However, in most of the cases, they are motivated by their selfish wills. This violates the system of rights. Therefore, there must be some coercive force to ensure the exercise of these rights. The State translates socially recognised claims of moral rights into terms of law. It accords them legal recognition. It acts like a coercive agency to prevent the operation of selfish wills of the individuals. A proper definition of the term 'right' should involve all the three ingredients. However, in the realm of political theory, the most important ingredient is the fact of political recognition that connects the element of disinterested claims of the individuals with the sovereign authority of the State. Gilchrist says: "Rights arise, therefore, from individuals as members of society and from the recognition that for society there is ultimate good which may be reached by the development of the powers inherent in every individual."[6] However, the view of Laski is better when he says, "Rights, in fact, are those conditions of social life without which no man can seek, in general, to be himself at his best. Since the State exists to make possible that achievement, it is only by maintaining rights that its end may be secured."[7] Rights, therefore, have a three-fold nature:

- **(i) Ethical:** When we deal with claims of the individuals based on their real wills. They are recognised by the community.
- **(ii) Legal:** When translated into law by the state rights are legal.
- **(iii) Political:** In politics are concerned with 'moral rights' which would be legally enforceable if law were what it ought to be.

Claim Aspect *Vs.* Duty Aspect

In the development of the concept of rights in recent times the 'claim aspect' has overshadowed the 'duty aspect'. There is a marked tendency to inflate the notion of rights. The rights are not merely asserted defensively against State action. They are rather interpreted as legitimate claims on the government to satisfy human needs. The distinction between rights as 'liberties' and rights as 'claims' has become an important matter to

5. $. *Ibid.*
6. R.N. Gilchrist, *Principles of Political Science*, p. 135.
7. Laski, *op. cit.*, p. 91.

social and political theory.[8] It puts a premium on the ideal relationship between rights and duties. The 'claim rights' entitle their holder to limit the liberty of another person. The argument that duties and rights are logically linked seems to be water-tight in some rights. However, there are uses of the word 'duty' which do not imply correlative rights.[9] This may be seen in the form of distinction between 'special' and 'general' rights. Special rights arise out of specific undertakings and agreements between individuals. They presuppose the existence of general rights. One needs a special right or a claim to justify a limitation on another's freedom. In the absence of such a right everyone has the general right not to be coerced.[10]

THEORIES OF RIGHTS

Among the various explanations of rights which have been offered from time to time we can distinguish five main theories as under:

1. The Theory of Natural Rights,
2. The Legal Theory of Rights,
3. The Historical Theory of Rights,
4. The Idealistic Theory of Rights, and
5. The Social Welfare Theory of Rights.

1. The Theory of Natural Rights

It holds that rights are rationally deducible from man's nature. They have their universal application irrespective of the difference of place, time and environment. Nature is the author of certain rights that have a universal, rational, eternal and immutable character. The Stoics of ancient Greece upheld the right to equality as given to us by Nature. The Roman thinkers like Polybius and Cicero emphasised that the laws of the State must conform to the Law of Nature. Though the principles of the law of nature may be understood by rational power, they are of a universal and eternal character. Thomas Hobbes defined right to life as a natural right which even the sovereign of the State could not jeopardise. John Locke treated three rights relating to life, liberty and property as natural rights. Effective protection of the natural rights is the responsibility of the State. If the sovereign authority is incapable of fulfilling the trust of the people, the contract may be dissolved and a new sovereign may be chosen to secure effective protection of natural rights.

The doctrine of natural rights was incorporated into important declarations as those of American independence of 1776 and of French

8. D.D. Raphael, *Political Theory and the Rights of Man*, pp. 56-57.
9. N.P. Barry, *An Introduction to Modern Political Theory*, pp. 186-87.
10. H.A.L. Hart, "Are There any Natural Rights?" in Anthony Quinton (ed.), *Political Philosophy*, pp. 60-64.

Revolution of 1789, The Universal Declaration of Rights adopted by the General Assembly of the United Nations in 1948 is based on theory of Natural Rights when it says: "All human beings are born free and equal in dignity and rights." Thus, the whole idea of natural rights is based on the assumption that irrespective of his merit as an individual in his personal or moral capacity, man is at least equal to all others in human worth. Even convicted criminals have the right not to be treated in cruel or in-human ways by the jail staff.[11]

Implications of 'natural rights':[12]

1. Historical affirmation: There is an historical affirmation that man pre-existed society.

2. Moral and metaphysical assumption: There is a moral and metaphysical assumption that man is a creature who possesses certain rights by virtue of the general nature and plan of the universe and of the part which he has to play in carrying out the plan of the universe.

3. Formation of society: In order that these rights may be preserved, he forms society.

4. Rights brought by men: Rights, then, are not created by society, but are brought by men into society.

5. Purpose of society: The purpose of society is to secure man's rights.

6. Right to rebel: If it does not do so, the individual has a right to rebel.

7. Man has no right to rebel: Because society is formed to secure his rights, as a whole. Even if on a particular occasion society appears to violate one of the rights, it does so only that it may better secure them as a whole; or it may better secure the rights of the most of its members even if it does not secure the rights of a particular member at a particular moment, or of a particular member at any moment.

Criticism of the Theory of Natural Rights

1. It is incorrect to say that rights may be available in the pre-political stage. To say that some rights are created by Nature is to say that some rights are available to man just after his birth. But, there are no rights unless there is some machinery to give them effective recognition or protection.
2. Rights are created in a well-organised social system. A man living in a forest or in some unknown island has no rights of his own. Robinson Crusoe had no rights until he met Man Friday.[13]

---

11. Barry, *op. cit.*, p. 192.
12. C.E.M. Joad, *Guide to the Philosophy of Morals and Politics*, p. 545.
13. Benn and Peters, *Social Principles and the Democratic State*, p. 97.

3. It is impossible to prepare a list of natural rights. Cicero, Hobbes and Locke, did not offer a precise definition of the term 'natural right', nor did they prepare a catalogue of such rights. There "is no official, or complete, or generally agreed upon list of natural rights."[14]
    1. To treat rights as pre-political is to make them absolute or beyond the control of the State. It becomes like a dogma at the hands of anti-statists. The new notion is that the State may impose reasonable restrictions on the exercise or enjoyment of any right that a man possesses. The rights must be associated with the usefulness or utility to the community. Therefore, Jeremy Bentham scoffed at the doctrine of natural rights by calling them as "rhetorical nonsense upon stilts'. Laski also rejected the case of natural rights though he realised the significance of this theory in a different way when he says that rights "are not natural in the sense that a permanent and unchanging catalogue of them can be compiled, rather they are natural in the sense that under the limitations of a civilised life, facts demand their recognition."[15]

2. Legal Theory of Rights

It holds that a right is a creation of law. If there is no law, there is no right. Custom may sanction some right, but as there is no law to enforce it, it is no right. Hobbes advocated this theory. In his view people made a social contract and thereby established a Leviathan to protect their rights by the force of law. Bentham holds that rights are the creatures of law and of organised society. John Austin says that every right, whether divine, legal or moral, "rests on a relative duty; that is to say, a duty lying on a party or parties other than the party or parties in whom the right resides. And manifestly that relative duty would not be a duty substantially if the law which affects to impose it were not sustained by might."[16]

1. *Limitation of legal theory*: To say that law alone creates right is to dismiss the importance of custom in the life of a community. People have so many rights because of the force of custom behind them. The law of the State protects the system of rights. But to dismiss the value of custom altogether is not justified.
2. To say that law is the creator of rights and that the state is the possessor of legal sovereignty is to make the State omnipotent

14. E. Asirvatham, *Political Theory*, VIII ed., p. 163.
15. Laski, *op. cit.*, p. 91.
16. Austin, *The Province of Jurisprudence Determined*, edited by H.A.L. Hart, p. 285 n.

and the people helpless in fighting for their rights in the event of any encroachment upon them by the action of the State. It deprives the people of their right to resist state absolutism.

3. Legal theory discards the role of ethical considerations. "It does not help us to make the State what it should be."[17]

3. Historical or Prescriptive Theory of Rights

In the creation of rights it takes the factor of time. Every right is based on the force of long observance. On account of its long observance the essential sanction behind a right is a tradition or custom, As R.M. MacIver says a law is nothing else than an action of the State in the form of the crystallisation of the age-old custom into a legal sanction. A better affirmation of this view may be found in the ideas of Edmund Burke in his theory of prescriptive institutions. According to him the people have a right over anything that they exercise or enjoy uninterruptedly over a fairly long passage of time. MacIver condemned the philosophy behind the action of French revolutionaries, who desired to uproot the established system of institutions and suddenly erect a new one in its place.

Limitations of Historical Theory

Rights do not have an eternal character just by virtue of their force of long observance, otherwise the system of slavery would have been in practice even in modern times. Times change and with it changes the whole pattern of social life. The system of rights also undergoes a change. The rulers may abolish a particular system of rights and instead impose a new one in the light of new conditions without bothering for the factor of prescription or long observance. For example, the British rulers finished the rights of the Indian people to burn alive a widow, to settle disputes in a panchayat, to excommunicate a person by the caste or community panchayat. They introduced a new system of rights that had to be accepted by the people of India. However, no one can deny that rights are created by the passage of time. History "cannot be ignored, but history cannot be relied on alone."[18]

4. The Idealistic Theory of Rights

According to Idealism man's rational will issues in the form of claims and leads to the creation of a system of rights when moral recognition of such claims is converted into legal sanction. T.H. Green begins with the assumption that human consciousness thinks of the goodness of

17. Asirvatham, *op. cit.*, p. 167.
18. Hocking, *Law and Rights*, p. 7.

the 'self' as well as of other human beings. Thus, he recognised that a claim conducive to common interest brings about a system of rights. In the words of Barker: "Human consciousness postulates liberty: liberty involves rights; rights demand the state."[19] As Bernard Bosanquet said, "It is a claim which can be enforced at law, which no moral imperative can be; but it is also recognised to be a claim which ought to be capable of enforcement at law; and thus it has a moral aspect.... A typical right unites the two sides."[20]

Idealistic theory looks at rights from a highly moral point of view. Rights are rooted in the mind of man. They are powers granted to him by the community so that he may realise a common good of which his good is an intrinsic part. A right must establish two things (i) the individual claiming it must be able to convince society that in doing so he is not interfering with like claims of his fellow beings, and (ii) he must be able to convince society that his claim is absolutely necessary for the sake of his self-development. Thus, a right "is a freedom of action possessed by a man of virtue of his occupying a certain place and fulfilling a certain function in a social order."[21]

Limitations of Idealistic Theory

1. The idealistic interpretation of the origin and nature of rights is too abstract to be understood by a man of average comprehension.
2. The whole idea of the 'best possible development of a man's personality' is so vague that the state cannot prescribe a particular pattern that may be equally relevant for all.
3. This theory seems to sacrifice social good for the sake of individual good.

However, the merit of idealistic theory lies on the theoretical plane. It furnishes a safe test to rights which can be applied at all times. Here in it is superior to the legal, historical, and social welfare theories. The one absolute right of all human beings is the right of personality.[22]

5. The Social Expediency or Social Welfare Theory

It implies that the rights are the creation of the society. They are based on the consideration of common welfare. They make what is conducive to the greatest good of the greatest number. They are the conditions of social good. Claims not in conformity with the general welfare fail from

19. Barker, *op. cit.*, p. 23.
20. Bosanquet, *The Philosophical Theory of State*, p. 188.
21. N. Wilde, *The Ethical Basis of the State*, p. 12.
22. Asirvatham, *op. cit.*, pp. 175-76.

being rights as they would not be recognised by the community. Jeremy Bentham developed the principle of utility to show that the system of rights is beneficial both to the individual and to the society. Laski reinterprets the premises of Benthamite utilitarianism in his positive liberalism. As he says: "We are making the test of rights utility; and that, it is clear, involves the question of those to whom the rights are to be useful. There is only one possible answer. In any State the demands of each citizen for the fulfilment of his best self must be taken as of equal worth; and the utility of a right is, therefore, its value to all the members of the state."[23]

Limitations of Social Welfare Theory

1. It dwells on the factor of social welfare which is a term too vague to be put into a precise form. The Benthamite formula of 'greatest good of the greatest number' may mean different things to the liberals, the socialists and the Marxists.
2. If carried to extremes, the point of individual welfare may be lost, as it seeks to sacrifice individual good at the altar of social welfare. N. Wilde believes that if rights are created by the consideration of social expediency, the individual is without an appeal and helplessly dependent upon its arbitrary will.[24]

However, the essential merit of social welfare theory lies in its linking up the idealistic version of rights with its utilitarian counterpart and thereby making it a commendable affair so far as liberal political theory is concerned.

6. The Marxian Theory of Rights

It links up the case of rights with the prevailing economic system of the society. It holds that rights cannot be understood in isolation from the pattern of social classes and struggle going on between them as a necessary consequence of the laws of dialectical materialism. The dominant class owns the means of production and distribution. It creates a system of rights to keep itself in power. The dominant class claims the right to exploit and oppress the dominated class who has no control over the' means of production and distribution. Until the capitalist system is replaced by the system of socialism the working class cannot have rights. After the successful revolution the proletariat has a new kind of social life in which its rights shall be associated with the set of duties so as to consolidate the new socialist order. The people would have rights like

23. Laski, *op. cit.*, p. 92.
24. Wilde, *op. cit.*, p. 124.

those relating to work and social security. They would also be tacked with duties like obedience to law and protection of the socialist system. With the advent of the socialist system the society would be able to dispense with the idea of rights prevailing in the bourgeois society.[25] Thus, Marxian theory of rights is unique in telling us about the meaning and nature of rights.

Criticism of Marxism

1. As every system whether pre-feudal, feudal, bourgeois or socialist, has its own system of rights, it cannot be accepted that the whole system of existing rights would disappear with the establishment of a socialist society.
2. To say that rights must be tacked with duties is a good thing, but to destroy the whole system of rights in the name of the fulfilment of duties by the role of an omnipotent state is equally bad.
3. Milovan Djilas and Stojanovic of Yugoslavia have rabidly denounced the Russian political system for allowing no meaningful rights to the people.

KINDS OF RIGHTS

1. Moral rights: Moral rights are the claims of the individuals based on the conscience of the community. These are the claims recognised by the good sense of the people. For example, a teacher has the moral right to be respected by his students. But such rights cannot be enforced by the courts. Their enforcement depends upon the good sense of the community. It only when moral rights are converted into legal rights, that they become enforceable by the action of the State.

2. Civil rights: Civil rights relate to the person and property of the individuals. As they relate to the essential conditions of a civilised life they are civil or social rights. They include a number of rights like those relating to life, personal liberty, thought and expression, property, religion and the like.

(i) *Right to life*: Right to life is most important of all the civil rights. The enjoyment of all other rights depends upon it. It implies that no person can take the life of another, and a person has the right to save his life even by killing another if his opponent makes an attempt to kill him. It is called 'right to self-defence." Suicide is a crime.

(ii) *Right to personal liberty:* The right to personal liberty includes right to live as a free citizen. A person cannot be detained

25. J. Plamenatz, *Karl Marx's Philosophy of Man*, p. 312.

without a proper cause. He cannot be punished physically or economically unless he is held guilty by a court of competent jurisdiction. The trial of the accused must be free and open.

(iii) *Right to think and express*: It also comes in this category.

(iv) *Right to keep arms and property*: In legal parlance, it means equality before law and its equal protection for all.

(v) *Right to religion*: It is also a civil right.

3. Political Rights: Political rights relate to a man's participation in the affairs of the State. They include right of giving vote, fighting elections, taking public employment, supporting or opposing the government and changing it by constitutional means. Political rights enable a person to send petitions to the government for the redressal of certain wrongs, following or abandoning a particular policy, making or unmaking a particular law, and expressing views for the creation of a healthy public opinion. Democracy is regarded as the best form of government because it ensures all such rights.

Chart 12.1

Kinds of Rights

- *Rights relating to Liberty*
  - *Civil Right to*
    - (i) Personal freedom
    - (ii) Personal security
    - (iii) Personal property
    - (iv) Religion
    - (v) Speech and expression
    - (vi) Formation of unions.
    - (vii) Movement throughout the country
    - (viii) Residence or settlement in any part of the country
  - *Political Right to*
    - (i) Vote
    - (ii) Contest elections
    - (iii) Form political parties and groups
    - (iv) Hold public meetings
    - (v) Criticise and change government by constitutional means
  - *Economic Right to*
    - (i) Work
    - (ii) Rest and leisure
    - (iii) Form trade unions
    - (iv) Carry on some profession or trade
    - (v) Avail social insurance
    - (vi) Bargain freely for adequate remuneration
    - (vii) Enjoy status of partners in control of industry
- *Rights relating to Equality*
  - Right to be treated equally and on equal footing with others in matters of
    - (i) Legal protection
    - (ii) Corrective justice
    - (iii) Taxation
    - (iv) Admissibility to honours and offices of public employment
- *Rights relating to Fraternity*
  - Rights to
    - (i) Education
    - (ii) Public assistance
    - (iii) Public employment

4. Economic rights: Economic rights relate to a man's vocation, his engagement in a gainful employment so as to solve the problem of food, clothing and shelter. It includes right to earn livelihood by proper means and the right to work. The right to rest and leisure makes a person take relief for the sake of maintaining and increasing his efficiency. The workers must have a right to form unions and associations for protecting and promoting their interests. They should have right to bargain freely for remunerative work. They should have some share in the management of industry. The socialists include right to social insurance and self-government in industry in economic rights.

5. Human rights: 'Natural rights' and civil rights have assumed more significance since the formulation of the Universal Declaration of Human Rights by the Human Rights Commission and their adoption by the General Assembly of the United Nations in December, 1948. The Declaration incorporates a host of rights that have a necessary connection with moral and civil rights pointed out above. It says that all human beings are born free and equal in dignity and rights; they are endowed with reason and conscience and should act towards one another in a spirit of brotherhood. It speaks of the right to security in the event of unemployment, sickness, disability, old age, or other conditions of destitutehood beyond one's control.

'Particular Rights of Citizen Stressed by Laski

1. The right to work: It means right to be occupied in producing a share of the goods and commodities that are essential for the community.

2. The right to adequate wages: It means that all those who work must be given sufficient wages to maintain themselves.

3. The right to reasonable hours of work: It means that he should be asked to put in that amount of work which does not exhaust him completely and thereby make him unfit to discharge his duties as an active member of the community.

4. The right to education: It means that he should be given that minimum of education which is essential for the performance of his duties.

5. The right to share in political power: It means that he should have right to vote, to be elected, and also remove a corrupt government and run machinery of the state according to the provisions of the Constitution.

6. The right to form associations and organise public meetings: Every citizen must be provided with judicial safeguards so that justice may be secured without fear or favour.

7. The right to property: It is limited only to the extent that is necessary for the development of his personality and does not prove detrimental to the interests of the society.

8. The right to industrial self-government: It means that he, as an industrial unit, must somehow be given the power to participate in the making of those decisions which affect him as a producer, if he is to be in a position to maximise his freedom.

9. The right to speech and expression: It means that he should have the right to ventilate his grievances and organise public opinion in that matter.

10. The right to equality before law: It is so that he may get justice without discrimination. It must not be harder upon the poor than upon the rich.

RIGHTS OF A CITIZEN IN A MODERN STATE

A. Civil Rights

1. Right to life: The right to life is a basic civil right given to each and every citizen. Without life and security of a person other rights are of no use. Green regarded it as the most fundamental of all rights. The state must provide protection to the individual against the foes, internal and external even against himself because he must be prevented from committing suicide.

2. Right to family: The family is the hope and cradle of civilisation. Its right implies the right to marriage, right to the custody and control of the children and the right of inheritance. The right to family is great importance for the continuation of the human race. The right includes the liberty to rear and bring up children in the way the parents like.

3. Right to property: Right to property is based on the assumption that owning property is a natural instinct in man and it provides incentive to hard work. Since early days of human society the idea of property has been a supreme factor in the evolution of modern civilisation. The right to property means the freedom to the individual to enjoy his property. It implies that the individual has the right to acquire, hold and dispose of property without any restriction or hindrance. It also means that he is free to alienate property by way of gift, exchange or will.

4. Right to worship: The right to worship is right to freedom of religion and conscience. It guarantees to every citizen the right to liberty, belief and worship. It means that everyone is free to progress and follow any religion and perform the necessary rites connected with his religious practices. The modern secular states remain neutral between different religious faith and permit the citizens to enjoy the right to profess, to propagate and practice any religion. The Constitution of India also guarantees this right to all the Indian citizens.

5. Right to work: The individual is born in the world in which if it were orgaisned rationally he would live only on his labour. It is the duty of the State to provide him with a job. If State fails to provide him with a job, his development will stop. The socialist states strongly advocate right to work. They plead that society should provide him with work or it should feed him. Right to work does not mean the right to particular work. Laski says, "A Prime Minister who has been overthrown has not the right to be provided labour of an identical character. Society cannot afford each man the choice of the effort he will like. It cannot in any ultimate way afford under emphasis occupation which carry with them special dignity. It means supply of goods and sources to maintain life." If a man is deprived of right to work he is entitled for an equal reward or compensation. Right to work carries with it the right to an adequate wage for one's labour. The wage earner needs the food which can keep him physically fit. He needs clothing and shelter which can enable him to start life. A worker needs those small comforts which make life a thing of some interests. Proper service conditions are necessary for good life of the workers.

6. Right to contract: Right to contract enables the individual to enter into contracts freely with others. An individual can enter into agreements with others regarding subjects of mutual interest. But the State can regulate or ban contracts those which are against the interests of the society.

7. Right to speech: The right to freedom of thought and expression alongwith the freedom of speech and press has been highly valued by all the democratic states. It is considered as fundamental for the development of human personality. Therefore, poets, philosophers, and political scientists have passionately pleaded for freedom of thought and expression. J.S. Mill strongly advocated for the liberty of thought and speech. According to Bury, "It is one supreme condition of mental and moral progress." Laski opines, "To allow a man to say what he thinks is to give his personality the only ultimate channel of free expression and uncitizenship the only means of moral adequacy."

Freedom of speech and expression is also the cornerstone of democracy. A government can always learn more from the criticism of its opponents than from the eulogy of its supporters.

8. Right to free movement: While governments in democratic states pass various laws to regulate the life of the individuals and society, they see to it that there is no arbitrary restriction on the free movement of the individual.

9. Right to equality: Right to equality is given great importance in the modern welfare states. The right means the absence of legal discrimination against anyone, individual group, class or race. Democracy can only exist and flourish in a society of equals.

10. Right to education: This right is considered very necessary to the citizens. Every developing state spend sufficient amount for the education of its citizens. Schools, colleges, universities, research centres are established by the state. The state provides proper educational atmosphere in these institutions. The education makes people perfect citizens. Without education there will be a mockery of peoples government. Education alone can provide conditions for developing all faculties of mind and body.

B. Political Rights

The political rights are those legal rights which enable the citizens to take part in the work of the government. The following are the important political rights given in all modern welfare states:

1. Right to vote: Right to vote enables a citizen to choose his representatives in the elected bodies as parliament or legislative assembly. This right to vote is also called 'franchise' is both a condition and product of democracy. Modern democracies because of their large areas and populations are not direct but indirect representative democracies. Every adult citizen has the right to express his opinion by casting a vote at the time of election what person he desires should undertake the task of the government. The right to vote should be as wide as possible irrespective of sex, property, race, creed, religion and education. One man one vote ought to be the maxim of a democratic government. Aliens, bankrupts, paupers, criminals and minors are denied the right to vote.

2. Right to be elected: The right to be elected is a corollary to the right to vote and most of the democratic states grant to their citizens the privilege of contesting elections to the different legislative bodies. It has been argued by some that it would be desirable to prescribe a qualification demanding experience of work on a representative body. Laski suggests a representative must possess adequate knowledge of the working of a local body.

3. Right to public work: In a democracy, every citizen has the right of equal eligibility for any office executive, administrative or judicial and to be protected against discrimination on grounds of religion, race, caste, sex, descent, place of birth or residence. The Indian Constitution ensures to all citizens in India equality of opportunity in matters of appointment to any office under the state. It does not mean that academic, professional and other qualifications cannot be laid down for filling the various posts.

4. Right to petition: The right to send petition for the redress of grievances is an old and valued right of the people. The right entitles every citizen to send petition either individually or collectively to the competent authority for the redress of grievances. In a democracy, the government cannot ignore the legitimate desires and grievances of the people because they are the ultimate sovereign. The government must always be above to the grievances of the people and promptly respond to their needs.

5. Right to criticise the government: This right is available only in free and democratic states. This right is beneficial not only for the people but also for the government. Public criticism of the government policies keep the government alert and efficient. A responsible opposition party in the legislature is therefore considered essential. The role and importance of healthy public opinion in a democracy cannot be over emphasised. Democracy is really a government by criticism for truth only comes by the clash of opinions.

6. Right to resist: The citizen has the right to resist the authority of the State if he honestly feels that a particular law or action of the government is inimical to his moral sense of justice. But the resistance of this type is only a moral right and not a legal right. Obviously no State can permit an action which defies the authority and may jeopardise even its very existence.

MEASURES FOR PROTECTION OF RIGHTS

1. Constitutional safeguard: The rights of the people must be enshrined in the Constitution of the State so that they may have the character of fundamental rights. By doing so the State accords them constitutional protection and empowers the courts to issue prerogative writs for their enforcement.

2. Rule of law: Another safeguard is the rule of law as available in Britain. There is no written Constitution in Britain and yet the people enjoy their rights because in the words of Dicey, this country is known for having the 'rule of law.' It has two essential features: (i) every citizen is under the same law of the land irrespective of his social, economic or political status, and (ii) a person cannot be arrested without sufficient cause and he cannot be made to suffer in body or in goods unless declared guilty by a court of competent jurisdiction after a fair trial.

3. Free and honest press: There should be a free and honest press in every country so that the people may have a straightforward dissemination of news and views. The press would highlight if there is any encroachment upon the rights of the people. Thus, a healthy public opinion may be created for the protection of their rights against encroachment of any kind.

4. Decentralisation of powers: Concentration of powers creates conditions under which the rights of the people are in jeopardy. But decentralisation of powers creates conditions that minimise the possibility of the abuse of power.

5. Independent and impartial judiciary: The existence of an independent and impartial judiciary is also necessary so that if the people feel aggrieved by any action of the state or some other institution, they may move the courts for the protection of their rights. In democratic countries the courts are given special power of issuing prerogative writs for the enforcement of constitutional provisions.

6. Extension of state's activities: It is suggested that the State should not extend its area of activity into the legitimate domain of voluntary groups and associations.

7. Eternal vigilance of the people: If the people are apathetic or indolent, their rights can never be secure. It is well said: "It is the proud spirit of the citizens, less than the letter of the law, that is their most real safeguard."[26]

QUESTIONS FOR EXERCISE

1. Discuss briefly but clearly the term rights. Also discuss various theories put forth in this regard.
2. Describe the theories of rights. Which of them do you prefer? Give reasons for your views.
3. Define the term "right". What particular rights should an individual have according to Laski?
4. Analyse Laski's Theory of Rights.
5. Write short note on Laski's concept of rights.
6. Examine T.H. Green's views on Rights.
7. What are natural rights? Discuss theory of natural rights.

---

26. Laski, *op. cit.*, p. 104.

13

Concept of Liberty

Liberty is essential for a man's personality. Liberty is not one but manifold. Such as natural liberty, civil liberty, political liberty, personal liberty, economic liberty and national liberty. Liberty is the most cherished ideal of life of a man. Liberty or freedom is the central problem of politics. History shows that freedom is the basic thing that goes to make up the ethos of man and civilisation. Without it no one can attain happiness which is the true end of man's life. Men want to be free to live their own lives in their own way. Rights are means to an end and that end is liberty. Freedom means absence of restraints. Liberals pleaded for the freedom of an individual from the authority of the State. The Marxists fought for the freedom of proletariat from bourgeoisie. The right to liberty is one of the most important rights because it contributes to the evolution of a man's individuality.

History has amply shown that liberty is the basic thing that goes to make up the ethics of man civilisation. Without it no one can attain happiness which is the true end of all human beings. Men want to be free to live their own lives, in their own way and the attainment of that ambition constitutes liberty. The purpose of rights is enabling men to live, to enjoy life and to develop to the full potentialities of their individual personalities. Rights are only means to an end and the end is liberty. Men want to be free to live their own lives in their own way and the attainment of that ambition constitutes liberty or freedom.

DEFINITION OF LIBERTY

In order to understand the essence of the word liberty it is necessary to examine some definitions :

1. *Seeley*: "Liberty is the opposite of over Government."

2. *Laski*: "I mean by liberty the absence of restraints upon the existence of these social conditions which a modern civilisation are the necessary guarantees of the individual happiness."

3. *Liber*: "It is the faculty of willing to the power of doing what has been willed without influence from any other source."
4. *D.D Raphael*: "Freedom means absence of restraints, a man is free so far as he is not restrained from doing what he wants to do or what he would choose to do if he knew that he could."
5. *Ramsay Muir*: "By liberty I mean to secure enjoyment by individuals and by the natural and spontaneous groups of individuals. Such as a nation, church, trade, union, of the power to think their own thoughts and to express and act upon them using their own gifts in their own way under the shelter of the law, provided they do not impair the corresponding right of others."

In brief liberty is the affirmation by an individual or a group of his or its own essence. The ideal of liberty has made its powerful appeal to man in all ages. John Locke was a great exponent of liberty.

Thus liberty means man's *right to do what is worth doing*. Social life is regulated by a set of principles or norms that make man's life civilised. These restraints distinguish between good and bad, right and wrong, moral and immoral, legal and illegal. Thus liberty means man's right to do what he wants for the sake of making the best possible development of his personality by following a course that is good, or right, or moral, or lawful. In fine, the real meaning of liberty should be understood with this point in view that the liberty of an individual is relative to that of others.[1] Sidgwick holds that freedom, when employed without qualification, signifies primarily the absence of physical coercion or confinement. A is clearly not a free agent if B moves his limbs, and he is not free if he cannot get out of a building because B has locked the door. But in another part of its meaning — which from our present point of view is more important — freedom is opposed not to physical constraint but to the moral restraint placed on inclination by the fear of painful consequences resulting from the action of other human beings."[2]

NEGATIVE ASPECT OF LIBERTY

The meaning of liberty has two dimensions — negative and positive. In a negative sense, liberty implies the absence of restraints as far as possible. All restraint is bad, because it effects curtailment or diminution of individual freedom. These should be as little as possible as liberty lives within restraints. Here the burden of argument is to accept the fact of restraints with a sense of compulsion. John Stuart Mill says that "all restraints *qua* restraints is an evil...leaving people to themselves is always

1. Barker, *Principles of Social and Political Theory*, p. 145.
2. Sidgwick, *Elements of Politics*, p. 45.

better than controlling them."[3] In order to make his meaning more clear, Mill divides man's action into two parts — self-regarding and others-regarding. The State has no right to interfere with the liberty of man if his action affects himself alone. Professing any religion, worshipping the deity, and reading a book are examples of man's strictly self-regarding actions. However, the state may intervene in the liberty of a man if he harms liberty of his fellow-beings. If a man does something that has its effect on others, it pertains to the realm of others-regarding. As Mill puts it, "The sole end for which mankind are warranted, individually or collectively, in interfering with the liberty of action of any of their number, is self-protection. That the only purpose for which power can be rightfully exercised over any member of a civilised community against his will is to prevent harm to others. His own good, either physical or moral, is not a sufficient warrant.... Over himself, his own body and mind, the individual is sovereign."[4]

F.A. Hayek says that every individual has some assured area of personal freedom with which others cannot interfere. The element of 'choice' should be taken as decisive.[5] A man is really free when he is not subjected to coercion of any kind. Coercion means subjection to the arbitrary will of others. It occurs when an agent's actions are made to serve the will of another, not for his own but for other's purposes. It implies *action* in the sense that a person, who is coerced, chooses to be what he does. It occurs only when one person threatens with the intention of thereby getting the other to act in conformity with his will."[6]

POSITIVE ASPECT OF LIBERTY

In the present times individual liberty is sought to be reconciled with the growing authority of the State. If the State desires to achieve the goal of public welfare restraints are essential. Human actions cannot be divided into water-tight forms as was done by Mill more than a hundred years back. Man lives in society, his actions have an effect on the liberty of others. There can be nothing like a strictly private or self-regarding sphere. Man cannot be allowed to commit suicide or read obscene literature. As L.T. Hobhouse points out, "There is no side of a man's life which is unimportant to society, for whatever he is,' does, or thinks may affect his own well-being, which is and ought to be a matter of common concern, and may also directly or indirectly affect the thought, action and character of those with whom he comes into contact."[7]

3. Mill, *Essay on Liberty*, pp. 150-51.
4. *Ibid.*, pp. 72-73.
5. Hayek, *The Constitution of Liberty*, p. 13.
6. *Ibid.*, pp. 12-13.
7. L.T. Hobhouse, *Liberalism*, p. 65.

CONTRIBUTION OF T.H. GREEN

The meaning of liberty in its positive aspect is a contribution of T.H. Green. He defines liberty as a positive power of doing or enjoying something that is worth doing or worth enjoying in common with others. As man is a social creature, his life should be regulated by certain social bonds. Liberty of the individual should be considered in relation to the norms of goodwill. Paraphrasing the meaning of Green, Barker says: "Liberty can only be liberty for this goodwill; it can only be liberty for the pursuit of objects which such a will presents to itself. It is, therefore, no negative absence of restraints any more than beauty is the absence of ugliness. Inhering as it does in the goodwill and in that will only, it is not a power of pursuing any and every object, but a power of pursuing these objects which the goodwill presents to itself. In a word, it has two qualities. It is positive — a freedom to do something, not a freedom from having something done to one. It is determinate — a freedom to do something of a definite character, something which possesses the quality of being worth doing, and not any and everything."[8]

Today the meaning of liberty has come to involve within itself both the individual and social sides of man's existence. As the social life requires a network of regulations, the idea of liberty has been bound with the necessity of due restraints. Liberty has come to have a derivative value arising from the supreme value of the moral personality acting and developing its capacities as such. The liberty which the state upholds and makes a principle of its action must be a liberty relative to and, regulated by the nature of moral personality. As like Prof Leo Strauss says: "There is no relation of man to man in which man is absolutely free to act as he pleases, or as it suits him.... By virtue of his rationality man has a latitude of alternatives such as no other earthly being has.... The sense of the latitude of this freedom is accompanied by a sense that the full and unrestrained exercise of that freedom is not right. Man's freedom is accompanied by a sacred awe, by a kind of divination that not everything is permitted. Restraint is, therefore, as natural or as primeval as freedom."[9] To quote Sir John Seeley, "We may say then that liberty is primarily the absence of restraint or the opposite of the government, but in a secondary sense, which is also convenient, it is the absence of excessive restraint or the opposite of over-government."[10]

8. Barker, *Political Thought in England*, p. 24.
9. Strauss, *Natural Right and History*, pp. 129-30.
10. Seeley, J. *Introduction to Political Science*, p. 120.

Thus liberty has both its negative and positive dimensions. The negative view disfavours the case of restraints on the liberty of man as far as possible. Mill and Hayek subscribe to this view. The positive view appreciates the system of reasonable restraints in the name of public good. Green and Strauss subscribe to positive view. As Prof Isaiah Berlin of the Oxford University has pointed out the real meaning of liberty involves both sides, and the two cannot be separated from each other. In some area of a man's life he must be free from the restraints of any kind so that he may wish to determine the course of his action without any direction from others. As Berlin affirms: "The extent of my social or political freedom consists in the absence of obstacles not merely to my actual, but to my potential, choices to my acting in this or that way if I choose to do so."[11] The State may impose some fetters on the freedom of man, but no fetter should be like one killing his area of choice. "Liberty is increased when sovereignty is put into right hands."[12] N.P. Barry says: "The old lag may deliberately commit a crime in order to recapture the security of prison life, but it would be absurd to describe his resulting condition as one of liberty."[13]

KINDS OF LIBERTY

Liberty implies "a condition of freedom especially opposed to political subjection, imprisonment, or slavery."[14] However, it is a multiple concept having following varieties:

1. Natural Liberty: Natural liberty implies complete freedom for a man to do what he wills. Hobbes called it 'licence' by the liberty of the woods. It means no restraint of any kind whatsoever on the doing of a man. In the world of nature all creatures live according to their will. So should be the pattern of a man's life. Let a man do what he wills.

Criticism

Liberty lives within restraints. Therefore, the idea of natural liberty is an arrant nonsense; it cannot prevail in a society of human beings. As a social creature, man should lead a life regulated by social restraints. Rousseau begins with the assumption that 'man is born free, he is everywhere in chains' but he ultimately stresses the point that "what man loses by the social contract is his natural liberty and an unlimited right to everything he tries to get and succeeds in getting; what he gains is civil liberty and the proprietorship of all he possesses."[15]

11. Berlin, *Four Essays on Liberty*, pp. xxxix-xl.
12. *Ibid.*, p. 166. The element of choice is very important in the meaning of liberty.
13. Barry, *op. cit.*, p. 160.
14. *Encyclopaedia Britannica*, Vol. 13, 1967 Ptg., p. 1029.
15. Rousseau, *Social Contract*, Book I, Ch. VIIL.

Kinds of Liberty

- *Natural Liberty*
- *Social/Civil Liberty*
  - *Personal*
    - (i) Freedom of choice in strictly private matters
    - (ii) Security of health, honour and person
    - (iii) Freedom of thought, expression and faith
    - (iv) Freedom of movement
    - (v) Use and enjoyment of private property
  - *Political*
    - (i) Right to take part in the affairs of the State
    - (ii) Right to exercise franchise
    - (iii) Right to have free supply of news
    - (iv) Right to fight free and fair elections
    - (v) Right to send petitions to the government
    - (vi) Right to support or oppose governmental policies and actions
  - *Economic*
    - (i) Right to have some gainful employment
    - (ii) Freedom from want
    - (iii) Right to produce and distribute goods
    - (iv) Workers' right to participate in the management of industry
    - (v) Establishment of industrial democracy
  - *Domestic*
    - (i) A responsible and respectable position of wife and children
    - (ii) Freedom of entering into matrimonial alliance
    - (iii) Responsibility of the parents for seeking moral and mental development of family members
  - *National*
    - (i) Freedom from colonial subjection or achievement of independence
    - (ii) Exercise of patriotism
  - *International*
    - (i) Renunciation to war
    - (ii) Abandonment of the use of force
    - (iii) Pacific settlement of disputes among nations
    - (iv) Limitation on the production of armaments
- *Moral Liberty*

2. Social Liberty: Liberty lies in its civil or social variety in personal, political, religious, economic, national and international spheres. It relates to man's freedom in his life as a member of the social organisation. It refers to a man's right to do what he wills in compliance with the restraints imposed on him in the general interest. This kind of liberty consists in the rights and privileges that the society recognises and the State protects in the spheres of private and public life of an individual. Following are its sub-varieties:

(i) *Personal Liberty*: According to Laski Private liberty "is that aspect of which the substance is mainly personal to a man's self. It is the opportunity to be fully himself in the private relations of life."[16] According to Blackstone, this kind of liberty consists in three directions — (i) personal security not only of health and life but also of reputation, (ii) personal freedom especially of movement, and (iii) personal property or the free use and enjoyment and disposal of all acquisitions.

(ii) *Political Liberty*: Political liberty refers to the power of the people to be active in the affairs of the State. It is integrally connected with the life of man as a citizen. It consists in the provisions for universal adult franchise, free and fair elections, and freedom for the avenues that make a healthy public opinion. Its existence shows that the people may curb, control and change their government.

(iii) *Economic Liberty*: Economic liberty pertains to the individual in his capacity as a manual or mental producer or worker engaged in some gainful occupation or service. It means security and opportunity to find reasonable significance in the earning of one's daily bread. The individual should be free from the fear of unemployment and insufficiency which saps the whole strength of personality. It includes freedom from want and right to produce and distribute goods. It stands for the establishment of industrial democracy enabling the workers to participate in the management of industry. Economic freedom is, however, a matter of controversy. The liberals desire a free and competitive economic system. The socialists advocate the system of state controls, even nationalisation of private property in the public interest. The Communists seek to abolish private economy. They define economic freedom as man's emancipation from evils like unemployment and exploitation.

16. Laski, *op. cit.*, p. 146.

Absence of unemployment and provisions for social security are the marks of economic freedom in the country.

(iv) *Domestic Liberty*: L.T. Hobhouse talks of domestic liberty which means a responsible and respectable position of the wife and children in the family, freedom for the members of the family to have marriage of their choice, and responsibility of the parents to seek moral and mental development of the members of their family.

(v) *National Liberty*: National liberty is another name for national independence. It rejects the colonial or imperial subjection of one nation by another. Freedom struggles are national movements. The Americans gained national liberty in 1776 and the Indians in 1947. Love for one's country is so deep-seated in human hearts that millions of people lay down their lives for the sake of protecting the honour and security of their motherland.

(vi) *International Liberty*: The ideal of liberty covers the world as a whole. In the international sphere, it implies renunciation of war, limitation on the production of armaments, abandonment of the use of force and pacific settlement of international disputes. This ideal is based on the assumption that as the world becomes free, the use of force becomes' irrelevant. There is no sense in aggression if it is not to issue in national subjection in one form or another.

3. Moral Liberty: Moral freedom is contained in the idealistic interpretations of thinkers from the ancient Plato and Aristotle to the modern Rousseau, Kant, Hegel and Green. Though a person may have all kinds of freedom, he lacks the essential quality of a human being if he does not have moral freedom. Moral freedom lies in man's capacity to act as per his rational self. Every individual has a personality of his own. Unless he seeks best possible development of his personality and desires the same thing for others and pays sincere respect for the real worth and dignity of his fellow beings, he is not free in the moral sense. Kant calls it the "fulfilment of the will to categorical self-imposed imperative of duty' and the 'autonomy of the rational will.' To Hegel such freedom has its objective realisation in the State. It has its place in the observance of complete loyalty to the State. It is necessarily connected with man's self-realisation that has a meaning only in the context of the common good.

J.S. MILL'S VIEWS ON LIBERTY

Liberty or freedom is the central problem of politics. The purpose of rights is to enable men to live, to enjoy life and to develop to the full potentialities of their individual personalities. Rights are only a means to an end and the end is liberty. Men want to be free to live their own lives in their own way and the attainment of that constitutes liberty or freedom. The rights and duties arise only if the citizens are provided with the environment in which they are truly free to be themselves. Liberty is free choice of creation of an individual. It is freedom from restraints.

J.S. Mill has been the great champion of liberty. In his famous *Essay on Liberty*, he strongly pleaded for the liberty of the individual against legislative interference as well as against the public opinion. An individual needed protection not only against the tyranny of magistracy but also against the tyranny of society. The growth of democracy and the increasing legislative power of the state tends to reduce individuals to a common type and to, "*swamp them in the tyranny of the collectivism*". Social progress depended upon giving to each individual the fullest opportunity for the fullest development of his personality. Hence, Mill forcefully pleaded for the freedom of the individual.

According to Mill an individual is sovereign over his body and mind. He should be left free in all that concerns himself alone. Society has no right to impose any restraint over the individual because restraint as such is an evil thing. Mill divided the actions of individuals into two parts; self-regarding and others-regarding actions. The self-regarding actions include those matters which affect the doer only, having no concern with others. The individual was to be free in doing those things which affected him alone. But his independence was to be restricted in those cases in which his action had a direct or indirect bearing on others. As it is difficult to divide actions into water-tight compartments the principle was to be followed in a general way. Regarding the relation of the State to liberty Mill's analysis implied three propositions:

1. An increase in the power of the State is prejudicial to liberty,
2. A distinction can be drawn between the part of human life in which it is chiefly the individual that is interested, and the part which chiefly interests society and that liberty is infringed if the State interferes with the first part, and
3. The most valuable element in human life is spontaneous choice, anything which is done by a compulsory power diminishes the scope of that choice and thus infringes liberty.

Criticism of Mill's Concept of Liberty

1. Individual freedom: Mill assumed that the individual is sovereign over his body and mind and therefore he should be left free in all that concerns himself alone. This is not a sound proposition. Neither it is a self-evident truth nor is it in harmony with the facts of total life. Mill, himself admits that, "there can be circumstances under which it may become legitimate for others to intervene in a purely personal matter i.e., where one is about to commit suicide. No one will call it an attack upon one's safety".

2. Division of human action: Mill's division of human action into two self-regarding and other-regarding is a misnomer. Individuals are not isolated beings in a society. The action of each individual directly or indirectly definitely affects others. Therefore, it is not possible to set apart a sphere of conduct which may concern the individual alone.

3. Nature of energy: Critics have also pointed out that, "in his argument he is adamant to identify the individual's energy with genius or originality and to forget that energy may be mere electricity — not strength of character; but weakness consequently need to be repressed rather than encouraged".

Contribution of Mill

Mill not only propounded the negative conception but forcefully pleaded for positive freedom also. He favoured freedom of speech, thought and action. He believed in the toleration of opinions and unhampered freedom of discussion. He was convinced that in the struggle of ideals ultimately the truth will triumph.

HAROLD LASKI'S VIEWS ON LIBERTY

Laski was a consistent believer in the dignity of human personality. In thought and action, he was an uncompromising individualist. He contended that the individual must consult his conscience before deciding to obey or disobey the particular command of the sovereign, The State which insists upon an unquestioning obedience to its orders by the citizens reduces the states of moral slaves. Laski criticised the modern society because it prevents a large majority of people from securing the material foundations of a spiritually enriched life. Laski revised some of the well-known dogmas which Mill stated in his *Essay on Liberty*. He discussed them in the context of an international situation when the success of Fascism was posing a serious danger to the ideal of freedom in all countries. He always remained a consistent champion of human freedom in all its variegated aspects.

Meaning of Liberty

According to Laski, 'Liberty' means the eager maintenance of that atmosphere in which men have an opportunity to be their best selves. He regarded rights as an essential condition of liberty. Without right, there can be no liberty because in that case men are the subjects of law unrelated to the needs of personality. Freedoms are opportunities which history has shown to be essential for the development of personality. Freedoms are inseparable from rights. If the rights are not guaranteed liberty becomes uncertain and illusory. Giving a very comprehensive definition of liberty, Prof Laski says, "Liberty is the eager maintenance of the atmosphere in which men have the opportunity to be their best selves. It is a product of rights. Without rights, there can be no liberty because in that case men are the subjects of law unrelated to the needs of personality. Liberty, therefore, is a positive thing. It does not merely means absence of restraints."

No Classification of Human Actions

Laski did not approve of Mills classification of human actions into two parts *i.e.*, self-regarding actions and other-regarding actions. According to him all conduct was social in the sense that whatever a man did, affected the other members of the society. Laski therefore, lays emphasis upon the relationship of the individual's liberty with the society. He is convinced that personal liberty cannot be enjoyed in isolation from society. He maintains that liberty also, "involves restraints because the separate freedom I use not freedom to destroy the freedoms of those with whom I live".

Three different aspects of liberty:

1. Private or individual liberty,
2. Political liberty, and
3. Economic liberty.

Three conditions for the realisation of liberty:

1. There should be no special privileges in society. Freedom cannot exist in the presence of special privileges.
2. Another condition for the realisation of liberty is the presence of rights. There cannot be liberty where the rights of some depended upon the pleasure of others.
3. The third condition for the realisation of liberty is the existence of a responsible Government whose incidence of action should be unbiased.

Thus, Laski was a great champion of a positive liberty. He attached great significance to human rights. But there was shift in his attitude later on.

MARXIST VIEWS ON LIBERTY

The Marxist interpretations regarding the meaning and nature of liberty hinge on the nature and scope of economic liberty available in the pattern of social life. The liberals define liberty as a bundle of rights that enable a man to seek the best possible development of his personality. They do not bother for the kind of social life of man. The Marxist view of liberty covers the case of man's life in the society he lives and the conditions he is subjected to. There is no liberty for a man of the 'dominated' class in a bourgeois society. In it all privileges are available to the members of the 'dominant class' by virtue of having the ownership of the means of production and distribution. After the occurrence of a socialist revolution conditions change with the change of society.

Abolition of Capitalism

In the Marxist view, there can be no real freedom unless the capitalist system is replaced with the socialist system. The bourgeois order with its system of private property and wage slavery throws man at the mercy of the blind forces of the market producers at all levels in society. The freedom of man "is crucified upon a cross of gold."[17] According to James Maritain, "Marx had a profound intuition which is to my eyes the great lightning flash of truth which traverses all his work of the condition of heteronomy and loss of freedom produced in the capitalist world by wage slavery, and of dehumanisation with which the possessing class and proletariat alike are thereby simultaneously stricken."[18]

Meaning of Freedom

While Marx takes liberty as synonymous with the end of exploitation of man by man in a class-contending society, he also integrates it with the 'glorious human values' possible only in the stateless era of social development. For him., the abolition of capitalism or the establishment of socialism only makes the truly human society, possible. As he says: "Every emancipation is a restoration of the human world and of human relationship to man himself"[19] The aim or purpose of human life is not to bear the pangs of exploitation and subjection and injustice but to

17. Caudwell, *The Concept of Freedom*, p. 75.
18. Cited in Harry Slochower, *No Voice is Wholly Lost*, pp. 220-21.
19. De Caute (ed.), *The Essential Writings of Marx*, pp. 187-88.

have a life of real freedom. This is possible only in a classless society. An alienated man has no freedom. Freedom can only be achieved by means of changing society so that the 'have-nots' of today are converted into the 'haves' of tomorrow. Huberman and Sweezy put it, "Freedom means living life to the fullest — the economic ability to satisfy the needs of the body in regard to adequate food, clothing and shelter, plus effective opportunity to cultivate the mind, develop one's personality, and assert one's individuality."[20]

The Marxist concept of liberty rejects 'free will' as the ingredient of liberty. Man is not only a social creature, he is also a conscious creature. He can understand the pattern of his social existence and then change it by means of his conscious revolutionary social activity (praxis). A man can know the implications of his free or unfree life only when he is conscious of the objective laws of nature and social existence. Knowledge makes possible the mastery of man over nature and society, but this knowledge is useless without man's revolutionary social activity. Thus, freedom as the laws of nature and society comes as a result of practical revolutionary activity based on such knowledge of the laws of historical development.[21]

Universal Principle

Marxist interpretation of freedom is universal. It has implications to all. It has its different implications to the people of different classes in a bourgeois or class-ridden society. There it means right to exploit and oppress the working class at the hands of the feudal or capitalist lords. It means bearing the condition of exploitation and subjection by the people of the working class. According to Marx, it signifies the freedom of the wolves in a society of sheep with shepherdship in the hands of the wolf. This is no freedom. Freedom means freedom for all in an equal measure. All people should be free from the pangs of exploitation, coercion, subjection, injustice, alienation etc. According to Marx, this is possible only in a socialist society that is committed to convert itself into a Communist way of life. Freedom implies activity aimed at creating real conditions for the all-round development and flowering of man's individuality. The full significance of this fact lies in the all-round development of all members of the society.

Criticism of Marxist View

The Marxist view of liberty was not appreciated by the liberal thinkers who identify liberty with constitutional government, political democracy

20. Huberman and Paul Sweezy, *Introduction to Socialism*, p. 76.
21. M. Petrosyan, *Humanism*, p. 179.

and orderly administration based on common law system. By the argument of their free-market liberalism Joseph Schumpeter and Milton Friedman reject the Marxian contention.

Louis Fischer

Arthur Koestler and J.K. Galbraith describe the socialist system as a condition of perfect regimentation of life under the iron rule of a small section of the Communist leadership. Their whole argument boils down to two important propositions. First, that competitive capitalism is a necessary condition of political freedom. Second, a socialist society is so constructed that it guarantees no political freedom.[22]

LAW AND LIBERTY

Relationship

The exponents of negative liberty regarded every law as an infringement of liberty. They argued that law obliges and every obligation is the loss of liberty, therefore every law is in the intimate analysis opposed to liberty. The exponents of such a view restrict the sphere of state activity to the minimum. To them, the State is a policeman whose only role is to maintain peace and order in the society. The State is a necessary evil. One of the greatest individualists of the 19th century Herbert Spencer summed up the negative liberal viewpoint when he said, "The State exists because crime exists in the society otherwise there would be no need of a State".

Liberty is the condition necessary to the fulfilment of man's personality. It is the spontaneous expression of man's individuality and fulfilment. It implies free choice — a choice to live the life according to one's own free will Laws on the other hand, place a restraint upon man's freedom. The laws of the state are backed by the physical force. The breach of law results in physical penalties. There are two different and divergent schools of thought with regards to the relation between law and liberty.

Law and Liberty are Antagonist

The Individualists and Anarchists maintain that law and liberty is antagonistic to each other. All laws contradictory to liberty. Law and liberty cannot be reconciled because the more there is one, the less there is of the other. For the supporters of this view liberty means absolute liberty, no restraint and restriction of any kind. According to J.S. Mill laws of the State are always an infringement on the individuality of man.

22. C.B. Macpherson, *Democratic Theory*, p. 143.

As a great champion of individual's liberty, Mill regarded an individual to be sovereign. Man's liberty is restricted and his initiative crushed by the least interference from outside. The individualists maintain that the state is a necessary evil and it should leave man alone. The Anarchists argue for a stateless society and assert that it only in the anarchist society an individual would be able to develop his full nature and to realise all that he has in him to be. According to William Godwin, "Law is an institution of most precious tendency". Therefore, they want to abolish the State with its entire legal system to free the man in full and final. Syndicalists are also hostile to the institution of state. They think that law is negation of liberty.

The Idealist View

The collectivists and idealists believe that liberty lies in the obedience to the State. There is no antithesis between liberty and law. Law is the condition of liberty. The laws of the state do not curtail liberty but promote and maintain it. If the law punishes the criminal or murderer, it defines the rights of the people. Some laws add to the creative faculties of man. If laws direct us to send our children to schooling, it is no restraint on our liberty. It creates conditions which enhance our happiness and present more opportunities to enjoy liberty. If there is no peace and order in the society, no individual will be able to do anything. Factory legislation has added to the realisation of liberty by the workers. The factory laws endeavour to provide better conditions of work by regulating hours of work, wages, sanitation etc. Therefore, state laws are not the negation of liberty as thought by some of the thinkers.

Liberty is the Product of Law

Law guarantees liberty and safeguards individual liberty. Law and liberty are not contradictory. Law paves the way of collective liberty by imposing restraints on individual liberty. The modern welfare states seek the maximum development of the individual by enacting various laws. By arranging free and compulsory education for all the children these laws of the State strive for real liberty. If the law imposes any restraints on the strong to protect the weak from their exploitation, it should be regarded as the guardian, custodian and not the grabber of liberty. Laws of the State provide equal opportunities for development of all. Thus, laws create and protect true liberty. According to Cicero, "We are bound in order to be free." Happy life can be expected in a society based on law. It creates those conditions in which an individual gets full opportunities for evolution. In the absence of the laws the weak will be exploited by the strong and the freedom of the former will be totally wiped out. Hence, it is said that "Liberty is the product of law".

However, every law enacted by the Parliament is not justified. If the law goes beyond what is necessary and spoils the life of spiritual enrichment, it is an invasion on the liberty of man. If the law means the evolution of man's individuality it is desirable. If it grabs the liberty instead of guaranteeing it such laws should be resisted. Unjust and oppressive laws should be resisted. For instance, a law imposing arbitrary restrictions on family freedom or laws upholding unjust claim of capitalists are the enemies of liberty and not its protector.

To conclude, the laws must be passed after wide publicity consultations. They must be based on the consent of the people who are affected by them. There should be continuous vigilance on the government so that unwanted laws are not passed. There should be perfect harmony between liberty and law.

Methods to Safeguard Liberty of the Individual

All those rights which guarantee liberty are safeguarded by the government. The right to liberty is the most essential and primary right. What is the use of life to a person if he lives under conditions or restrictions which kill all his initiative, imagination, stagnate his intellect, starve him to death, make him a social leper or outcast, deny him the means to know in short dwarf his physical, mental, moral, economic and political being.

Safeguards to Liberty

The modern state safeguards liberty in a number of ways. In order to enable all the citizens to enjoy the full fruit of liberty it is essential and desirable to provide certain safeguards.

1. Vigilance: Vigilance is the price of liberty. The people should be fully conscious of their rights and duties. A government is a human agency. Those who are given powers are liable to misuse them. They may encroach upon the rights and liberty of the people. But if the citizens are alive to their rights, they will not tolerate any in roads on their liberty. They should be conscious and guardian of their rights. They should have the courage to protect and resist if a willful invasion is made on their liberty by the government. In the words of Prof Laski, "Liberty is never real unless the government is called to account when it invades the rights of the people". The people must be prepared to safeguard their rights at all costs. Indifference or apathy on the part of the people may result in the loss of liberty and the development to an autocratic government. Therefore, constant vigilance matters above everything else. The real safeguard of one's liberty is to fight for it. People who are not vigilant enough about their rights and liberties soon lose them.

2. Fundamental rights: The rights should be well-defined in the Constitution of the State to avoid possibilities of encroachment upon individuals rights and liberties. If government encroaches upon these rights they can have an access to legal remedies. The Constitution is a custodian of the rights and liberties of the people. All democratic countries of the world allow fundamental rights to their citizens. Part III of the Constitution of India covers fundamental rights and liberties of the people and the constitutional remedies for their enforcement. Similarly the Constitution of USA contains a list of rights. Right to equality, Right to Liberty, Right against exploitation, Right to freedom of religion, cultural and educational right and right to constitutional remedies are given to all citizens of India by the Constitution.

3. Independence of the judiciary: An independent and impartial judiciary is a great safeguard of individual liberty. The judiciary should administer justice fearlessly. It must take stern action against those who violate the rights of others. To become the custodian of the liberties of the people, it should be independent and impartial. The judges should not be subservient to the executive or the legislature. Law itself is an important condition of liberty. If the people can secure speedy and impartial justice, their liberty is duly guaranteed. The judges should be appointed free of nepotism and they should be paid adequately.

4. Democracy: Democracy is the government by consent. In it sovereignty belongs to the people. The government is carried on in accordance to the wishes of the people. Liberty can best flourish under a democratic form of government. Democratisation of power ensures freedom. It checks the authorities from becoming autocrat because persons in authority are bound to face the electorate at the time of elections. In democracy laws are supposed to be made in accordance with the wishes of the people. They are also given an opportunity to participate semi-autonomous bodies. The more there is democratisation of powers the more is the liberty for the citizens. In democracy the citizens are legally permitted to fight for their liberties. As people have a strict check on the working of the government they will never allow a government to abuse its power.

5. Spirit of toleration among the people: A democratic system where liberties are given to the people cannot be successful unless people have toleration spirit. The majority must respect the rights of the minority.

People should realise that others have equal liberties. The majority must tolerate the healthy criticism of the minority. At the same time, the opposition should not oppose only for the sake of opposition.

6. Absence of privileges: According to Prof Laski freedom cannot be achieved for the masses in the presence of special privileges guaranteed to a small section of the society. There can be no liberty where the right of some depends upon the pleasures of others. It is only when equal opportunities are given to all that a man can really free. In a society where class privileges and social and economic differences exist there can be hardly any freedom for those placed in a position of inferiority.

7. Presence of rights: There can be no liberty where the rights of some depend upon the pleasure of others. No group of persons should be strong enough to take away the rights of ordinary persons.

8. Existence of responsible government: A condition for the realisation of liberty is the existence of responsible government whose incidence of action should be unbiased. It is very difficult to achieve but every effort should be made to achieve it as far as possible.

9. Separation of powers: According to Montesquieu and Blackstone, separation of powers is an effective safeguard for individual liberty. In the interest of individual liberty three powers of the government — executive, legislative and judicial should be vested in three separate and distinct organs each independent of the other. Combination of powers in the same person or set of persons might result in abuse of powers and loss of individual liberty. Power corrupts man and absolute power corrupts man absolutely. Thus in the interest of liberty it is essential to have separation of powers.

10. Checks and balances: It is necessary for the realisation of liberty that the three wings of the government are not divided into three water-tight compartments. There should be check of one department over the other for better results. Each department should work in co-operation with other for satisfactory results. There should be complete harmony between executive and legislature, though they should be independent of each other.

11. Decentralisation of power: If liberty of the people is to be safeguarded it is necessary that the powers of the government is decentralised. The central government should do the work of national' importance only. The rest of the work must be done by the local bodies. Local affairs must be managed by them. This system will enable people to participate more in the affairs of the government. It will ensure better safeguard of liberties.

12. Economic equality: In an economically divided society or where there is a wide gap between the haves and have-nots, it shall only be liberty of the rich and not of the poor. Though perfect economic equality is not possible yet there should be as little economic disparity as possible. Equal opportunities of development and education should be available to all sections of citizens in a country.

13. Freedom of press: No democratic system can be successful unless the press and other agencies are free to criticise the policies of the government. The press moulds public opinion. It keeps public opinion alive. It helps in forming sound public opinion. People read news and views and form their own opinion. Press is a powerful check on the working of the government. It criticises any such action which is against the liberty of the people. In Western countries the power of the press is of great significance because the people are educated and understand their rights and obligations.

If the above safeguards are provided then there is no possibility of misuse of authority and denial of liberty to the people. Thus, the price of liberty is eternal vigilance on the part of the people.

LIBERTY AND AUTHORITY

Are liberty of the individual and authority of the State exclusive of, inimical to, or complementary to each other? Different views are available on this issue:

1. The classical individualists: John Stuart Mill, Adam Smith and Herbert Spencer take liberty of the individual incompatible with the authority of the State. The two are anti-thetical. But as State is a 'necessary evil, there should be as little authority of state as possible so that the individuals may have the maximum possible amount of freedom. The individualists appreciate the. system of *laissez faire* implying maximum possible liberty of the individual in the midst of minimum possible area of state interference.

2. The anarchists: They go a step ahead in denouncing State as an unnecessary evil that should go root and branch. Authority of any kind is bad, because it restricts liberty of the individual. Great anarchists like Proudhon Bakunin and Kropotkin advocated that there should be no authority — whether economic, political or religious — so as to emancipate man from the yoke of the capitalists, the State and the religion respectively.

3. The Marxists: State is an instrument of exploitation and oppression by one class over another. It deprives the class of the have-nots to enjoy liberty in the midst of numerous restraints imposed by it to protect and promote the interest of the class of the 'haves'. Its authority shall survive during the transitional stage so as to deal with all reactionary and counter-revolutionary forces. But when the socialist system is finally established, the State authority shall wither away entailing complete emancipation of man.

4. The democratic socialists: To them the State is a welfare agency that may restrict liberty of the individuals in the name of public welfare. Liberty lives within restraints. The State makes laws for the protection of individual liberty. The violators of laws are punished. The liberals support the view that law protects liberty of the individuals. Hobbes and Locke say that the distinction between the state of nature and civil society is that in the latter there is a system of restraints imposed by the sovereign authority in the form of laws. Positive liberals like Hobhouse and Laski take the point to the extent of appreciating more and more reasonable restraints in the public interest.

5. The Fascists: They adulate the system of restraints to any extent whatsoever. In their view, liberty of the individual lies in rendering complete obedience to the authority of the State. Fascists take inspiration from the idealistic interpretation of Rousseau and Hegel that the State can do no wrong. Mussolini of Italy and Hitler of Germany justified their totalitarian systems as the best safeguards for individual liberty. Fascist view is based on the assumption that man is a social creature and the development of his personality is possible only in a society of his fellow beings. The State represents the general will of the community. Hence, the liberty of the individual can never be anti-thetical to the authority of the State. A German idealist Treitschke said that 'man should fall down and worship the State'.

Conclusion

Liberty by its very nature involves restraints. The freedom of a man does not amount to the destruction of the freedom of others because there are rules and regulations to ensure the conditions of minimum freedom common to all. The uniformities of the rules ensure liberty. They are less terrifying than the uncertainties the individuals would experience by their absence. Historic experience has led to evolution of rules of convenience. As Laski says, there promote right living and compel obedience to them. This is a justifiable limitation of freedom. Thus, the "rules of convenience" imposed by some authority make conditions of freedom. There can be no liberty in the absence of authority. State intervention is necessary in the sphere of individual liberty in order to keep it within reasonable limits. However, the authority of the State should not be absolute so as to menace, even destroy liberty as happens under a Fascist or a Communist system.

QUESTIONS FOR EXERCISE

1. Define Liberty. Discuss the various forms and kinds of liberty.
2. Distinguish clearly between Positive Liberty and Negative Liberty.
3. What do you understand by liberty? Mention some of the theories of Negative and Positive Liberty.
4. Examine critically J.S. Mill's and Harold Laski's views on liberty.
5. What is the Marxian concept of 'freedom'? Do you agree that freedom is a product of free society? Can freedom exist without economic equality in society?
6. Discuss the various methods in a modern State to safeguard liberty of the individual.
7. "External vigilance is the price of liberty." In the light of the statement discuss the main safeguards of liberty.

14

Concept of Equality

Equality like liberty is an important theme of normative political theory. Like liberty, it is also a subject that cannot be studied in isolation to other related themes like fraternity and justice. The concept of equality constitutes a concomitant of the principle of liberty, on the one hand, and of justice, on the other. Hence, great thinkers as well as revolutionaries have treated it as an integral part of their movement for liberty and social transformation. John Locke held that the "Law of Nature teaches all mankind who will but consult it, that being all equal and independent, no one ought to harm another in his life, health, liberty or possessions."[1] The Founding Fathers of the American nation adopted a Declaration of Independence in 1776 that *inter alia* said, "...all men are created equal, that they are endowed by their creator with certain unalienable rights." Likewise, the National Assembly of France adopted the Declaration of the Rights of Man and Citizen in 1789 which, *inter alia*, said that "all human beings are born free and equal in dignity and rights."[2]

Difficulty in Defining Equality

According to Laski, no idea is more difficult to be defined in the whole realm of political science than the concept of equality.[3] As Ernest Barker says, "Equality is a Protean notion; it changes its shape and assumes new forms with a ready facility."[4] It is so because equality has become like a multi-dimensional concept. It possesses more than one meaning. The controversies surrounding it arise partly because the same term is employed with different connotations. It may either purport to state a fact, or convey the expression of an ethical judgement. It may affirm

1. Locke, *Second Treatise of Civil Government*, Ch. II, paras 18-19.
2. See Benn and Peters, *Social Principles and Democratic State*, p. 107.
3. Laski, *op. cit.*, Ch. 3.
4. Barker, *Principles of Social and Political Theory*, p. 151.

that men are, on the whole, very similar in their natural endowments of character and intelligence. It may assert that while they differ profoundly as individuals in capacity and character, they are equally entitled to consideration and respect as human beings and that the well-being of society is likely to be increased if it so plans its organisation that, whether the powers are great or small, all its members may be equally enabled to make the best of such powers as they possess.[5]

Definition of Equality

1. *Oxford English Dictionary*: Equality implies (i) the condition of having equal dignity, rank or privilege with others, (ii) the condition of being equal in power, ability achievement of excellence, (iii) fairness, impartiality, due proportion, proportionateness. Here equality is defined in the light of equal conditions guaranteed to each for making the best of himself.

2. *Barker*: Equality implies that "whatever conditions are guaranteed to me in the form of rights, shall also, and in the same measure, be guaranteed to others, and that whatever rights are given to others shall also be given to me."[6]

3. *Laski*: Undoubtedly, it implies fundamentally a levelling process. It means that no man shall be so placed in society that he can overreach his neighbour to the extent which constitutes a denial of the latters citizenship.[7]

4. *Tawney*: In very simple terms, the idea of equality refers to the equality of rights and opportunities so that each member of the civilised community may have the best possible scope for the development of his personality. It obtains in so far as, and only in so far as, each member of a community whatever his birth or occupation, or social position, possesses in fact and not merely in form equal chances of using to the full his natural endowments of physique, of character, and of intelligence.[8] In other words, it desires a state of life in which the strong and the weak share same privileges for the development of their personality irrespective of any artificial distinction like that of wealth, religion, colour of the skin, domicile, language, descent, sex and the like.

In defining Equality one may say with Laski, "It means that my realisation of my best self must involve as its logical result the realisation by others of their best selves. It means such an ordering of social forces

5. R.H. Tawney, *Equality*, p. 22.
6. Barker, *op. cit.*, p. 151.
7. Laski, *op. cit.*, p. 153.
8. Tawney, *op. cit.*, pp. 103-04.

as will balance a share in the toil of living with a share in its gain also. It means that my share in the gain must be adequate for the purpose of citizenship."[9]

POSITIVE AND NEGATIVE EQUALITY

1. Positive equality: In a positive sense, equality means the provision of adequate opportunities for all. It does not mean simply identical treatment for all as men differ in their needs and capacities and also in their efforts, they require different opportunities for their self-development. The native endowments are by no means equal. As Benn and Peters say, 'The goal of 'equality of opportunities' is achieved only when there is an appropriate opportunity for each; what is to be equalised is not the opportunity to enter professions or to be successful in business but the opportunity to lead a good life, or to fulfil one's personality."[10]

2. Negative equality: In a negative sense, equality means no discrimination on some artificial ground like that of religion, caste, wealth, creed, domicile, descent, sex and the like. However, discrimination can be made if the reason behind it is valid. For example, very hazardous jobs cannot be given to the females. But discrimination on the basis of caste cannot be justified by any rational standard. Thus, as Laski points out, there should be no arrangement whereby the authority of few is qualitatively more than that of the many.[11]

The Doctrine of Desert

The *doctrine of the desert* means that the principle of equal opportunities for all should be qualified by the maxim of 'deserving'. Though the doors of progress must be open for all in an equal measure, but due consideration must be given to the factor of talent or ability that a person has in comparison to others. J. Rees says that "natural inequalities of physical strength, beauty and so on are acceptable social inequalities, because they are a product of pure convention, seem to turn upon the assumption that conventional inequalities are *alterable* while natural ones are not, and it is that seems to live behind the contemporary doctrine of the equality of opportunity."[12]

A contemporary admirer of the doctrine of desert like John Rawls says the "meritocracy follows the principles of careers open to talents and uses equality of opportunity as a way of releasing men's energies in pursuit of economic prosperity and political domination.'[13]

9. Laski, *op. cit.*, p. 153.
10. Benn and Peters, *op. cit.*, p. 119.
11. Laski, *op. cit.*, pp. 153-54.
12. John Rees, *Equality*.
13. Rawls, *A Theory of Justice*, p. 107.

Limitations of the Doctrine of Desert

The doctrine of the desert makes sense on a theoretical plane. But when we try to look into its practical implications the difficulty arises. A discrimination in the name of talent or special merit may not be wholly fair and impartial. It may destroy the whole sanctity of the principle of equal opportunities. Some other criteria may be adopted in a poor and backward country. Therefore, the Constitution of India prescribes special reservations and safeguards for the upliftment of socially and educationally backward sections of the community. The State may provide special benefits to the persons belonging to Scheduled Castes and Scheduled Tribes. Though, such an arrangement is violation of the ideal principle of equality, it may be justified on two grounds:

1. It is meant for the benefit of those sections of the society who have suffered the pangs of social injustice for many centuries. Now some special facilities must be given to them for the sake of the betterment of their lot.
2. Reservation is a temporary affair. It may be abolished after some time when the contemplated goal of social justice is achieved. Hence, it is known by the name of 'compensatory' or 'protective discrimination'.

KINDS OF EQUALITY

1. Natural equality: Natural Equality implies that Nature has made all men equal. In ancient times, the Stoics of Greece and the Roman thinkers like Polybius and Cicero contradicted the principle of natural inequality of mankind as advocated by Plato and Aristotle. Cicero said: "For no one thing is like as equal to another one as we human beings are like and equal to one another." The Stoics and the Romans took the argument of the 'law of Nature' that was equally applicable to all people irrespective of their country or race. Identifying the 'law of Nature' with the 'law of God' the Christian thinkers upheld the principle of natural equality of mankind as sanctioned by the Biblical injunction of the 'Fatherhood of God and brotherhood of man'. In modern times, Rousseau and Marx were the best exponents of the case of natural equality of mankind. However, though the natural equality of mankind is a very noble idea which constitutes one of the two foundations of democracy (the other being liberty), in practice things are not so. It is like an ideal to say that 'all earth is surface',[14]

14. A. Appadorai, *The Substance of Politics*, p. 81.

2. Social equality: The social or civil equality is an actuality. It implies that the rights and opportunities of all are equal so that each may have the best possible development of his personality. In the world of law we come across the principle of equality before law and its equal protection for all. From the President or Prime Minister at the top to a constable or a watchman at the bottom the law of the land is applicable to all. The judicial system protects the rights of all irrespective of anybody's social and economic position. The noted English jurist Dicey defines it as one of the two essential principles of the 'rule of law'.[15]

3. Political equality: Political equality means the access of all to the venues of power. All citizens should have equal voice in the management of public affairs, or in the holding of public offices irrespective of their differences in matters of religion, caste, creed, race, wealth, sex, language. Every adult citizen should have rights like exercising franchise, fighting elections, securing a public employment, opposing or supporting some official policy or activity, changing the government by constitutional means and the like. There is no political equality, if there are severe restrictions on the freedom of franchise, thought and expression, or where such privileges are available to a very limited section of the community. Hence, Laski insisted on the abolition of the privileges of the Lords in England. Carl J. Friedrich rightly feels that "political equality is increased by the degree to which democratic legitimacy is embodied in the political order."[16]

4. Economic equality: Economic equality implies that there should be no concentration of economic power in the hands of few persons. The distribution of national wealth must be such that no section of the people becomes over-affluent to the detriment of others. No section of the community must be forced to reach the margin of starvation or economic want. There should be 'a specific civic minimum' in the realm of economic benefits accruing to all. It implies 'equality of proportions'.

Criticism

But economic equality has different implications according to different thinkers. The classical liberals take it as equal opportunities to all in the spheres of production, consumption and distribution of goods with least possible intervention of the State. It means economic freedom to all subject to rules and regulations imposed by the State in public interest so that the rich may not exploit the poor. The Marxists seek to establish a

15. A.V. Dicey, *An Introduction to the Study of the Law of the Constitution*, p. 202.
16. Friedrich, "A Discourse on the Origin of Political Inequality" in *Nomos*, IX, p. 222.

'classless society' in which all property would be under the control of the state and the ideal of economic equality would mean complete absence of the exploitation of man by man just by the use of economic power. As a positive liberal or a democratic socialist, Laski says: "State divided into a small number of rich and a large number of poor will always develop a government manipulated by the rich to protect the amenities represented by their property."[17]

5. Legal equality: Legal equality has three implications:

(i) All citizens are alike in the eye of the law of the land. Only the head of the State may be its exception.

(ii) The protection of the life and property of each citizen is guaranteed by law. This facility is available to all without discrimination of any kind.

(iii) Justice is available to all at a low cost and without undue delay so that everyone irrespective of his social or economic position may get it according to the established procedure of the land. But if law guarantees different sets of privileges for persons belonging to different positions in the society there would be no violation of the principle of equality. For example the privileges of a Member of Parliament cannot be made equal to the privileges of a Cabinet Minister by the system of law. This is equality at equal levels. It implies that the privileges of one must be legally equal to the privileges of others if they stand at the same level. L.T. Hobhouse rightly asserts that it "is in the spirit of modern law to hold certain fundamentals of rights and duties equally applicable to all human beings."[18]

6. International equality: International equality means that all nations of the world must be treated equally without any consideration for any nation's demographic, geographical, economic, or military potential Each member-state of the United Nations has one vote in the General Assembly. This is equality in the international sphere. But with the growth of internationalism, this term has acquired some more implications. It is also desired that nations must not resort to force. They must make use of pacific means of the settlement of their disputes. Evils like those of slavery and racial segregation must disappear from the face of the earth. There should be distribution of scientific and technological achievements among all nations of the world so as to usher in a new international social and economic order.

---

17. Laski, *op. cit.*, pp. 157-58.
18. L.T. Hobhouse, *The Elements of Social Justice*, p. 104.

LIBERAL *VERSUS* MARXIST INTERPRETATIONS

Liberal Doctrine

The central theme of Liberal view is that "equals should be treated equally, unequal's unequally, and the respects in which they are considered unequal must be relevant to the differences in treatment that we propose."[19] However, with the assimilation of the socialist content in the philosophy of liberalism, the real meaning of equality has been integrated with the consideration of social good as a result of which the concept of social equality has become all-pervasive. John Rawls suggests two essential points inherent in the notion of equality:

1. Each person is to have an equal right to the extensive basic liberty compatible with similar liberty for others.
2. Social and economic inequalities are to be arranged in a way so that they are both (a) reasonably expected to be to every-one's advantage, and (b) attached to position and offices equally open to all.

The liberal doctrine of equality stands on the premise of the 'equality of adequate opportunities' available to every member of the society. All people have liberty to compete in the midst of equal opportunities with the result that those who can make best use of their chances may go ahead of others, inequality in the midst of equal opportunities is thus a valid affair. It is egalitarianism. J.H. Schaar thus explains the meaning of egalitarianism: "The doctrine of equality of opportunity is the product of a competitive and fragmented society, a society in which individualism, in Tocqueville's sense of the word, is the reigning ethical principle. It is a precise symbolic expression of the liberal-bourgeois model society, for it extends the market-place mentality to all the spheres of life. It views the whole of human relations as a contest in which each man competes with his fellows for scarce goods; a contest resting upon the attractive conviction that all should be allowed to improve their conditions as far as their abilities permit.... Thus, it is the perfect embodiment of the liberal conception of reform; the fundamental character of the social-economic system is altered in substance."[20]

Marxist Interpretation

The Marxist view of equality is different. It studies the whole case of liberty and equality through the prism of class war. Equality cannot exist in a society ridden with class contradictions. The class of the 'haves' enjoys

19. Rawls, *op. cit.*, p. 61.
20. Schaar, "*Equality of Opportunity and Beyond*" in *Nomos*, IX, p. 237.

all liberty. It is not available to the poor, weaker and backward sections who have to undergo the pangs of exploitation and oppression. The existence of a classless society is the *sine qua non* of the existence of the real conditions of liberty and equality. All kinds of artificial distinctions can be eliminated only when the dictatorship of the proletariat removes all kinds of contradictions in the society. Only then the real meaning of equality shall prevail that "lies in the existence of identical conditions and opportunities for the free development of the individual and the fulfilment of the requirements of all members of the society, the equal position of people in society being understood differently in different historical epochs."[21]

View of Stalin

In a speech delivered in 1934 at the Seventeenth Congress of the Communist Party of the Soviet Union, Stalin declared that "equality in the sphere of requirements and personal life is a piece of reactionary petty-bourgeois stupidity worthy of a primitive sect of ascetics, but not of a socialist society organised on Marxian lines, because we cannot demand that all people should have the same requirements and tastes, and that all people shall live their individual lives in the same way.... By equality, Marxism means, not equality in personal requirements and personal life, but the abolition of classes, *i.e.*, (a) the equal emancipation of all toilers from exploitation after the capitalists have been overthrown and expropriated; (b) the equal abolition for all private property in the means of production after they have been transformed into the property of the whole society; (c) the equal duty of all to work according to their ability and the equal right of all toilers to receive according to the amount of work they have done (*socialist* society); (d) the equal duty of all to work according to their ability and the equal right of all toilers to receive according to their requirements (*communist* society). And Marxism starts out with the assumption that people's tastes and requirements are not, and cannot be, equal in quality or in quantity, either in the period of socialism, or in the period of communism.... It is time it was understood that Marxism is opposed to levelling."[22]

Distinction in Liberal and Marxist Views

In the view of the liberals, a classless society under the dictatorship of the proletariat is the model of a single-interest society that guarantees no liberty and hence no equality of any kind to its members. It is a totalitarian

21. *A Dictionary of Scientific Communism*, p. 85.
22. Emile Burns (ed.), *A Handbook of Marxism*, pp. 937-38.

set up. Real equality prevails in an open society having different interests living in competition with each other. Thus, equality means equal rights and opportunities to all to play their part in a competitive pattern of life. The distinction between the rich and the poor subsists due to the fact that they have different capacities and different levels of merit to play their part in the competition of life. The Marxist view condemns the model of a liberal society. It desires a thoroughly new social and economic system free from exploitation and oppression of man by man in any form. A liberal or bourgeois society cannot ensure the boons of equality to its members. As Lenin says: "Under the guise of equality of the individuals in general, bourgeois democracy proclaims the formal or the legal equality of the property-owner and the proletarian, the exploiter and the exploited, thereby grossly receiving the oppressed classes."[23]

LIBERTY AND EQUALITY

Historically speaking, the glorification of liberty precedes that of equality. Until recent times many thinkers can be seen assigning a higher and superior position to the former. For example, ancient Greek and Roman ideals of liberty were not coupled with the notion of equality, as not all men were free in slave societies. The Stoics preached the principle of natural equality of mankind, though it received limited response. When thinkers like Polybius and Cicero of the Roman period repeated the Stoic doctrine, they did so just to make their political philosophy in consonance with the changing conditions of the empire. The idea of difference between a Greek and a barbarian and subsequently between a Roman and a non-Roman continued until Christianity became the official religion that preached the doctrine of "Fatherhood of God and brotherhood of man".

Liberty remained a privilege of the aristocratic section of the society. John Locke described liberty as a natural right, but he excluded the case of right to equality. The American Declaration of Independence of 1776 for the first time, incorporated the idea of equality. It saw its shining repetition in the slogan of 'Liberty, Equality, Fraternity' during the days of French Revolution of 1789. Since then the relationship between liberty and equality has been a matter of negative and positive approach.

23. Lenin, *Collected Works*, Vol. 31, p. 145.

Kinds of Equality

Natural	Social	Political	Economic	Legal	International
All are born equal, hence no discrimination on any artificial ground as religion, race, creed, caste, sex, wealth, place of birth, domicile, language, colour of the skin etc.	Equality of rights and opportunities subject to genuine grounds of discrimination.	Equality of participation for all in the management of public affairs 1. Universal adult suffrage 2. Open recruitment to public offices for all 3. Free and fair periodic elections 4. Free press and mass media agencies 5. No special rights to any section of the community.	Non-concentration of national wealth in few hands, equality or proportions 1. Guarantee of a specific civic minimum 2. Provision of special safeguards to protect the interests of the weaker sections of the community 3. Placing of private sector under social control.	Fundamental rights available to all in an equal measure 1. Equally before law 2. Equal protection of law for all 3. Equality at equal levels 4. Availability of justice at a low cost and without undue delay.	No discrimination among states on the basis of demographic, geographical, economic or military potential 1. Equal treatment to all nations 2. Distribution of scientific and technological knowledge among all nations 3. Eradication of gigantic evils like slavery and racial segregation 4. Renunciation of the use of force 5.Pacific settlement of international disputes by free and frank discussions and negotiations.

1. The negative view: Liberty and equality are incompatible terms. Matthew Arnold spoke strongly about the incompatibility of the attitude of equality with the spirit of humanity and a sense of dignity of man as man which are the marks of a true civilised society. Lord Birkenhead declared that the doctrine that 'all men are equal' is a poisonous doctrine. Sir Ernest Benn writes that economic equality is a 'scientific impossibility'.[24] It is based on the Aristotelian notion that mankind are unequal by nature; that equals should be treated equally and unequals unequally. F.A. Hayek says: "From the fact that people are very different, it follows that if we treat them equally, the result must be inequality in their actual position, and that the only way to place them in an equal position would be to treat them differently."[25] Lord Acton of England and Alexis de Tocqueville of France subscribe to the view that liberty is a privilege of the few that cannot be reconciled with the liberty of all that means equality. Richard Norman says that equality "can be reached only by massive external intervention in people's live."[26] The pursuit of equality has in practice led to inequality and tyranny. Bringing about a condition of equality results in the coercion of the many at the hands of the few. To quote Joseph and Sumption, "A society in which the choices fundamental to human existence are determined by coercion is not a free society. It follows irresistibly that egalitarianism must choose between liberty and equality"[27] Following are some statements of negative view:

1. *Thomas Carlyle*: Aristocracy and priesthood, a governing class and a teaching class..there did no society exist without these two vital elements, there will none exist.
2. *Hitler*: The parliamentary principle of decision of majority, by denying the authority of the person and placing it instead in the number of crowd in question, sins against the aristocratic basic idea of nature.
3. *O.Y. Gasset*: Society is always a dynamic unity of two component factors — minorities and masses. The minorities are individuals or groups of individuals which are especially qualified. The mass is the assemblage of persons not specially qualified.

2. The positive view: It takes liberty and equality as compatible terms. In the ancient period the Stoics and the Roman lawyers reiterated that 'all are equal in the eye of nature'. The Christian thinkers repeated the same

24. See Tawney, *op. cit.*, p. 19.
25. Hayek, *The Constitution of Liberty*, p. 87.
26. Richard Norman, "Does Equality Destroy Liberty?" In Keith Graham (ed.), *Contemporary Political Philosophy*, p. 85.
27. K. Joseph and J. Sumption, *Equality*, p. 47.

point by replacing nature with God. In present century, it has seen its reaffirmation at the hands of many positive liberals. Hobhouse says that 'liberty without equality is a high sounding phrase with squalid results'. In the words of Tawney, 'a large measure of equality, so far from being inimical to liberty, is essential to it'. While lamenting over the 'religion of inequality', he says that the people "accepted the *mana* (a mysterious wisdom) and *karakia* (a magical influence) of social and economic inequality in the same way that primitive people accepted the ritual of tribal society, There is no rational justification for social inequality; its survival is a matter of prejudice."[28] So says Barker: "It remains to add that equality is not an isolated principle. It stands by the principle of liberty and fraternity."[29]

Following are two statements in favour of positive view:

1. *Kant:* 'Treat every man is an end in himself and not as a means'. Each man is to be, at it were, free from certain conspicuous structures of inequality in which we find him.
2. *Bernard Williams*: The notion of inequality is invoked not only in connections where all men are claimed in some sense to be equal, but in connections where they are agreed to be unequal as in situations of need and merit.

Evaluation of the Two Views

If the aim of normative political theory is to seek and analyse the avenues relating to the development of human personality, it is required that the ideals of liberty and equality should have a simultaneous flow. Both are necessarily connected with the supreme worth and dignity of human personality and the spontaneous development of its capacities.

The positive view is really convincing. While paraphrasing the ideas of Laski, Deane says: "Liberty and equality are not in conflict, nor even separate, but are different facets of the same ideal.... Indeed, since they are identical, there can be no problem of law or to what extent they are or can be related to. This is surely the nearest, if not the most satisfactory, solution ever devised for a perennial problem in political philosophy."[30]

28. Tawney, *op. cit.*, p. 13.
29. Barker, *op. cit.*, p. 159.

QUESTIONS FOR EXERCISE

1. Define equality and discuss its various forms.
2. What do you mean by the term equality? Discuss its various forms.
3. Discuss the relation between liberty and equality. Are they contradictory?
4. "Liberty and equality are not opposed to each other but supplementary to each other", Laski. Comment.
5. Do you agree with the view that there can be no political liberty without economic equality? Give reasons in support of your answer.
6. "Equality and liberty are inconsistent with each other". Discuss. What do you understand by liberty? Discuss relation between liberty and equality.
7. Define equality. Do you agree with the view that political liberty in the absence of economic equality is a myth?

15

Law and International Law

According to Barker, "the essence of the State is a living body of effective rules; and in that sense, the State is law."[1] As the State — the fundamental subject of politics — is a legal association or 'a juridically organised nation' a study of the basic concepts of political theory should begin with a discussion of the idea of law. The state is distinguished from society, nation, and other associations by virtue of its being the exclusive possessor of a 'coercive power'— a power that issues forth in the form of law. The State is like a nation organised for action according to certain specific and well-set rules. Every State is known by the system of law it maintains due to its highest coercive sovereign power. In this sense there is no 'international law' to regulate and correct the behaviour of the sovereign nations. But international law is a law having its sanction in the behaviour of the civilised peoples of the world. Law demands its effective and honest implementation which leads to the issue of justice. The function of the State is to enforce law in a just manner. In the words of Lord James Bryce "There is no better test of excellence of a government than the efficiency of its judicial system, for nothing more nearly touches the welfare and security of the average citizen than his sense that he can rely on the certain and prompt administration of justice. Law is respected and supported when it is treated as the shield of innocence and the impartial guardian of every civil right.... If the law be dishonestly administered, the salt has lost its flavour, if it be weakly or fitfully enforced, the guarantees of order fail...if the lamp of justice goes out in darkness, how great is the darkness."[2]

1. Barker, *Principle of Social and Political Theory*, p. 89.
2. Bryce, *Modern Democracies*, Vol. II, pp. 421-22.

MEANING OF LAW

The term 'Law' has been used in a variety of senses. For instance, in the realm of physics, the laws of motion and gravitation denote the sequence of cause and effect. Social and customary laws guide the behaviour of men in their collective life. Moral laws relate to the question of intrinsic right and wrong, good and bad. They have necessary relationship with the issues of motive and conscience. In a democratic society law is a technique with a purpose — it is the sum of the social influences regularly recognised and applied by the State in the administration of justice.[3]

Definition of Law

1. *Etymologically*: The word 'law' comes from the old Teutonic root 'lag' which means to lay, to place, to set, or to fix something in an even manner. Law is, something positive or 'imposed'. In a deeper sense, the word' 'law' originates from the Latin word 'jus' that is essentially connected with another Latin word 'jungere' implying primarily a bond or a tie. If so, the term 'law' denotes 'primarily a joining or fitting that readily glides into the sense of binding or obliging'.[4] It conveys the idea of 'a valid custom to which any citizen can appeal, and which is recognised and can be enforced by a human authority'.[5] In the field of political theory, however, we are concerned with laws that regulate man's behaviour as a member of an organised society and which, for the most part, "deal with external conduct and are enforced by a system of compulsions."[6]

2. *The Oxford English Dictionary*: Law is 'a rule of conduct imposed by an authority'.

3. *Positivists*: They treat law as the 'command of the sovereign'.

4. *The Marxists*: They regard it as 'an expression of society's general interests and needs emerging from a given material means of production'.

5. *Benn and Peters*: These authors describe law as[7]:

   (i) the normal expression of conventional morality, or of that which the State should enforce, or

   (ii) a system of rules by which the interests of a dominant class are safeguarded, or

   (iii) a system of rules held to be binding or obligatory, or

   (iv) a system of rules aimed at realising justice, or

   (v) a system of rules discoverable by reason, or

3. Rodee, Christol and Anderson, *Introduction to Political Science*, p. 80.
4. Barker, *op. cit.*, p. 94.
5. *Ibid.*
6. E. Asirvatham, *Political Theory*, VIII Ed., p. 381.
7. Benn and Peters, *Social Principles and the Democratic State*, p. 57.

(vi) a command of the sovereign, or
(vii) what the judges decide in the courts, or
(viii) a system of rules backed by coercive sanctions.

6. *A.L. Lowell*: In the most widely understood sense, 'the term law' signifies a "body of rules enforced by the courts."[8]

7. *Henry Sidgwick*: "Law in the sense in which we are primarily concerned with it, is a body of rules intended to control the conduct of members of a political society, for the violation of which penalties may be expected to be inflicted, by the authority of the government of that society; and which, therefore, may be regarded as imposed by the government."[9]

SOURCES OF LAW

1. Custom: The earliest form of law is traceable in the well-established practices of the people. These practices, gradually developed because of the utility that inhered in them. In due course, a practice became a usage. After a sufficient standing usage was hardened into a custom. Primitive communities attached great significance to the observance of their customs. The law of today is based on the customs of the people. It is a translation of an age-old established practices into specific written terms by the State.

2. Religion: Law finds its sanction in the religious books of the people. The words contained in the holy books and their interpretations made by the priests and divines constitutes the religious law of the people. Most of the principles of religious law have been translated by the states in terms of specific rules.

3. Adjudication: In response to the growth of civilisation as the process of social organisation became more and more complex the force of customs declined. The 'wisest men of the community' delivered verdicts to settle the meaning and nature of custom. These decisions formed precedents for future guidance even if they were handed down by tradition. Subsequently, they were put in writing as the interpreter and enforcer of the customs of the people. As judges became the 'wisest men of the community', their decisions came to have a special sanctity. These were given in writing. They constituted the case-law.

4. Equity: Equity is an informal method of making new law or altering an old one depending on intrinsic fairness or equality of treatment. It means equity or natural justice in cases where the existing law does not apply properly and judgement has to be given according to commonsense or

8. A.L. Lowell, *The Government of England*, Vol. II, p. 473.
9. Henry Sidgwick, *Elements of Politics*, p. 33.

fairness. Equity arises from the fact that as time passes and new conditions of life develop, positive law becomes unsuitable or inadequate to the new situations. To make it suitable, either the old law should be changed, or it should be adapted by some informal method. In the absence of a positive law, judges decide cases on general principles of fairness, reasonableness, commonsense and natural justice. The principles of equity supplements the premises of law when they are put into specific terms by the State.

5. Legislation: Legislation is the most prolific source of law. It means placing of a specific rule on the statute book of the land. It reflects the will of the State declared by its law-making organs. It may be in the form of a royal decree, or an ordinance promulgated by the head of the State, or assented to by him after being passed by the legislature. It has the validity of the law of the land. It is to be implemented by the executive and enforced by the judicial departments of the State. Today, legislation has become the most important source of law that has outplaced the significance of other traditional forces like custom and religion. Uncertainties and ambiguities which used to get easily accommodated in the spheres of religious and customary law have been sufficiently removed by the codification of law.

6. Standard works: An important source of law may be traced in scientific commentaries of leading thinkers, jurists and statesmen expressing their views on important points of law. These when recognised, are treated as binding by virtue of being the decisions of the 'wisest men of the community'. The opinions of these great men of the community are accepted by the courts and also incorporated into the law of the land. For example, the works of Coke, Littleton and Blackstone in England and of Kent and Story in the United States. These standard works compile, compare and logically arrange legal principles, customs and decisions of the 'wisest men of the community'. They decipher important principles for the guidance of the people in future possible cases.

KINDS OF LAW

1. Natural and positive law: Being authored by nature or some supernatural agency the law of nature is abstract. Being a creation of man the law of state is concrete. It is called positive law, for its terms are quite specific and binding. Moreover, while the Natural law has its sanction in respect for or fear of some supernatural power, the positive law is enforced by the sovereign authority. Thus, it is called deterministic or imperative law.

2. National and international law: A law formulated by the sovereign authority and applicable to the people living under its territorial jurisdiction is called national (municipal) law. It determines private and public relations of the people living in a State. International law regulates the conduct of states in their intercourse with each other. The essential point of difference between the natural and international law lies in that while the former has the force of a sovereign authority on its back, the latter derives its sanction from the good sense of the civilised nations of the world.

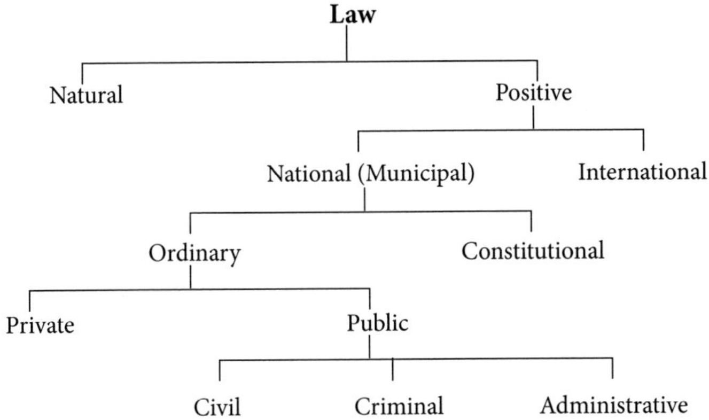

3. Constitutional and ordinary law: Both constitutional and ordinary law are laws of the State. They differ from each other in respect of sanctity attached to them. The constitutional law has a higher status being a part of the Constitution of the land. The ordinary law occupies a lower place. It has to keep itself in consonance with the constitutional law which may be partly written by some constitutional convention and partly unwritten on account of being in the form of well-established practices. In a country like the United Kingdom there is no difference between the constitutional and ordinary law because there is unwritten constitution.

4. Civil and criminal law: The civil law deals with a civil wrong committed by a person going to harm the interests of another such as non-payment of dues or the violation of the terms of a contract. The criminal law relates to a criminal act of a person like theft, robbery and murder.

5. Private and public law: The private law is concerned with the relationship between individuals. Public law involves the relationship between the people and State. It is concerned with the organisation of the State, the limits on the functions of the government, and the relations between the State and its citizens.

6. Administrative law: It determines relations of the officials to the State. It fixes the organisation and determines the competence of the administrative authorities. It indicates to the person the remedies for the violation of the rights.

7. Case-law or law made by the courts: In certain situations the court gives its own opinions to clarify or explain the meaning of a legal provision. A new kind of law comes into existence known as case-law out of such interpretations made consciously or unconsciously. It has its place in the decisions of the courts.

THEORIES OF THE ORIGIN AND NATURE OF LAW

1. The natural theory: It considers law as eternal, universal, constant, rational and immutable. It can be understood by the rational faculty of man. It is universal. It prevails everywhere. It has its validity at all times. It is same at all places and under all circumstances. It cannot be changed by any power on earth. As nature is the author of this law, it is based on right reason. Positively, it is in the nature of a call and a command to one's duty. Negatively, it is a warning against the performance of some deceitful or evil act. Thus, natural law is higher law. The civil law must conform to it in order to be valid.

With the advent of Christianity in the medieval period the law of nature (*jus naturale*) became the law of God (*jus divina*) as contained in the Bible. In early modern times social contractualists like Spinoza, Hobbes and Locke referred to it. Instead of taking it as a creation of nature or God, they regarded it as 'a system in which reason moves progressively from higher order to lower order to lay down some prescriptions.' Analytical jurists like Bentham and Austin, who defined law 'as the command of the sovereign' rejected the law of God. As N.P. Barry observed, "The difficulty with the natural law theories of the absolutist kind is that of securing agreement on the ends which men ought to pursue. Natural lawyers often write as if their prescriptions were as necessary as the laws that govern the physical world, but clearly that is not so. Natural law relates to human conduct and has, therefore, quite a different logic from scientific law; it is normative law; it is normative not predictive or discipline and is, therefore, concerned with demonstrating those rules of *behaviour* which ought to be followed. But men's needs and desires change and actions which were regarded as universal by one generation must not be acceptable to another."[10]

2. Imperative theory of law: It has its affirmation in the works of Bodin, Hobbes, Bentham, Austin and Dicey. It uses the word 'law' in a positive

10. N.P. Barry, *An Introduction to Modern Political Theory*, p. 25.

sense. It maintains that the laws are 'commands' of a determinate political authority. It is known by the name of 'legal positivism'. It designates that only those norms "are juridically valid which have been established or recognised by the government of a sovereign State in the forms prescribed by its written or unwritten constitution. No Divine Law and no Natural Law is valid, according to legal positivism, unless so recognised by the State or its government."[11] As Hobbes says: "Covenants without sword are but words, and they are of no strength to secure a man at all."[12]

Limitation of Imperative Theory

1. It lays too much reliance on positivism. Law is regarded as something put in very set or positive terms by the State whose violation is visited with punishment.
2. It ignores the force of rules emanating from religion or custom or backed by the force of public opinion as these are not backed by the authority of a determinate human superior (sovereign).
3. It makes the meaning of law rigid and introduces an element of conservatism in juristic conclusions on the subject of law and State.
4. By emphasis on the force of command it confuses the distinction between the law as expected to be observed by the people and the order that may even provoke the people to destroy the political system. As Laski points out, to think of laws as simply a command is even for the jurist "to strain definition to the verge of decency."[13]

3. Historical theory: It treats law as a result of silent forces at work in society neither authored by nature (or God), nor a deliberate creation of the State. Law is the result of the inevitable but imperceptible social development. It is independent of, and anterior to, the State. The function of the State is not to create law but merely to recognise and enforce it. According to Gustav von Hugo and Savigny, law is the organ of folk right that moves and ever grows like other expression of the life of the people; it is formed by custom and popular feeling through the operation of silent forces and not by the arbitrary will of a legislator. In his *Ancient Law* Sir Henry Maine has sought to prove how modern law originated and developed from the ancient Roman habits, practices and institutions. So says Bryce: "Law cannot be always and everywhere the creation of the State, because instances can be adduced where law existed in a community before there was any State."[14]

11. Arnold Brecht, *Political Theory*, pp. 182-83.
12. Hobbes, *Leviathan*, Ch. 17
13. Laski, *A Grammar of Politics*, p. 51.
14. Bryce, *Studies in History and Jurisprudence*, Vol. II, p. 249.

Merits and Demerits

Historical theory holds that the law of the State is found in the process of historical evolution of the people. The sanction behind law is the pressure of the will of the people. Such a view has its strong and weak points.

Merits: (i) It analyses the role of historical forces that play their part in the sphere of legal obligation.

(ii) It contributes to the understanding of the nature of law by emphasising that legal systems change and they should undergo modifications in order to meet new conditions.

Demerits: (i) It errs in ignoring or reducing the element of 'command' to the point of a mere metaphor.

(ii) It assumes a conservative character because of its reverence for the past and its distrust for deliberate efforts directed at reforms of the law and legal systems.

4. The sociological theory of law: An extension of the historical theory it insists that law is the creation of social forces and must be studied in the light of social needs. The State does not create law. It only imputes legal value to a rule or practice that grows out of social needs. Sociological theorists include Duguit in France, Krabbe in Holland, Roscoe Pound and Justice Holmes in the United States and Laski in England. They contended that the obligations of the people are based on the fact that men live in society and they must so live in order to survive and that life in society requires a certain manner of conduct. Law is the totality of general or particular, written or unwritten rales which spring from men's feelings or 'sense of right.' Justice Holmes suggests that one should consider not only what the laws are as they appear in the constitutions, statutes, and judicial decisions but also what effects they have produced in the past, how they operate today, and how they may be improved by deliberate human effort in time to come.

Merits: This theory has the merit of emphasising the role of social needs in the sphere of legal obligation. Law exists to serve social purposes and the people obey it because of their "sense of right".

Demerits: It ignores what the advocates of imperative theory so strongly affirm. We cannot lose sight of the role of forces that lie behind law and which is a result of the will of the sovereign authority. To say that law is prior or anterior to the State is to misunderstand the significance of the analytical theory of law. We cannot detach law from the fact of the existence of a coercive power vested in the State. The idea of law being prior, or anterior, to the existence of political authority is untenable.

5. Marxian theory of law: According to Marx, the economic structure constitutes the real basis upon which the political and juridical superstructures are built. Legal relationships are footed in the material conditions of life. Laws merely express the will and the interests of the dominant class. As Marx says: 'Law is an expression of society's general interests and needs as they emerge from a given material means of production." According to Lenin, law is an expression of what is expedient for the construction of socialism and to fight for it. As law is enforced through the courts, judiciary acts like an instrument of class domination. As a noted Soviet jurist A.Y. Vyshinsky says: "A court of whatever sort is an organ of the class dominant in a given State depending and guiding its interests."[15] So says Afanasyev: "Law is the totality of *obligatory* standards and rules of behaviour of people in society. These rules are expressed in corresponding laws which are safeguarded by the State and its numerous instruments of compulsion and education. Law, like politics, arose with classes and the State. It is the will of the ruling class expressed in legal forms and it defends the political and economic interests of the ruling class."[16]

Merits: (i) Its merit lies in its integration of the principle of legal obligation with the general character of the society.

(ii) It puts emphasis on economic structure of society that has its decisive impact on the organisation and working of political and legal institutions.

Demerits: (i) It denounces the State and law as being instruments of exploitation and oppression by one class over another. This may not convince the advocates of a liberal-democratic order.

(ii) It rejects the 'rule of law' that is regarded as the hallmark of a democratic order.

(iii) It may prevail only in a Communist country where the pattern of the government is totalitarian.

RELATION OF LAW AND LIBERTY

1. The anarchists and the syndicalists: These are rank anti-authoritarians. The anarchists like Proudhon, Bakunin and Kropotkin and syndicalists like Sorel and Pelloutier frankly denounce the State as an instrument of exploitation and oppression. They cherish a classless and stateless society in which there is no law to limit or destroy the liberty of the individual. The dominant class controls the State and uses law as an instrument to protect and promote its interests. The Parliament and the courts are the agencies that perpetrate the rule of the class of the

15. A.Y. Vyshinsky, *The Law of the Soviet State*, p. 500.
16. V.G. Afanasyev, *Marxist Philosophy*, pp. 372-73.

exploiters and the oppressors. Law is the instrument that kills liberty of the individuals. In the final stage of social development there should be no state, no law, no authority of any kind to exercise coercion.

2. The individualists: John Stuart Mill, Herbert Spencer, Adam Smith etc., take state as a necessary evil. They cherish minimum possible interference of the state in the liberty of the individual. Spencer treats law as a 'sin' and legislators as 'sinners' who destroy the liberty of the individual by imposing limitations of law on it. Individualist thinkers support the case of minimum possible control of law so as to allow maximum possible liberty to the individuals.

3. The socialists: They treat law and liberty as complementary terms. To them State is a 'welfare agency'. It can ensure a better and just social order by its legal mechanism. Law imposes restraints that are essential for the sake of social welfare. Though the capitalist class exploits the working class, the state may eradicate the evil of exploitation by making necessary laws. As no freedom is absolute, the State may impose necessary restrictions on the use and enjoyment of rights of the people. It may make laws for the regulation of working conditions or maintenance of social security. It may even make laws for the nationalisation of private property in the public interest. As Laski says, law comes very close to the world of liberty that demands observance of common rules that bind the conduct of men in their civilised collective life.

4. The idealists: They worship State as a moralising agency. Every law represents general will of the community. Every law of the State must be observed by the people. A man is free when he obeys the law of the State. If a man does not do so, he may be coerced. Rousseau and Green hold that the State can use force to create freedom. According to Hegel, State cannot do anything opposed to the real interest of man.

5. The fascists: They give a practical expression to the idealistic version given above. "Nothing against the State', says Mussolini. The State must make law to protect the interest of the individuals. The real interest of individuals lies in rendering complete obedience to it. It is impossible to think of a law that is anti-thetical to public interest. The State can do no wrong. Man should fall down and obey law so as to worship the State.

Conclusion

It is rightly said: 'No restraint, no liberty'. Thus, law is required to impose due restrictions on the behaviour of man so that he may not be a source of nuisance to the liberty of others. At the same time, law destroys liberty of the individuals as in a fascist or a communist country. The problem of legal obligation finds its proper solution in the affirmation that based on the general will of the people the State should devise its legal machinery in a way so that obedience to law is sincerely associated with the consent of the people. If they refuse to obey a law which they denounce as a 'black' or a Draconian measure people rise in revolt. To conclude: "So long as the actions of the State are in the interest of the common good, the disobedient individual can be forced to be free, for even when he is being compelled, he is constrained in his own true interest."[17]

LAW AND MORALITY

Distinctions

Law and morality differ from each other in their content, sanction and definiteness:

1. While law is concerned with the outward actions of man, the morality is concerned with his inner motives.
2. While law is concerned with the regulation of the objective behaviour of man, morality has its connection with the subjective aspect of the same.
3. While the purpose of law is to restrain a man from doing a crime like theft or burglary, the purpose of morality is to save him from committing a sin like speaking untruth or practising ingratitude. Thus, law and morality differ in respect of their application.
4. While law is universal in character and applicable to a large number of people in a uniform measure, morality has its application to individual cases. It differs from man to man and from group to group.
5. While law is quite specific and its terms are very clear, morality is rather ambiguous and uncertain.
6. While the law is mandatory and is backed by the authority of the sovereign, the morality has an optional character having its source of sanction in the good sense or conscience of the people.

As the people rise in revolt when law breaks a celebrated norm of their morality, Laski has rightly said that even the 'sovereign' British Parliament cannot make a law that undermines the norms of a civilised behaviour. Law should protect morality of the people, but it may do otherwise if it is so desired by the enlightened sections of the community.

17. Asirvatham, *op. cit.*, p. 192.

"In order that a law may be valid, it is enough that it should satisfy the canon of declaration, recognition and enforcement by a constituted authority acting on behalf of the community."[18]

Prof R.M. MacIver is, however, correct in his affirmation that law cannot cover total sphere of morality in view of the fact that "to turn all moral obligations into legal obligations would be to destroy morality."[19]

INTERNATIONAL LAW

International law is common to all states. It incorporates the experience of many centuries during which peoples have lived together and have done business with each other. It may be spoken of as the moral code of states, for it is the body of rules upon which they have agreed so that they may survive. Some writers contend that in reality international law is a law among states — not over them. The difference is a fundamental one. It involves the basic nature of the State system. As Palmer and Perkins put it, "Indeed, international law must be studied with the realisation that it not only presumes the sovereignty of states but also seeks to preserve sovereignty — that, in general, It has been the friend rather than the enemy of sovereignty."[20]

Definitions of International Law

1. *Oppenheim*: It is "the name for the body of customary and conventional rules which are considered legally binding by civilised states in their intercourse with each other." He added that it is "a law for the intercourse of states with one another, not a law for individuals" and that it is "a law between, not above, the single states."[21]

2. *Ellery C. Stowell*: "International law embodies certain rules relating to human relations throughout the world, which are generally observed by mankind and enforced primarily through the agency of the governments of the independent communities into which humanity is divided,"[22] International law is "generally defined as law applicable to relations between states."

3. *Phillip C. Jessup*: "The recent trend in the West, particularly in the United States, is toward a less technical view of the law. The increasingly influential school of international law created by Myres S. McDougal of Yale University regards law as a process of decision into which all relevant

18. Barker, *Principles of Social and Political Theory*, p. 117.
19. MacIver, R.M., *The Modern State*, p. 157.
20. Palmer and Perkins, *International Relations*, p. 266.
21. L. Oppenheim, *International Law* (New York: Longmans Green & Co., 1905).
22. Ellery C Stowell, *International Law* (New York: Holt, 1931), p. 10.

factors, and not merely technical norms, enter. It virtually identifies law with policy and calls the study of law "a policy science."[23]

4. *Charles C. Fenwick*: International law is primarily "the body of rules accepted by the general community of nations as defining their rights and the means of procedure by which those rights may be protected or violations of them redressed.[24]

ATTITUDES TO INTERNATIONAL LAW

The Communist Attitude

The Communists regard traditional international law, as an instrument of the capitalist, imperialist West, designed to preserve the *status quo*. A standard Soviet definition of international law was given in 1948 by A.Y. Vyshinsky, who called it "the sum total of the norms regulating relations between states in the process of their struggle and co-operation, expressing the will of the ruling classes of these states and secured by coercion exercised by states individually or collectively."[25] This definition was also presented in the textbook on international law published in 1957 by the Institute of State and Law of the Soviet Academy of Sciences, with the addition of a reference to "peaceful coexistence" as coming within the purview of international law. Although Y. Korovin in 1961 went so far as to insist that "Contemporary international law may be defined as the international code of peaceful co-existence."[26] A year later, a statement by G.I. Tunkin head of the Treaty and Legal Department of the Soviet Ministry of Foreign Affairs, reaffirmed the more typical Soviet view that international law reflects "the struggle and co-operation of states, and, first of all, of states of the two systems."[27] It is this Soviet stress on antagonism rather than co-operation as the primary characteristic of the relations between the states of 'the two systems' that sets narrow limits to the role of international law in world affairs."[28]

Attitudes toward international law appear to reflect the difference in the ideologies and policies within the Communist world, "from the relative moderation of the Yugoslav government at one end of the spectrum to the intransigence of the Communist regime in mainland China at the other."[29]

23. Phillip C. Jessup, *Transnational Law* (New Haven: Yale University Press, 1956).
24. Charles G. Fenwick, *International Law* (New York: Century, 1924), p. 34.
25. "Mezhdunarodnoie Pravo i Mezhdunarodnaia Organizatsiia" *Sovetskoie Gosudarstvo i Pravo*, No. I (1948), p. 22; quoted in Lissitzyn, pp. 16-17.
26. "International Law Today," *International Affairs*, July 1961, p. 19.
27. "XXIIS, ezd KPSS i Zadachi Sovetskoi Nauki Mezhdunarodnogo Prava," *Sovetskoie Gosudarstvo i Pravo* No. 5 (1962), pp. 12-13; quoted in Lissitzyn, p. 17.
28. Lissitzyn, p. 17.
29. *Ibid.*, p. 35.

The official position of the Chinese Communists toward international law is still in the process of formulation. In general, like the Soviet leaders, they follow the Marxist Leninist approach, with perhaps even more emphasis on the struggle between systems and on the political rather than the legal approach to foreign affairs. In the words of Anthony R. Dicks, "When it becomes necessary to raise legal questions, the Chinese government some times make skillful use of traditionally accepted international rules, suiting them to its own characterisation of the facts of the situation. At other times, the generally accepted rules are sidestepped by a varying combination of orthodox and Marxist argument. Like the Soviet Union, the Chinese People's Republic has chosen an extremely nationalist and conservative formulation of state sovereignty as the most effective legal safeguard of her freedom of action."[30]

International Law in Developing Nations

The developing nations of Asia and Africa exhibit a distrust of traditional international law, a belief that the traditional norms are not binding on them, and a strong desire for the development of international law to meet the needs of the modern world. These nations want to be sure that international law does not become an instrument for the preservation of the *status quo* which may stand in the way of measures to promote de-colonisation, self-determination, human rights, and the social use of natural resources. They are inclined to give more emphasis to the "progressive development of international law" than to its codification. Unlike the Communists, they have a positive view toward international law. In most instances they are inclined to accept, or at least to abide by, its traditional norms. Most of them are ready to join international organisations, become parties to multilateral conventions and treaty arrangements, and play as active a role as possible in international life. Yet, as Oliver Lissitzyn has pointed out there is among the developing nations, "a perceptible current of discontent with traditional international law."[31] Judge Radhabinod Pal, a distinguished Indian jurist who wrote a famous dissent in the Tokyo War Crimes Trials and who was a member of the International Law Commission of the United Nations, wrote that they ought not "to be bound by rules of international law which they have not helped to create and which very often ran counter to their interests."[32] "There is also, a desire to incorporate in it [international law] certain principles that have been usually regarded in the West as political rather

30. Anthony R. Dicks, "Chinese Attitudes to International Law (1)," a memorandum dated October 9, 1964, privately distributed by the Institute of Current World Affairs, New York, p. 16.
31. Lissitzyn, p. 38.
32. Quoted in "Future Role of the International Law Commission in the Changing World," *United Nations Review*, IX (September 1962), p. 31.

than legal and that, by their very generality and flexibility of application, lend themselves to manipulation. The non-Western nations tend to use such principles as weapons in their effort to do away with the remnants of Western domination in both political and economic spheres."[33] The new states, place great stress on the concept of self-determination, which they advance vigorously in their anti-colonial crusades and in their efforts to assert their economic and social, as well as political, independence. This orientation is reflected in the Declaration on the Granting of Independence to Colonial Countries and Peoples, adopted by the General Assembly of the UN in December, 1960, which affirmed that "aly peoples have the right to self-determination."

BRANCHES OF INTERNATIONAL LAW

1. Public and private international law: To distinguish it from what is known as "private international law," a branch of the law which deals entirely with the relations of persons living under different legal systems, the international law is at times spoken of as "public international law." Private international law applies when justice requires that the law of some outside jurisdiction be applied in a particular case. Frequently the nationality of a person is the issue. As Professor Edwin D. Dickinson stated, "There is a host of problems concerning the adjudication and regulation of matters of private right and duties which arise uniquely from the continuing movement of persons or things from one nation to another and from the increasing ease with which relationships of agreement, family, property, enterprise, or the like may be consummated across national frontiers."[34] Private international law is a term more current in Europe than in the United States. American lawyers commonly use "conflict of laws" to mean the same thing in relation to the laws of states of the United States.

2. Admiralty and administrative law: Admiralty law, which is the law of maritime commerce, resembles private international law as a large part of it is concerned with differences between separate national jurisdictions. In the United States, the system of admiralty or maritime law which prevails by general consent in all commercial states has no inherent force of its own. It is operative only to the extent that it has been adopted by American customs or law.

Administrative law, consists of the body of rules growing out of the regulations adopted by international administrative agencies, as for example, the Universal Postal Union.

33. Lissitzyn, p. 39.
34. Edwin D. Dickinson, *Law and Peace* (Philadelphia Press, 1951), p. 59.

3. International comity: The term "international comity" has been the subject of much controversy. When the courts of one state gave force to the laws of another state in order to render justice to the parties involved, they did so as a matter of comity or grace. Some writers would abandon the term entirely as it has been applied in private international law. It is used in public international law to explain the practices which states more or less consistently observe, even though they are not legally bound to do so. Comity thus influences the growth of international law.

SUBJECT MATTER OF INTERNATIONAL LAW

International law proper, public international law, is divided into the law of war and the law of peace. Hugo Grotius called his great pioneering work *On the Law of War and Peace;* Oppenheim's classic treatise consisted of one volume on peace and one on war. It was believed that public international law is made up of two separate and distinct branches, with the law of war being necessary to regulate the rights and obligations of belligerents and neutrals when the law of peace is no longer applicable. But today the boundary lines between war and peace are becoming more obscured. The new techniques and new weapons of destruction have made conventional laws of war inadequate, if not obsolete.

The International Law Commission listed 25 topics in the field of international law: (1) Subjects of international law; (2) Sources of international law; (3) Obligations of international law in relation to the law of States; (4) Fundamental rights and duties of States; (5) Recognition of States of Governments; (6) Succession of States and Governments; (7) Domestic jurisdiction; (8) Recognition of acts of foreign States; (9) Jurisdiction over foreign States; (10) Obligations of territorial jurisdiction; (11) Jurisdiction with regard to crimes committed outside national territory; (12) Territorial domain of States; (13) Regime of the high seas; (14) Regime of territorial waters; (15) Pacific settlement of international disputes; (16) Nationality, including statelessness; (17) Treatment of aliens; (18) Extradition; (19) Right of asylum; (20) Law of treaties; (21) Diplomatic intercourse and immunities; (22) Consular intercourse and immunities; (23) State responsibility; (24) Arbitral procedure; (25) Laws of war. Each one of these 25 topics raises fundamental questions of international conduct and obligations each has been the subject of careful examination and discussion.

EXPANDING SCOPE OF INTERNATIONAL LAW

In recent years, there has been a marked tendency to develop principles of international law to apply to questions, which in the past would probably have been regarded as outside the scope of international law. An outstanding example is the effort of the UN General Assembly and a Special Committee of the Assembly to develop "principles of international law concerning friendly relations and co-operation among states."

Other fields of international law expanding in scope and significance are: international constitutional law, international administrative law, international labour law, international commercial law, international corporation law, international anti-trust law, international tax law, and international economic development law. As Professor Wolfgang Friedmann has pointed out, these new fields "are developing from a far-reaching interpretation between public and private law," and may in fact be evolving "the form and authority of new international norms."[35]

The subject matter of international law is expanding rapidly in volume as well as in scope. This is illustrated by the formidable achievements in the codification of international law, the development of international legislation. The number of treaties and other international instruments, etc. The major contributors to international law are, of course, the United Nations and its affiliated agencies. "Despite the U.N.'s political paralysis, its various sub-groups have probably created more international laws in the past 20 years than enacted in all previous history."[36]

1. International law in outer space: The advent of the space age has moved international law, beyond the territorial sphere. In 1959 the General Assembly created a Committee on the Peaceful Uses of Outer Space. In September 1963, this committee was urged to continue its "efforts to find solutions in the legal field in order to match the continuous scientific and technological progress in outer space."[37] Three months later the General Assembly unanimously adopted a Declaration of Legal Principles Governing the Activities of states in the Exploration and Use of Outer Space.[38] In it, it was stated that outer space and celestial bodies are not subject to national appropriation and are free for exploration and use by all states. It recommended that consideration be given to incorporating principles governing space activities "in international agreement form, in the fixture as appropriate."

2. Laws of war: Laws of war on land and sea have been formulated through various codes and conventions, particularly by the conventions drafted at the Hague conferences of 1899 and 1907 and in many Geneva conventions. Following aspects of warfare were dealt with

35. Wolfgang Friedmann, *The Changing Structure of International Law* (New York: Columbia University Press, 1964), pp. 152-87.
36. *Time*, May 28, 1965.
37 U.N. Document A/AC 105/PV. 20. October 10, 1963, p. 6.
38 General Assembly Res. 196 (XVIII), December 13, 1963.

in these documents: privateering, blockade, prize courts, the care of sick and wounded, protection for medical personnel and facilities, the qualifications of lawful combatants, the treatment of prisoners, forbidden weapons and agencies, the powers of military commanders in occupied enemy territory, the status of spies, the beginning of hostilities, the use of merchant vessels as warships, naval bombardments, the use of submarine mines, the right of capture in maritime warfare, the rights and duties of neutrals, and the use of poison gases. On some of these subjects the agreements were largely nullified by sweeping reservations. On others the agreements were never ratified. In the convention on the treatment of prisoners of war[39], the law is detailed and explicit. However, a substantial part of the laws of war is still based on custom and usage.

The laws of war have helped to humanise warfare. Even the totalitarian states have more generally observed them than disregarded. However, they have not tried to prevent the most inhuman practices, such as unrestricted submarine warfare and the use of flame-throwers, napalm, and atom bombs. Laws of war have never been adequately revised to cover the new and more terrible weapons of destruction that were developed during World Wars I and II and in intervening years. They have not been adapted to meet the needs of the atomic age.

3. Laws of neutrality: Before the First World War an important offshoot of the laws of war, the laws of neutrality, were concerned with the forms of neutrality and of neutralisation, the proclamation of neutrality, and especially the relations between neutral states and belligerent states and between states and individuals. The problems involving the rights and duties of neutrals were the maintenance of the inviolability of the territorial jurisdiction of neutrals; the obligation of neutrals not to permit the use of their territory as a base for military operations; the regulation of the rights of asylum and of internment; the conditions under which enemy ships may enter and leave neutral ports; the obligation of a neutral state not to furnish military assistance to any belligerent or to permit enlistment of troops for a belligerent state; and the neutrals' obligation to enforce its neutrality laws.

In World War I traditional laws of neutrality lost much of their meaning. They were flagrantly disregarded. They appeared to be largely inapplicable to the use of such new weapons as the aeroplane and the submarine. Woodrow Wilson insisted on the rights of the United States as the greatest neutral state. This led to strained relations with Great

39. James Wilford Garner, "Laws of Warfare," *Encyclopaedia of the Social Sciences* (New York: The Macmillan Company, 1937), XV, 363.

Britain over interference with American ships, goods and nationals and to the American declaration of war upon Germany. Germany's use of the submarine was, to the President, a clear violation of America's rights as a neutral power. Traditional laws of neutrality have never been satisfactorily revised since that time. During World War II, they seemed quite anachronistic. Writing before World War II, Phillip C. Jessup declared that "it may well be argued that in the present or future condition of world solidarity, neutrality is an anti-social status."[40]

4. The laws of peace: The subject matter of the international law of peace embraces the bulk of the matters with which the international lawyer usually deals. In a brief chapter on "The Law of Nations", Professor Dickinson delineates "six grand aspects or divisions of the subjects":

1. *The law relating to the nation-state*: It is "the traditional and principal subject of law in the international system," with particular attention to "its birth, recognition, life and death."

2. *Nationality*: It deals with "the principles which determine human allegiance to the nation, including the severance of allegiance and the protection of nationals abroad."

3. *National laws*: It is "the law of the national domain or homeland, including such earthy business as acquisitions, transfers, boundaries, internal authority and external responsibility."

4. *Laws of jurisdiction.*

5. *Laws of intercourse and agreements.*

6. *The settlement of disputes*: International law is rather well-developed in these areas. At the same time, however, there as "characteristic weaknesses," "important gaps," and "extraordinary paradoxes in the law".

It is due to the character of the international society where "The law has developed among the members of an organised community of basically dissimilar subjects."

INTERNATIONAL LAW AND MUNICIPAL LAW

While International law is largely concerned with relations between states, municipal law controls relations between individuals within a State and between individuals and the State. Both are similar because of their sources in custom and express agreement. However, both have substantial differences in legislative machinery and judicial processes. Both are usually applied by national courts. It results in complete decentralisation of the judicial function in international law and effective centralisation

40. Philip C. Jessup, "Neutrality," *Encyclopaedia of the Social Sciences* (New York: The Macmillan Company, 1937), XI, 364.

in municipal law. Most municipal laws are enforced by a responsible executive unknown to international law. Traditional international law always depended for its enforcement upon the initiative of the injured party.

In the event of a conflict between international law and domestic law, Oppenheim held that the national courts could not apply the law of nations, for "the latter lacks absolutely the power of altering or creating rules of municipal law."[41] On the other hand, Clyde Eagleton insisted that "to admit that international law is ultimately dependent upon domestic law and courts, or that municipal law may override international law, would be to deny international law outright, and no state makes such a denial"; the "decisions of the courts putting its [the state's] own law above international law are not final, but may be reviewed and reparation may be demanded by an international tribunal."[42] After World War I, the constitutions of Germany and Austria specifically made international law a part of municipal law, and that court decision achieved the same result in the United States.

THE SOURCES OF INTERNATIONAL LAW

The sources of international law are treaties, custom, and general principles of law. The Statute of the International Court of Justice (Article 38) stipulates that the Court shall apply:

(a) international conventions, whether general or particular, establishing rules expressly recognised by the contesting states;
(b) international custom, as evidence of a general practice accepted as law;
(c) the general principles of law recognised by civilised nations;
(d) ...judicial decisions and the teachings of the most highly qualified publicists of the various nations, as subsidiary means for the determination of rules of law.

Here (d) merely indicates means by which (b) and (c) may be determined.

1. Treaty: Law as fixed by treaty or convention is a fairly objective one. This however, presents at least two difficulties. One is the matter of interpretation, and the other is that of knowing just when a rule becomes international law.

2. Custom: It is often difficult to prove that a particular rule has been accepted in practice by the community of states, even though the various

41. Oppenheim, 1, 26.
42. Clyde Eagleton, *International Government*, rev. ed. (New York: The Ronald Press Co., 1948), pp. 48-49.

states have never reached an explicit understanding to that effect. The rule must be proved by the presentation of evidence from judicial decisions, diplomatic correspondence, state papers, and the findings of research societies and private scholars.

3. The "general principles of law: These have been variously spoken of as justice, commonsense, and right reason. These are principles common to the great legal systems of the world, determined with some degree of objectivity. They make it possible for judges to fill in the gaps between the rules of "positive law".

ENFORCEMENT OF INTERNATIONAL LAW

Traditional international law recognised a right of self-help on the part of injured states. World public opinion has long exerted some pressure on states to observe the rights of other states and of individuals. However, no international organisation intervened to enforce the law. Each State was the judge in its own cause. While states possessed a right of action on behalf of themselves and their citizens, no right of action was lodged anywhere in the international community when a State mistreated its own nationals.

Thus, under traditional international law, self-help, or, more formally, unilateral action, was the ultimate means of enforcement.

NATURE OF INTERNATIONAL LAW

Austinian school, insisted that international law is not law at all but a branch of international morality. Other declare that the matter is one of definition. Still others staunchly defend the validity of the term. International law, unlike domestic law, is very limited in scope. The greater portion of international relations has not come within its jurisdiction at all. Traditional international law has applied only to those subjects on which states have agreed that it should apply. Economic discrimination, imperialism, and war were not necessarily violations of international law.

It is argued that international law is not true law, because it is not binding. It is impossible to reconcile the dogma of sovereignty with the idea of a law to which states must submit whether they like it or not. More generally, it is held that states enter the community of nations with the assumption that they accept its laws, and that the continued general observance of certain rules of conduct implies a tacit acceptance of those rules. J.L. Brierly, an English authority on International Law, argued that the views of Jean Bodin and Thomas Hobbes, the great champions of absolute and indivisible sovereignty, never meant to underwrite international anarchy, as some of their followers have done."[43] He added that "the doctrine was developed for the most part by political theorists who were not interested in, and paid little regard to, the relations of states with one another, and in its later forms it not only involved a denial of the possibility of states being subject to any kind of law, but became an impossible theory for a world which contained more states than one." Thus, individual states may be bound by international law even against their will, but law must rest upon the general consent of the community of nations.

Some writers believe that in the absence of centralised legislative, judicial and executive authority international law is not a true law. It cannot be true law because "it is not enforced". The assumption of non-observance has been pretty well demolished by jurists from the time of John Bassett Moore to the present. Quincy Wright had this to say on the point of enforcement: "A considerable failure of realisation is...to be expected of any rule of jural law. Its status as law depends not only on objective observation that persons and official agencies within the society generally conform to the rules but also on subjective assumption of a duty to conform by such persons and agencies. If that assumption is generally made in the society, the rule may be valid law even though its imperfect observance and enforcement makes it ineffective."[44]

As Eagleton complacently remarked, "the theorist who wishes to deny to the law of nations the title of true law does not in the least affect the actual conduct of affairs in that society, nor the fact that those affairs are regulated by rules as well enforced and observed as those of domestic law."[45]

THE ORIGIN AND DEVELOPMENT OF INTERNATIONAL LAW

International law had its beginnings in the pre-historic world. As stated emerged in the ancient world certain peoples, particularly the Hebrews and the Hindus, asserted ideals of justice and order in the relations of states.

1. Pre-Grotian International law. In the relations among the city-states, the Greeks made their greatest contribution to the law of nations. They also furthered orderly inter-state or international relations through their belief that these relations should be based upon certain rules. In their inter-city-state relations they acknowledged rules of warfare and

43. J.L. Brierly, *The Law of Nations* 6th ed., edited by Sir Humphrey Waldock (New York: Oxford University Press, 1963), pp. 7-16, 45.
44. Quincy Wright, *The Study of International Relations* (New York: Appleton-Century-Crofts, 1955), p. 220.
45. Eagleton, p. 53.

diplomatic immunity. They made considerable use of arbitration. They evolved a system of maritime law.

The Romans extended the authority of Rome by conquest and alliance until they achieved a world-state. Their legacy to international law was the ideal of a common citizenship and impartial justice everywhere, the idea of a universal law, and the breaking down of the old isolationism and the old contempt for foreigners. Roman jurists formulated the principles of the *jus gentium*, or law of peoples, a body of rules and usages believed to be applicable to all peoples and resting upon natural justice. These principles survived the fall of Rome and were accepted as part of the emerging international law towards the close of the Middle Ages. Thus, the way was prepared for the modern belief that definite legal principles should control the relations of states. International relations in the modern sense of the term began to develop with the rise of Britain, France, Portugal and Spain as nation-states. Regulations became imperative for the conduct of war, the preservation of neutrality, the use of the seas in both peace and war, and the fixing of boundaries in colonial claims. Agreements were made between states by treaty and conference. The principles of Roman law respecting private property were applied to boundary lines and colonial claims, and a law of war was slowly formulated.

There was a growing body of rules of conduct that states were approving by observance and commitment in the principles of Roman law, in practice and custom, and in what they called "natural law". Thus, international law was made by the actions and agreements of rulers. It was collected and systematised by scholars through researchers in the past and current relations of states. In the words of Pitman B. Potter, "International law as now practised by the states of the world, is largely the product of private scholarship, taken over later by the states more or less in spite of their natural instincts."[46]

The first of the important writers was Legnano, an Italian, whose study of the rules of war was written in 1360, and published in 1477. Six legal scholars produced notable works on international law in the 16th century. These included Vitoria, a Spaniard who "laid down the principle that the nations formed a community based upon natural reason and social intercourse," Suarez, also a Spaniard, who "first distinguished between reason and custom as sources of international law, a distinction followed ever since", and Gentilis, a British subject of Italian extraction,

46. Pitman B. Potter, *An Introduction to the Study of International Organisation*, 5th ed. (New York: Appleton-Century-Crofts, 1948), p. 58.

who added historical and legal precedents to natural reason and natural law as sources of international law.

2. Grotius (1583-1645) and natural law: Hugo Grotius was the man destined to become known as the "Father of International Law". Born in Holland in 1583, he took the degree of doctor of laws at the University of Leyden at the age of fifteen. In 1609 he published *Mare liberum*, where in he argued for freedom of the seas, a view then not generally held. Later he went to Paris, where he lived for ten years. In 1625 he published his great work *De jure belli ac pacis*, or *On the Law of War and Peace*.

With *De jure belli ac pacis*, particularly Part II, "the science of the modern Law of Nations commences.. .because in it a fairly complete system of international law was for the first time built up as an independent branch of the science of law".

Characteristics of Grotius' Laws

1. Grotius would hold states to practice the same rules which regulate the lives of individuals and make the violation of them a crime subject to punishment.
2. Basing his judgement upon researches in the scriptures, ancient history and the classics, Grotius formulated the "law of peace" which became the foundation of his whole system.
3. Grotius argued that states may properly punish other states which violate the law.
4. Grotius accepted natural law — or right reason — as the primary basis for determining rules for the rightful conduct of states.[47]

Grotius defined the natural law or law of nature as "the dictate of right reason which points out that a given act, because of its opposition to or conformity with man's rational nature, is either morally wrong or morally necessary, and accordingly forbidden or commanded by God, the author of nature."[48] It was a theoretical approach which sought to assert what ought to be the law rather than to list the rules to which men and states had actually committed themselves by custom or agreement. While Grotius did not ignore positive law, which he called "voluntary law", he kept it distinct from the rules which he took from natural law. His formulation of the rules of state conduct resting upon natural law dominated thinking on international law for two centuries.

3. Zouche (1590-1660) and positivism: Richard Zouche, an Oxford professor of civil law, published a little book in which he asserted views

47. Cornelius van Vollenhoven, "Hugo Grotius," *Encyclopaedia of the Social Science* (New York: The Macmillan Company, 1937), VII, 177.

48. Book I, Chapter I, Section X.

quite opposite from those of Grotius. Whereas Grotius has emphasised natural law and minimised customary law, Zouche reversed the order. He is sometimes called as the "Second Founder of the Law of Nations". Instead of using Grotius' term, *jus genium* or law of nations, he used jus *inter gentes* or law between nations, thus supplying the "inter" for the term "international law", first used by Jeremy Bentham a century and a half later.

4. The three schools of thought: Nearly two centuries after 1625, during the 17th and the 18th centuries, one finds three schools of thought:

1. *The naturalists*: They took their cue from Grotius but often went far beyond him to deny all positive law.
2. *The positivists*: They rejected Grotius' natural law and supported Zouche's customary law, some even outdoing Zouche and denying natural law lock, stock and barrel.
3. *The Grotians*: They accepted both natural and customary laws, although most of them given more importance to customary law than had Grotius.

The writers of the first two-thirds of the century showed the influence of Grotius. As scholars in considerable number delved into archives, they narrowed the field in which positive law was lacking. As states more and more frequently entered into law-making treaties, they lessened the need for appeals to natural law. Thus by the last third of the 19th century positivism had become the prevailing school of thought.

THE CODIFICATION OF INTERNATIONAL LAW

Legal scholars of the past half-century have accepted the separation of positive law and natural law. The most significant development was an expanded interest in the collection and systematisation of existing law and organised efforts to translate ideas of improved inter-state relations into the law of nations by multilateral agreements. These developments are commonly known as codification and international legislation.

Meaning of Codification

Code means to systematise the law in a certain field. In the words of Eagleton "the codification of international law, if it means anything at all, means systematic legislation."[49]

Beginnings of Codification

The earliest attempts at codification were not made until the I860,, the first being a precis formulated in 1861 by an Austrian jurist. Two years later, in 1863, Francis Lieber (1800-1872) prepared *A Code for the*

49. Eagleton, p. 207.

Government of Armies, which was used by the Union armies in the Civil War and by Germany in the Franco-Prussian War. In 1868 Bluntschli (1808-81) produced a more comprehensive codification, declaring that his intention was "to formulate clearly the existing ideas of the civilised world." In 1872 an American, David Dudley Field (1805-94), issued a *Draft Outline of an International Code*, and an Italian jurist, Pasquale Fiore (1837-1914), published in 1889 a code covering the whole field of international law. An English translation was published by Edwin M. Borchard in 1915 as *International Law Codified.*

Institutional Codification

In 1873 was founded the *Institut de Droit International,* and the Association for the Reform and Codification of the Law of Nations, which in 1895 changed its name to the International Law Association. The *Institut* issued a number of draft codes, the most being the *Manual of the Laws of War on Land*, published in 1880. A compilation of fifty-six "resolution" and "views" of the *Institut* was published in 1916 by James Brown Scott, Director of the Division of International Law of the Carnegie Endowment for International Peace. Like the *Institut* the International Law Association has concentrated upon the statement of law on particular topics founded in 1905. The American Society of International Law publishes a journal of notable excellence, *The American Journal of International Law*, but it does not emphasise codification.

The American Institute of International Law, devoted its energies almost exclusively to the drafting of codes, particularly as they embody practices in the Western Hemisphere. Founded in 1912 through the efforts of Alejandro Alvarez of Chile and James Brown Scott of the United States, this organisation was closely associated with the Union of American Republics and its Commission of Jurists. It enjoyed the financial support of the Carnegie Endowment for International Peace. In June 1950, the Inter-American Council of Jurists acknowledged the "notable contribution" of the Institute and asked for its continued co-operation. The Institute's part in the codification of "American international law" has largely taken the form of making recommendations to the official organs of the Inter-American System. A German organisation, *the Institut Fiir Internationales Recht* at Kiel, also did more in the direction of codification. Finally, a number of draft conventions were issued by Harvard University's Research in international law, set up in 1926 to aid the League of Nations in the work of codification. The first three of the drafts related to nationality, responsibility of states, and territorial waters.

Early Official Codification

Official codification began when the representatives of twelve states, assembled at Geneva in 1864, endeavoured to describe existing practice in respect to the care of the wounded in battle. Meeting on the invitation of the Tsar of Russia at Brussels in 1874, representatives of the leading powers drew up a draft code of the rules of war on land, which was never ratified. More ambitious ventures in codification were undertaken by the famous Hague Conferences of 1899 and 1907. The first conference approved a code of the law and customs of war on land and adapted to maritime war the principles formulated in the Geneva Convention of 1864 for the care of the sick and wounded in land warfare. The second conference of 1907 adopted conventions on the codification of the rights and duties of neutrals and on certain phases of the conduct of naval warfare. Both conferences also accepted many conventions that embodied new rules of international law. In 1900 the United States Government published *The Laws and Usages of War at Sea*, thus supplementing Lieber's rules of warfare on land. In 1909, the leading maritime powers sent delegates to a conference in London to work out a code of warfare on the sea, but the resulting Declaration of London was ratified by only a few states. World War I soon prevented other efforts. As Professor Fenwick says, "Until the creation of the League of Nations, attempts at codification were haphazard and infrequent."[50]

Codification of American International Law

Proposals for codification of "American International Law" were made at the Inter-American Conferences of 1889-90 in Washington and of 1902 in Mexico City. The Third Conference, meeting in 1906 in Rio de Janeiro, approved a convention for setting up a Commission of Jurists to draft codes of international public and private law. In 1912 the Commission agreed upon a report on extradition and set up six committees to study subjects for codification.

Revitalised by the Fifth Inter-American Conference at Santiago in 1923 the Commission submitted twelve projects of codification to the Havana Conference of 1928. "It was at Havana," says Professor Bemis, "that the United States made its last defence of the interventions still unliquidated in the Caribbean."[51] There was clash between the United States insistence on recognition of international duties and the Latin American insistence on international rights. The Havana Conference

50. Fenwick, p. 209.
51. Samuel F. Bemis, *The Latin American Policy of the United States* (New York: Harcourt, Brace, 1943), p. 252.

approved the Bustamante Code of private international law and invited the American republics to ratify it. The United States declined to do so. The Sixth Conference also directed the Commission of Jurists to continue its work.

When the United States accepted the Doctrine of Absolute Non-intervention at Buenos Aires in 1936 it seemed that the American republics might regain their interest. Yet the Mexico City Conference of 1945 "recognised that the frequent attempts to codify international law up to that time had largely failed."[52] At the Ninth Inter-American Conference, held at Bogota in 1948, the machinery was again revised as part of the general reorganisation of the Inter-American System. An Inter-American Council of Jurists was made one the three responsible to the governing body (the Council). The Inter-American Juridical Committee was made the permanent committee of the Inter-American Council of Jurists. All other juridical agencies were abolished. One of the four departments of the general secretariat of the Pan American Union was the Department of International Law and Organisation which began the publication of the Inter-American Juridical Yearbook "to present a survey of the development of inter-American regional law during the current year". It continues the issuance of the Law and Treaty Series.

In its first meeting in Rio de Janeiro in May and June, 1950, the Council of Jurists approved a draft statute which included a detailed plan for development and codification. It directed the new Council of Jurists to "establish relations of mutual co-operation with the International Law Commission of the United Nations."[53] Although the Judicial Committee continues its work on the projects set up at Rio, the American republics have really not accomplished very much, though they have made a good start.

Codification by the League of Nations

In 1924 the Assembly and Council set up a Committee of Experts to begin the task. A Codification Conference met at The Hague in 1930 to consider three subjects: nationality, territorial waters, and the responsibility of states for damage caused in their territory to the person or property of foreigners. One convention and three protocols were adopted, but the delegates clung tenaciously to the practices of their respective governments, thus the venture of the League of Nations into the codification of international law accomplished nothing.

52. Edward O. Guerrant, *Roosevelt's Good Neighbour Policy* (Albuquerque: University of New Mexico Press, 1950), p. 80.
53. The draft Statutes of the Inter-American Council of Jurists are printed in *Annals of the Organisation of American States*, II, No. 3 (1950), 278-90.

Codification by the United Nations

The United Nations Charter specifically provides for the codification of international law. The General Assembly early created a seventeen-member *ad hoc* Committee on the Progressive Development of International Law and its Codification, and assigned to it the duty of studying methods by which the Assembly could discharge its obligation under Article 13 of the Charter of "encouraging the progressive development of international law and its codification." In its report to the Assembly in September 1947, the Committee recommended the creation of an International Law Commission, to which would be assigned the dual task of studying subjects of law not yet highly developed and the "precise formulation of the law in matters in which there was extensive practice, precedent and doctrine."[54]

The Committee recommended that the International Law Commission "consider ways and means of making the evidence of customary international law more readily available by the compilation of digests of State practice, and by the collection and publication of the decisions of national and international courts on international law questions."[55]

The General Assembly, established the International Law Commission on November 21, 1947, adopted a statute for its government, and later elected fifteen members of the commission for three-year terms. In 1956 the membership was increased to 21, and in 1961 to 25.

The ILC prepared a Declaration on the Rights and Duties of States. It formulated some though not all of the principles of law underlying the Nuremberg War Crimes Trials. It drafted a Law of Treaties. The Nuremberg Principles assert that both individuals and governments are to be held responsible for "crimes against peace," "war crimes," and "crimes against humanity." Neither of the two formulations here achieved the status of international law.

On December 18, 1962, the 17th Session of the General Assembly adopted a compromise resolution,[56] recognising the paramount importance in the "progressive development of international law and its codification" of the following seven principles: (1) refraining from the use or threat of force; (2) peaceful settlement of international disputes; (3) non-intervention in matters within the domestic jurisdiction of another state; (4) sovereign equality of states; (5) equal rights and self-determination of peoples; (6) co-operation among states in accordance

54. *International Organisation*, I (September 1947), 492.
55. *Yearbook of the United Nations* 1946-1947 (New York: United Nations, 1947), p. 259.
56. General Assembly Res. 1815 (XVII), December 18, 1962.

with the UN Charter; and (7) fulfilment in good faith of obligations assumed in accordance with the Charter. In 1963 the 18th Session of the General Assembly decided to establish a Special Committee on Principles of International Law Concerning Friendly Relations and Co-operation among states to study the first four principles and prepare a report on its conclusions and recommendations.[57]

The U.N. Secretariat has drafted conventions on certain aspects of the status of the U.N. The International Court of Justice has prepared an agreement on its own status in the Netherlands. The Human Rights Commission drafted the Universal Declaration of Human Rights, two covenants on human rights, and the Convention on Genocide.

THE LIMITATIONS OF INTERNATIONAL LAW

Basically, all the limitations of international law are inherent in the present character of international society, in which the concept of a legal order is not generally accepted but is, in fact, regarded as actually inapplicable in the most vital areas of international relations. These limitations consist of the following:

(1) the incompleteness of the legislative function;
(2) various and serious limitations in the judicial function;
(3) the lack of effective enforcement;
(4) limitations on the scope and functions of international law; and
(5) widespread misunderstanding of the nature and purpose of the law.

The Judicial Function

The problem of the judicial function may be said to be made up of the limitations arising from the following conditions:

1. Nature of international judicial machinery: International law, for the most part, is enforced by national courts.

2. Lack of compulsory jurisdiction: International law does not require any state to submit its disputes to an international tribunal against its will.

3. Ambiguity of the law: The ambiguity of the law arises in part from the lack of a judicial hierarchy and from the doubtful character of the rule of state decisions. It is also due in part to the vague and general terms in which international agreements are frequently expressed.

4. Subjects as judges: Another serious defect in the judicial function is that the subjects of international law have also been its judges. Individual

57. General Assembly Res. 1966 (XVIII), December 16, 1963.

states or their agencies possess the right to interpret the law which they are under obligation to enforce.

5. Limitation of justiciable disputes: As states are not subject to compulsory jurisdiction, they distinguish between "justiciable" and "non-justiciable" disputes.

The distinction between justiciable and non-justiciable disputes is unknown to domestic law.

The Narrow Range of International Law

In discussing what he calls one of the "most serious shortcomings of the present system," Brierly asserted that "it is because the demands that international law makes on states are on the whole so light that its rules in general are fairly well observed." He pointed to the whole field of economic relations as one in which the individual states have exclusive jurisdiction over matters which often provide the causes of international disputes. Other areas he mentioned are immigration, naturalisation, a state's treatment of its own nationals, and the choice in a form of the government. "Law will never play a really effective part in international relations," declared Brierly, "until it can annex to its own sphere some of the matters which at present lie within the 'domestic jurisdictions' of the several states".[58]

International Law and International Relations

International law is only one aspect of international relations, and by no means the most important one. The great issues of international politics, involving issues of peace or war, are largely outside its purview. International law, is still in a very primitive stage of development. Professor Dickinson, a friendly critic, described it this way: "...as regards its institutions and procedures of adjustment the law of nations has been a jungle law imperfectly ameliorated by a fragmentary and hesitant progress in the direction of legal order."[59] In Professor Brierly's judgement, "the system is still at what we may describe as the *laissez faire* stage of legal development." Nevertheless, it represents a positive attempt to build an international legal order, in the absence of which peace and sanity in the international community are in constant jeopardy.

UTILITY OF INTERNATIONAL LAW

Warning against what he describes as the swing from overestimation to underestimation of international law, Professor Josef L. Kunz recalls that at the close of World War I "there was everywhere, in victors, neutrals,

58. Brierly, pp. 74, 75.
59. Dickinson, p. 76.

and vanquished, not only the will to achieve a better world through international law, but also the firm conviction that it could be done." After World War II came the flowering of the new "realism" with its emphasis on politics and power. International law was not even mentioned in the Dumbarton Oaks Proposals, and it barely escaped exclusion from the UN Charter. Whereas the Permanent Court of International Justice was busy in its early years, the International Court of Justice has had very little business. Kunz protested against this "underestimation" of international law; he declared that the law is not "sterile" and that it must necessarily play an important role in international relations.[60] Professor Dickinson, followed a rather severe critique of international law with a volume of essays entitled *Law and Peace*, in which he affirmed his faith in international law as a realistic approach to peace.[61]

Belief in international law as a basis of enduring peace was also expressed by Senator Robert A. Taft. He contended that the veto power in the Security Council of the United Nations "completely dispels the idea that any system of universal law is being established, for surely nothing can be law if five of the largest nations can automatically exempt themselves from its application."[62] "It seems to me", he wrote, "that peace in this world is impossible unless nations agree on a definite law to govern their relations with each other and also agree that, without any veto power, they will submit their disputes to adjudication and abide by the decision of an impartial tribunal.,..."[63]

Kelsen asserted categorically that "it is the essential characteristic of the law as a coercive order to establish a community monopoly of force"; in 1944 he proposed a Permanent League for the Maintenance of Peace, "with compulsory jurisdiction" for an international court and with the four guarantor states — the United States, Great Britain, China and the Soviet Union — as "the power 'behind the law."[64] Jessup declared that "until the world achieves some form of international government in which a collective will takes precedence over the individual will of the sovereign state, the ultimate function of law, which is the elimination of force for the solution of human conflicts, will not be fulfilled."[65]

60. "The Swing of the Pendulum: From Overestimation to Underestimation of International law," *The American Journal of International Law*, XLIV (January 1950), 135-40.
61. "International Law: An Inventory," *California Law Review*, XXXIII (December 1945), 506-42; see also, the same author's *Law and Peace*.
62. Robert A. Taft, *A Foreign Policy for Americans* (Garden City, N.Y.: Doubleday & Company, 1951), pp. 39-40.
63. *Ibid.*, p. 40.
64. Kelsen, *Peace Through Law*, p. 66.
65. Jessup, *A Modern Law of Nations*, p. 2.

Professor Dickinson's approach was more cautious and perhaps more realistic while he admitted that "world law has yet to assure the order and decency which exclude violence and supplant anarchy," he was convinced that "there is a vast body that is useful, indeed indispensable, and contained in its practices and principles are great potentialities of growth." He advanced suggestions for the expansion and improvement of the law and of what may be called the international judicial system, but he took care to warn that labours on this front should be accompanied by accommodation at the highest levels. "Every day of peace is a time for the extension of law" — a time for moving forward on "a vast and complicated front."[66]

QUESTIONS FOR EXERCISE

1. Define law and explain its sources.
2. What are the kinds of laws? Explain.
3. Assess the merits and demerits of various theories about the origin and nature of law.
4. Discuss the relation of (i) Law and Liberty; (ii) Law and Morality.
5. What is International Law? Discuss its utility in better international relations.
6. What are the sources of International Law? Discuss its limitations.

66. Dickinson, *Law and Peace*, Chapter IV.

16

Concept of Property

Man seeks to acquire property. He needs property for his development. The concept of property is crucial to modern political theory. It is the basis of modern state and society. Nothing has played such a vital role in the development of State, civilisation and culture. Many of the laws relating to property are much fuller, precise and more exacting than even laws relating to life and liberty. In the 20th century the right to property became very controversial. The Marxists are against the institution of property. The Anarchists condemn private property. For them property is theft and the root cause of all prevailing evils and crimes in the society. It divides the society into two warring factions — haves and have-nots. The haves or capitalists exploit the have-nots — the workers. Liberals advocate the right to private property. According to them it emancipates man from the care of morrow the ghost of starvation and the dread of want. It enables him to lead a comfortable life and seek intellectual attainments.

MEANING OF PROPERTY

The word property is derived from the Latin word '*Proprites*' which means 'one's own'. Thus, whatever one owns is his property. Ownership and, control of material goods is property. Property is the control by man over things or on appropriation of material objects recognised by the society.

Definitions of Property

1. *Asirvatham*: Property may be defined as the control by man over things or an appropriation of material objects recognised by the society. "It does not mean mere possession which confers only a delegated right". It calls for exclusive and permanent control over things.

2. *Sidgwick*: The property is "the complete right of exclusive use including the right to destroy and the right to alienate but not necessarily the right of bequest". Property is needed to satisfy physical wants and requirements of human beings.

CHARACTERISTICS OF PROPERTY

1. Complete control: Property is those material goods over which we have complete control. Complete control means the right to destroy and the right to alienate also.

2. Social sanction: Like all other rights, right to property also requires social sanction or recognition. A right is meaningless if it does not have behind it the sanction of society.

3. Natural right: John Locke believes that property is a natural right but others consider it a legal right. It exists within the State.

4. Creation of society: Socialists believe that property is the creation of society so the right to property is relative and not absolute. This means that the property should be used for the good of the society as a whole.

EVOLUTION OF THE CONCEPT OF PROPERTY

The origin of property lies in the instinct of acquisition in human beings. In the primitive society communal property was the universal order. There was no private property. Every thing was held in common by the society. But Hobhouse thinks that in the early society there was private property also. It included his weapons which he used in hunting and protecting himself from wild beasts and animals. Property in the form of domestic animals also came into existence when the animals came to be domesticated for milk, wool and ludes etc. Property in the form of land, factories, house came into existence with the evolution of society through various stages hunting, pastoral, agricultural, handicrafts, etc. Aristotle the father of political science considered slaves as a part of property. He supported the institution of private property on the ground that is natural and necessary. During middle ages Christianity advocated trusteeship of property.

PRIVATE PROPERTY

Property is usually equated with private property. It is the right of an individual to exclude others from some use or benefit of something. The issue of private property has made property a contentious moral issue. It was attacked by Plato as incompatible with the good life for the ruling class. It was defended by Aristotle as essential for the full use of human faculties and as making more efficient use of resources. Machiavelli was the first political thinker to say that property is the source of power. According to him, "Men forget more easily the death of their fathers than the loss of patrimony". Hence, Machiavelli warns the rulers not interfering with the property of the people.

Legal Theory of Property

Hobbes advocated the legal theory of property. Property is possible in the State. Locke considered property as a natural right. Individualists and utilitarians justified private property. But in the 19th century the institution of private property came under severe criticism. Proudhan called property a theft. Anarchists and Communists opposed the institution of private property, because it was responsible for all kinds of moral, physical and social immorality. Ownership of means of production should be in the hands of society. It should be used for the interests of socicty as a whole. The protagonists of various schools of thought disagree about the utility, role, place and functions of private property in society.

Liberal Theory of Property

Theory of property is an integral part of the philosophy of liberalism. As an economic, social and political doctrine liberalism arose in defence of capitalism, the capitalist market society and the interests of the capitalist class after the decline of feudalism. The right to property was needed to operate the capitalist market economy. Liberalism defended the right to property. Prof Laski, Adam Smith, Herbert Spencer, Jeremy Bentham, J.S. Mill, T.H. Green and other liberal theorists advocated the right to private property and the private ownership of the means of production. They defended capitalism and private property. They advocated freedom for trade and industry. They opinioned that trade and industry flourished well under free competition. The free movement of capital and trade and adjustment of prices on the basis of demand and supply would lead to the best economic adjustment in the economy. It stimulates production, keep wages and prices at their normal level, prevent excessive rates of interest, increase national wealth and promote individual and social welfare. They demanded free trade, freedom of occupation, unrestricted competition and along with it inviolable property rights.

Property as Reward

The liberal theory is based on the assumption that property is the reward for one's labour. A man is fully entitled to own what his labour and ability have produced. A man should have a right to ownership and private property. In the private market economy the forces of demand and supply automatically bring about the best equilibrium between production, prices and consumption. The right to property is inherent and natural. However, inequality in society is not because men were unequal by birth. Instead the liberals found a rational explanation of inequality in man's ability and capacity. In a free capitalist society any man working hard and having requisite ability can accumulate any amount of property as the reward of his labour and ability. It is in the interest of the society to respect the right to property and ownership. The liberal theory of property pleads for an exclusive and absolute right of the individual to property.

CONCEPT OF PROPERTY AND VIEWS OF JOHN LOCKE

At the hands of John Locke (1632-1704) the liberal theory of property received a great fillip. He began with the contention that the earth and its fruits were given by nature to mankind in common. Every person has a property in his own person. Labour creates property rights. The labour of the body and hands creates property rights.

Locke uses the term property in two senses:

(a) a narrow sense of goods and possessions,

(b) an extended one to cover life, liberty and estate.

Locke justifies the natural right to private property. Labour is the personal property of man. Whatever the man appropriates from the common property bestowed by nature becomes his private property. But the right to this property is not absolute and unconditional. It is subject to their remaining a sufficiency of fruits available for others which they too may appropriate. To waste is to offend against the common law of nature. No man has a right to take more than he can himself consume. No one has a right to waste property and one must leave enough for others. Money solved the problem of waste. It enabled man to store up wealth in a non-perishable form. It made possible a great increase in production and commerce. The State did not create property. It was created to protect it. One of its main purposes is the defence of established system of property rights. Without the express consent of the people the Government has no right to abridge or abrogate the right to property. Property is not only a natural right but a legal right as well.

The Main Points of the Liberal Theory

1. Private property is the real property: Earlier no difference was made between private and public property.

2. Private property is the reward of labour: Labour and ability are the personal and private property of man which is the result of his labour and therefore should be accepted as right.

3. Control of the State on economic system: The socialist liberal theory asserts that right to property should be used for public good. If right to property is to be utilised for public good then it is necessary that the economic system is controlled by the State.

4. Theory of compensation: Modern liberals accepted the institution of private property but they want that excessive property must be surrendered for public service. Property should not be confiscated by the State. If it is taken by force in public interest he should be paid compensation.

Defence of Right to Property

1. Economic ground: In the absence of the institution of private property production will suffer. Free competition is essential for the economic development of the society.

2. Psychological ground: The institution of private property is essential for an incentive to work. A man puts more labour because he gets better reward.

3. Ethical ground: Private property is the reward of labour and ability which he puts to earn more and more.

4. Logical ground: It is logical to give freedom to enterprises for better production.

5. Historical ground: History shows that private property was held by the individuals from the time memorial. Civilisation has developed due to institution of private property.

Though the liberals are in favour of institution of private property they want some restrictions on the right of private property in the interest of general welfare of the society as a whole. They are not in favour of abolishing right to property. They are confident that evils of private property can be checked through proper legislation.

THEORIES OF JUSTIFICATION OF PRIVATE PROPERTY

Ownership and control of material goods is property. It is the control of man over things or an appropriation of some material object recognised by society. Right to property requires social recognition. It is nothing if it does not have the sanction of society behind it. John Locke believed that property is a natural right but others consider it legal right. It exists within the State. Socialists believe that property is the creation of society so the right to property is relative and never absolute. This means that the property should be used for the good of the society as a whole. Following are various themes about justification of private property:

1. Natural theory: According to this theory the right to property is a natural right. It is prior to society and State. Natural theory is of two kinds. In the beginning, things belonged to none. Everything in nature was held in common. But after some time one who enclosed a piece of land became its owner. Thus, the institution of property came into existence.

2. Labour theory: It was supported by John Locke. He asserts that man has a natural right to that with which he has mixed the labour of his body and mind. He says, "The labour of his body and the work of his hands are his property whatsoever thus, he removes out of the State that nature hath provided and left it in, he hath mixed his labour with and joined it something that is his own and thereby makes it his property".

3. Legal theory: Hobbes and Bentham are the great supporters of this view. They maintain that there can be no right in the state of nature because rights are created and maintained by the State. According to this theory, the civil law is able to furnish not only the legal but the ethical basis for the institution of private property. "Property and law" writes Bentham, "are born-together". Before laws were made there was no property. Take away law and property ceases. "Rousseau adopts the general view that it is only in an institution made secure by the protection of the political authority that the foundation of property is to be found in law".

4. Idealistic theory: The idealists support private property on the basis of personality. In the words of Kant, "Property is necessary for the realisation of one's will". It is necessary for the fulfilment of personality. According to T.H. Green appropriation of property is an expression of will. It is an effort of the individual to give reality to a conception of his own good which is at the same time a common good. Property does not rest on contract or on supreme force. It is an instrument of self-expression and satisfaction.

Arguments for Private Property

1. Fundamental right: Individualists and liberals consider the right to property as the most fundamental right. According to Locke, political authority was established to support the right to property. Classical Economists like Adam Smith and Ricardo also supported the institution of private property. Liberal thinkers like J.S. Mill and T.H. Green support the institution of private property though they do not consider it as absolute. They put some limitations on it in the interest of the society.

2. Psychological and physical satisfactions: The possession of private property gives man a sense of security. It emancipates him from the ghost of starvation and the dread of want. Those who are without any property lead a very miserable life. They are always in the grip of uncertainties. In the modern industrial society they are no better than the slaves. Property enables a man to provide for the future and affords a sound basis for family independence.

3. Social status: Property gives a man a status in society which ultimately leads to happiness and contentment. Machiavelli rightly remarks, "Men forget more easily the death of their fathers than the loss of patrimony."

4. Peace and stability: A man of property is said to be a man of deliberation and prudence. As such he is not likely to be swept off his feet by every new fanged doctrine leading to violent change. This leads to political stability in the country. Peace and stability are the primary requirements for progress and prosperity.

5. Development of personality: Property helps the individual in the development of his personality. A man of property can develop his talents and faculties of mind to the maximum extent. It promotes a sense of independence. It emancipates him from the yoke of involuntary work and the drudgery of undesired activity.

6. Creative life: In the development of civilisation and culture property is an end. A man of property can devote his means to the fostering of art, culture, science, literature and technology. Thus, it enables him to have creative life.

7. Incentive to work: Private property provides an incentive to work. It is the reward of one's own labour. When one knows that he will get the reward of his efforts, he works sincerely and to the best of his capabilities and efficiency.

8. Support by history: Historical experience justifies the institution of private property. The states which have recognised the right to private property have progressed more and at much faster rate than the states which did not recognise this right.

Arguments against the Private Property

1. Division of society: The institution of private property has divided the society into two classes — haves and have-nots. The gap between the rich and poor is ever widening. Hence Laski says, "It remains historically obvious that a community divided into rich and poor when the latter are numerous, built upon the foundations of sands."

2. Anti-democratic: There can be no democracy in a economically unequal society. In capitalist societies, rich people have monopolies over the means of communication and transportation. They have full control over the three wings of Government. All the laws of the country favour the rich class.

3. Moral and physical evils: Private property is responsible for all kinds of moral and physical evils. It brings economic dependence for the poor. It brings superfluous luxury for the rich and laborious toil for the poor. It is responsible for spiritual and social immobility.

4. Offence against justice: Kropotkin condemns the institution of private property as an offence against justice. It allowed a few persons to enjoy what was created by the efforts of many. Human progress was the outcome of collective efforts and not individual efforts and consequently there was no justification for private property.

5. Exploitation: Property is a tool in exploitation of the poor. It is an instrument which is used to dominate and enslave the weaker classes of people. Millions of people remain ill-fed, ill-clothed and ill-housed. The growth of children is checked.

6. Economic and political evils: Property leads to over production, large scale production, use of a machinery, division of labour, technology etc. It leads to imperialism and colonisation. Thus, property is at the root of war and destruction.

7. Other rewards of labour: Private gain property need not be the only incentive to labour. Lord Haldane remarks that the desire to distinguish himself in the service of the State is as potent motive with the brain workers as the desire to amass a fortune. Plato claimed that the satisfaction derived from performing a congenial task or rendering public service was a great reward in itself.

The institution of private property has got its own merits and demerits. The individual should be given the right to property but it should be controlled and regulated by the state in the interest of the society as a whole. A striking balance must be maintained between the private property and social service.

MARXIST THEORY OF PROPERTY

For Marxists property is important for its productive value and not as the means of personal gratification. They view property in the totality of the economic system and social relationship of man in this system. The form of property has always been changing with the change in the mode of production and the relations it establishes in the society. In the primitive society there was no such thing as private ownership.

Origin of Ownership of Property

With the decline of primitive society, domesticating of animals instead of killing them became prevalent. Emergence of handicrafts changed the material conditions of society. People started owning tools, implements and domestic animals and land and slaves. This gave rise to the concept of private property. Once it came into existence, it continued unabated though its form changed with the march of civilisation. The capitalist private property is the capital. It is the means of production of wealth in an economic system. It comes into being by the transformation of the system of self-earned property into capitalist private property. A close associate of Karl Marx, Engels discussed about the origin of private property in his famous book, *The origin of the Family, Private Property and the State*. In primitive society there was no private property. It was the stage of primitive communism when forms of production were a few and they were possessed by society as a whole. No man exploited another. Men used to wander from one place to another in search of food. They depended on nature for their livelihood through hunting, fishing and fruit and root gathering. Whatever they got, they distributed it among them.

New forms of production were discovered as the civilisation advanced. People started domesticating animals instead of killing them. Agriculture developed gradually. This brought a revolutionary change in the life of society. The stronger compelled the weak to work on their land. The society was divided into haves and have-nots. There were two types of people, one the diligent, intelligent and frugal elite, and the other lazy, rascal, spending their substance. The former sort of people accumulated wealth and the latter had nothing to sell except their own skin.

Theory of Surplus Value

Surplus value is the difference between the value of a commodity produced by labour and the wages received by the labourer. According to Marx, as the value of a thing is due to labour alone the whole of the surplus value of the thing should be paid to the labourer. However, this is not done in actual practice. The capitalists give only a little to the labourer and pocket the rest of it. It is robbery on the part of the capitalists to keep any thing to themselves. His theory of surplus value Marx showed how the employers steal the value created by the labourers.

Evils of Capitalism

Marx attacked private property and capitalism from various angles:

1. Social evils: He condemns capitalism because it exalted the fortunate few at the expense of the oppressed many and cheated millions of people of the just fruits of their labour.

2. Moral evils: From the ethical point of view capitalism is exploitative, oppressive and dehumanising. It is unfair and results in inequality of wealth and income in society. It deprives the poor of the major part of their rightful earnings. The appropriation of surplus value is nothing else by a highway robbery.

3. Aesthetic evils: On aesthetic ground also capitalism is undesirable and harmful. Production under capitalism is hostile to art. It is responsible for ugliness and vulgarity. It fills the land with factories which give out smoke, stench and filth endangering health of the people. It raises mansions for the rich and hovels for the poor. All creative activities depend upon the whims of the capitalists. Hence, capitalism is dirty and vulgar. It is the sinister way of life under which men who value beauty, good manners and noble thoughts cannot hope to create or even live.

4. Economic evils: On economic grounds capitalism has failed to realise the material well-being of the masses. It has proved wasteful of material and natural resources. The resources of the country are not put to the best use of the economy. The majority of people have to go without bare necessities of life. Resources are used to produce articles and luxury goods few the privileged few. The goods produced on mass scale do not satisfy the wants of the common man. On account of over production and under production (Trade cycles) there are wide fluctuations in prices. The situation created under capitalism is something like — "water every where but not a drop to drink".

5. Psychological evils: On psychological grounds capitalism injures the spirit of man. The workers are worse off psychologically than materially. On account of wide economic disparities there is constant breast burning. Machines were built by men. The goods produced by them were meant to serve his needs and he was not to become a slave of the machine.

6. Political evils: Capitalism is all the more undesirable on political grounds. It distributes power and freedom unequally. It reduces democracy to mockery. It leads to imperialism, colonialism and global destructive wars. Marx condemned capitalism as defective from all angles — economic, political, ethical, psychological etc.

In "Communist Manifesto', the theory of communism was summed up in the abolition of private property. Private property is responsible for class war. It is a tool of exploitation in the hands of bourgeoise. It keeps proletariates at the stage of permanent misery. Marx and Engels advocate for the abolition of private property and for this they have advanced moral, economic, social, political reasons.

Methods to Abolish Institution of Private Property

Abolition of the institution of private property alone can restore human values. Marxist secure human freedom and evolve a national system of production and distribution to ensure satisfaction of social needs. Marx gives a revolutionary method to abolish institution of private property. The socialist revolution will take place under the leadership of organised and class conscious workers. Dictatorship of the proletariate will be established after the revolution. Means of production will be socialised. A socialist economy will take the place of capitalist economy. A classless society will be established. There will be no need of any State. The State will wither away. The institution of private property will wither away through Communist revolution. It will pave the way for a rational and humanistic reorganisation of production and distribution. However, Marx is not against personal property consisting of small consumer goods of every day life. The personal property is a genuine fruit of an individual's labour. The socialist property transforms the exploitative character of property into a development character.

Criticism of Marxist Theory of Property

1. Failure to achieve its object: The institution of private property is still there in Communist countries. The State has not withered away. The State has become still more powerful. The State instead of abolishing the institution of private property has given shelter to it.

2. Dictatorship of the proletariate: Marxist theory wants dictatorship of the proletariates through socialists revolution. It does not suggest any method to decide disputes among proletariates. In the absence of State there will be disorder and anarchy.

3. Classless society: The theory visualise a classless society. Classes can never vanish away from the society because there are inequalities among the people on the basis of ability.

4. No initiative: The theory of surplus value ignores other factors of production such as capital and organisation. This kills initiative because there is no place for incentive in this theory.

5. Miserable life: If institution of private property is abolished, the life will become miserable. Property gives joy and happiness to man. It gives security from the uncertainties of morrows.

However,, one cannot deny the value of Marxist theory. It is an attack on wide socio-economic disparity in modern society. But the establishment of a stateless and classless society is a distant dream.

LASKI'S THEORY OF PROPERTY

Laski's concept of property is both a critique of the existing economic order and a justification of the existing institution of property largely on the Fabian lines of argument. He did not reject the institution of property altogether. He rather gave its defence on national grounds. He modified the theory of private property under the influence of socialist ideas of the 20th century. He wanted that one should use right to property for social good.

Present System of Property

The present system of property is not conducive to healthy economic system. The number of those who own significant property is always small. Such ownership is not related to the performance of duties. The property may be inherited. The ownership of property involves the control of capital. It involves the power to direct the lives of workers. The development of industry in modern times has made the power of capital greater than in any previous age. In a society which is divided into haves and have-nots, the poor are denied the conditions which make their effective citizenship possible. The system is not conducive to a healthy economic system. The production is carried on wastefully and without plan. Wrong commodities are produced. Those produced are distributed without regard to absolute urgency. Goods are produced for the sole object of making profit and not for the well-being of the masses. Even harmful things are produced to reap dividends. Natural resources are ruined. Commodities are adulterated. Legislators are corrupted. Thus, the present property system has distorted the economic system and led to weakening of the society as a whole.

Moral Basis of Property

Laski is not against the institution of private property. Property provides a means of harmony in the shape of security. Men get a sense of security. They develop their creative impulse. The institution of private property is not bad as such but it is possessed by few capitalists who exploit others. It gives birth to the evils of capitalism. The capitalists use private property for private profit. They do not bother for the good of others. Their production is not according to the needs of the society. Distribution is rarely related to social urgency. There is wasteful expenditure. They exploit the people for their personal benefits. The hereditary property is justified only for the widows and the children of the deceased. Laski is against functionless property. No property is justified unless it is the result of the performance of socially useful functions. Moral basis of property lies where it results from personal efforts.

Theory of Reward

Liberals consider property a reward of one's labour. Laski examined several theories of right to determine the true basis of right to property. Rejecting the doctrine of equal rewards, he says, "There seems no justice in an equal reward for unequal effort, not does it seem just to reward equally where needs are unequal". Rejecting the liberal theory of rights, he maintains that when workers and capitalists do not have equal bargaining power the income should be decided on the basis of contract of demand and supply. He also rejects the theory that "each contributes to the society according to his powers and is rewarded according to his needs". He thinks that there is no rod which may measure the needs of the people. The theory does not seem to be practicable.

Laski's theory of property satisfies two conditions. It enables the individual to reach out towards his best self. It preserves and develops the necessary functions of the society, It reconciles the interest of the society as a whole, In it every one will meet his minimum basic needs and society will also not suffer. No one should get remuneration more than to meet the basic needs. Thus, one gets rewards for the services which one renders to the society.

Principles of Sound Theory

Laski did not favour the abolition of the right to property altogether. He wanted to construct a sound theory of property. This he believed could be done only on the basis of following principles:

1. Linking the right to property with the performance of functions.
2. Collective interest of the society, and
3. A more national hereditary system of property. In short, he wanted property to be linked with the service of the community.

Property and Industrial Organisation

Laski suggests that the capital must play a limited role in industrial organisation. The capitalists must not be allowed to control the industries. The industrial system of the country should not depend upon the lust of the capitalists for profits. Social elements should be given their due share in industrial management.

Suggestions for the Industrial Organisation

1. Industry must be made a profession: Just as the rules of a profession are made subject to the will of society by those engaged there in, so must the rules of industry be made by the working class.

2. No control by capitalists: There must be alteration of the character of the owner of capital. He should be paid a fixed dividend and should not be allowed to control the business in which his capital (property) is invested.

3. Control by industrial workforce: There should be an alteration in the character of control exercised in industry. The control should pass on from the functionless owner of capital to the industrial workforce.

4. Emphasis on social aspect: More emphasis should be laid on the social element in the industrial equation.

The New System of Property

In the new system of property suggested by Laski functionless property of the capitalist system will be converted into an instrument of social good. Only those who perform social functions should be allowed to have property. One will get reward for the services he will render to the society. There will be improvement in industrial system. It will eliminate capitalists. Even if private property is allowed only shareholders will be left. There will be self-government in industry. Under the influence of socialist ideology of 20th century Laski justified institution of private property for social good only. Property is socially useful labour. Only that property is moral which is earned by performing socially useful functions. Laski did not plead for abolition of private property but stressed the need for change of the system. Private property must not be so large in amount that its owner experiences power by reason of its sheer magnitude. On the contrary, it must never be so small that its possessor cannot be himself at his best. To conclude, in the words of Laski, "There is nothing inherently wrong in the notion of private property. There is a sense in which it may be so held as genuinely express personality and to contribute to its enrichment. It must be derived from self effort".

QUESTIONS FOR EXERCISE

1. Critically examine the liberal theory of property.
2. What do you understand by private property? Discuss the various theories about the origin of the concept of private property. Give arguments for and against the right to property.
3. What do you understand by the concept of property? Discuss various theories about the origin of the concept of private property. Give arguments for and against the right to property.
4. Discuss the Marxist Theory of Property. Do the citizens of communist countries own private property?
5. Critically examine the Marxist Theory of Property.
6. Examine the principles on which Laski attacks the institution of private property. What is the scheme suggested by him for its reorganisation?
7. Laski maintains that inheritance is always justified where "it means the provision of income for widowhood on the one hand and education of the children on the other. But the retention of property beyond that period cannot be justified in moral terms". Comment.

17

Concept of Justice

History of political philosophy is the history of quest for justice. Man has been continuously struggling for the maintenance of justice. But, thinkers differ in their concept of justice. It has been defined as the interest of the stronger, a virtue to be cultivated in society, or proportion between persons and things assigned to them, the rule of law as distinguished from rule of men, the participation of people in the political processes, abolition of discrimination and privileges based on birth, race, caste, creed or sex or the establishment of classless and stateless society. The concept of justice is not static but dynamic. It changes with time and circumstances. In common parlance justice means righteousness or virtue. It is identified with truth and morality. It is considered a standard bearer of the good. In ancient times, the object of justice was to get individual justice but in modern times we want social justice. In different social systems there are different concepts of justice.

MEANING OF JUSTICE

The term justice is derived from the Latin word which implies the idea of joining or fitting the idea of bond or tie. Primarily joining or fitting implied in the idea of justice was that between man and man in an organised system of human relations. Prof Barker extends the meaning of justice by including in it the idea of joining or fitting between value and value in a general synthesis of values —- the supreme values for a just system of human relations being liberty, equality and fraternity. Thus according to Barker justice is the reconciler and synthesis of political values. C.E. Herriam has defined justice as consisting in a system of understandings and procedures through which each is accorded what is agreed upon as fair. Actually the concept of justice is a relative concept. It is related to the social system of the society. When the social system changes, the concept of justice also changes. That is why Rawls writes, "The nature and aims of a perfectly just society is the fundamental part of the theory of justice". Regarding the place and value of justice Plato, Augustine, Acquinas etc., suggest that the concept of justice is absolute, eternal, and permanent. It does not change with time or changing circumstances. Like truth, justice is infallible and unchangeable though it is governed by certain specific rules. On the other hand, Aristotle, Bentham and Mill opine that 'justice' is a relative concept and is susceptible to change with changing times, conditions, values and circumstances.

SOURCES OF JUSTICE

1. Religion: Medieval christian writers believed the idea of justice is planted by God in the human mind. It is sacred and preserved through the authority of law. Saint Thomas said that there were four kinds of law corresponding to four forms of reason -— External law, natural law, divine law and the human law. Religion as a source of justice has lost much of its significance since the separation of church from the State. The norms of justice enunciated by religion ought to be applied without any legal coercion. If legal coercion is applied, it may not succeed at all. Religion as a source of ethical principles is an ultimate source of notice of justice. It cannot be considered as the immediate validating principle.

2. Nature: Stoics supported the idea of nature being of a source of justice. The stoic conception of 'Nature' combined their moral philosophy and religious beliefs. The word 'Nature' related to a spiritual world. For them Nature, God and Reason was one thing. They believed that men who lived in conformity with Nature also shared something of Reason and God. It implied three things — men must be free, men should be treated as equal, and men should be associated with their fellow men by the common factor of reason. Thus, the three cardinal sources provided by Nature for justice were Liberty, Equality and Fraternity. The Stoics identified justice with the rule of reason or God.

3. Economics: Some thinkers considered economics as the most important source of justice. The Marxists believe that economics is the source of justice. Positive law or the law of the State is enacted by the dominant ruling class. It represents their economic interests. It is imposed on society by the authority of the ruling class which also controls all the means of production. Marxists believe that the bourgeoise is the repository and dispensey of justice. When the revolution of the proletariate has succeeded in establishing a proletariat state class based justice will come to an end. The laws of the State will now reflect the wishes of the common people. The idea of justice and its content varies with the interests of the ruling class. It is only when the State has withered away and a stateless society is established without classes, that the interests of society as a whole will be served.

4. Ethics: The idealist thinkers Plato, Aristotle, Kant, Green, Barker believe that the true source of justice is to be found in ethics. Law be made by a properly constituted state authority. It should also fulfil the requirements of moral conscience. Law and ethics are not the same thing. Law is concerned with the external actions of human beings whereas ethics is concerned both with the external acts as well as internal motives of man. In spite of these differences ethics and law are related to each other in the sense that law seeks to secure the external conditions necessary for the moral action or the general framework of external order in which the moral conscience can act and determine itself most easily and most freely. Sanctioned and enforced by the general moral conscience the moral standard of community constitute the real basis of the idea of justice. The system of values accepted by a community should be the impersonal source of positive law enforced by the state.

DIMENSIONS OF JUSTICE

1. Legal dimension: Legal justice consists in codes enacted by the State and supplemented by customary rules observed by the community. In every country there is a general body of rules recognised and enforced by courts. The Constitution and Acts of Legislature determine the legal dimension of justice. The Constitution of India prohibits discrimination among the citizens on grounds of religion, race, caste, sex, place of birth or any of them. The laws of legislature prohibit *Sati* or child marriage. This is a legal way of promoting justice. Legal dimensions of justice requires laws of the State and faithful adherence to them. Those who do not obey them are punished by the courts.

The laws are framed by the legislative bodies which should be truly representative bodies. If the representative bodies make unjust or unreasonable law, the people should have right to oppose such law. The independent judiciary is a check on the legislative body. It does not allow legislature to make unjust laws. But the ultimate check should be the people. Strong public opinion will never allow legislature to behave irresponsibly.

The judicial system of the State should be simple and cheap. It should not be difficult to understand. A poor man cannot get justice if it is costly. The judiciary should be independent. The judges should be qualified and well paid. They should have secured service. The judiciary should be separated from the executive and legislature. The judges should not be allowed to accept legal profession after retirement.

Infliction of punishment is based on various theories of punishment such as Retribution Theory, the Deterrent Theory and the Reformative Theory. The Retribution Theory believes in immediate punishment and therefore the theory is rejected. The Deterrent Theory brings fear complex in the criminals. The most acceptable theory is the Reformative Theory as the aim of punishment is to reform the criminals and turn them into good citizens.

2. Political dimension: 'Political equality' within the State is the essence of political dimension of justice. It is concerned with the actual policies through which the political process realises the norms of justice.

Political justice lies in the relationship between the individual and the authority i.e., the State. There should be political equality. All citizens should have the same political rights and equal voice in government and an equal access to all offices of authority provided the necessary qualifications are fulfilled. This means democracy and adult suffrage. It is through the exercise of this right that democracy actually comes into existence. Only a democratic constitution ensures political justice to the people. The Constitution, the Parliament and the courts give shape to the legal dimension of justice. The political parties the interest groups in the country give shape to the political dimension of justice. They try to translate the legal norms of justice into political programmes. The political dimension has a great force in democratic countries. It is a guide to the legal authority. The preamble and directive principles enshrined in the Constitution of India are the best examples of political dimension of justice. They envisage the creation of a just social order in the country. The public opinion should always be respected. The views of the minority should not be ignored. The healthy criticism by the opposition should be welcome by the ruling party. A democratic form of government assures political justice to the people.

3. Social dimension: The socio-economic dimensions of justice is an extension of the legal and political dimensions of justice. In the ancient and medieval times, the societies were hierarchical. The division of the community into ranks, castes or orders was regarded as an expression of justice. In these societies there were the masters and the slaves, the lords and the serfs. While the masters and the lords were destined to rule from birth, the slaves and serfs were destined to serve and obey from their birth. It was considered as a natural phenomena of society. It was justified in terms of God's will, reason and morality. In India, the division of society into a caste hierarchy was sanctioned by the law of *Karma* and ordained by *Dharma*.

The aim of social justice is to protect the interests of minorities to eradicate poverty, unemployment and illiteracy from the society, It helps in removing social evils. It removes all those hindrances which hamper common good. Social justice gives protection to downtrodden and weaker sections of society. Equality before law and independent judiciary are necessary for achieving social justice. Social justice demands elimination of all discrimination between citizens on any ground. There should be freedom of conscience and free profession.

4. Economic dimension: With the advent of socialism we are laying more emphasis on the economic dimension of justice. Without economic justice, we cannot achieve the objectives of social and political justice. For economic justice there should be sufficient production of essential goods. Basic necessities of life must be available to all. Every one should get adequate food, clothing and shelter. There should be equitable distribution of wealth and income. Co-operation should replace cut-throat competition in society. There should be no exploitation of man by man. A just socio-economic order is possible only in a classless Communist society of the future. "Everyone should do according to his capacity and will get according to his needs". Economic justice means, socialism or economic democracy. As M.C. Chagla, former education minister said, "Freedom is meaningless if it prevents the achievements of economic justice. To a hungry man or to a man who is denied human dignity, political freedom is an empty word. The problem of today is how to bring economic and social justice without sacrificing the individual to the ever increasing power of the State".

NATURE OF JUSTICE

The term 'justice' is given different meanings by different people at different times. Its implications vary from man to man and from situation to situation. The idea of justice is a dynamic affair. Its implications change with the passage of time. What was justice in the past may be injustice today or *vice versa*. One may talk of moral justice or divine justice, but it will hardly be conformable to any set of empirical standards and, for this reason, not capable of practical application. Due to this, Potter said that "most men think that they understand the meaning of justice, but, in fact, *their notions prove* to be vague."[1]

1. Harold Potter, *The Quest of Justice*, p. 3.

Implications of Justice

The concept of justice has these important implications:

1. A just state of affairs: It is impossible to assess the justice of actions without a prior identification of the just state of affairs.[2]

2. Aligned with the conditions of morality: For instance, a fair race is one in which a person who wins morality deserves to win but one in which, there is no cheating, nobody jumps' the gun, or has an unfair advantage through the use of bad things like drugs.[3]

3. Proper distribution of favours and losses: It means that justice is primarily concerned with the way rewards and punishments are distributed among the individuals in a rule-governed practice and its intimate connection with fairness indicates that if a ruler were to boil his subjects in oil jumping in afterwards himself, it would amount to an act of injustice though there would be no inequality of treatment.[4]

4. It prevails in a congenial atmosphere that is provided by a democratic set-up: As N.P. Barry says, "Fair rules may be impartially enforced in regimes which allow little political participation and majority rule democracies may generate arbitrary treatment of individuals and minorities.[5]

Traditional and Trans-traditional Justice

According to Brecht, "not only do different individuals hold various ideas about the ideal state of affairs they would consider really just; every individual is capable of several such ideas. Our ideas and feelings of justice may be two-fold, or three-fold, or manifold in accordance with different systems of values to which we respond positively at different times, or even simultaneously. Justice, in the light of personal ideas, is or at least may be a barrel with several bottoms."[6] Brecht divides justice into two broad categories.[7]

1. **Traditional Justice:** It accepts the fundamental institutions which constitute the basis of our daily life. It takes them for granted. It does not question them. In so far as these institutions have been established by the positive law, written constitutions, legislation, judicial precedents and the like, the traditional idea of justice is positivistic.

2. David Miller, *Social Justice*, pp. 17-18.
3. Brian Barry, *Political Argument*, p. 103.
4. W.K. Frankena, "*The Concept of Social Justice*" in R. Brandt (ed.), *Social Justice*, P- 17.
5. N.P. Barry, *An Introduction to Modern Political Theory*, p. 116.
6. Brecht, *op, cit*., pp. 147-48.
7. *Ibid*., p. 148.

2. **Trans-traditional justice:** It detaches itself from the existing institutions, either in whole or in part. It criticises them according to principles which are taken from a trans-traditional scheme of evaluation.

These two levels are the subjective and objective aspects of the same theme of justice. In a normative sense, justice implies the idea of joining or fitting, the idea of a bond or a tie.[8] In an empirical context it has its relation with the concept of positive law with the result that law and justice become sister-concepts. The fundamental purpose of law is the quest for justice which is to be administered without passion as when it (passion) "comes at the door, justice flies out of window."[9] Viewed in this sense, justice implies the fulfilment of the legitimate expectations of individual under the existing laws and ensuring him the benefits promised there and to afford him protection against any violation of his rights or against any encroachment on his rights.[10]

THEORIES OF JUSTICE

1. The philosophical theory of justice: It is found in the religious injunctions, or in the highly abstract ideas of philosophers. Hindu scriptures identify justice with *Dharma* or righteousness that involves duties in the category of actions. Plato in his *Republic* treats justice as the principle of right ordering of human personality so as to have a right ordering of social classes. In the case of individual the principle of justice means that he should discover his place according to the best element of his personality (reason, courage, appetite). In the case of society it means that it should have three classes (ruling class, military class, economic class) and in each class individuals should be accommodated according to the best element of their personality. There should be no interference of one element or of one class into the domain of another. This shall open the way for proper division of labour and specialisation of functions. Here is the profile of a just man and a just society. Justice means proper ordering of the three elements of human personality and reorganisation of society in three classes in correspondence to these three elements of human personality.

Criticism

Critics of philosophical theory say that (i) it is too abstract to be understood by a man of average comprehension; (ii) It is too difficult to be put into practical terms.

8. Barker, *op. cit.*, p. 102.
9. C.K. Allen, *Aspects of Justice*, p. 34.
10. Bakhshish Singh, *The Supreme Court as an Instrument of Social Justice*, p. 33.

2. Natural theory of justice: Men should follow the principles of a moral life as sanctioned by the law of nature. The observance of the principle of natural equality of mankind is a precept of natural justice. Slavery is not a natural but a conventional institution. With the advent of Christianity the word 'Nature' came to have its substitute in God. Therefore, natural justice came to be identified with divine justice. The law of 'Nature' became the law of God. Not law of 'Nature' but law of God (as contained in the holy books) became the determinant of justice. Even in modern times, the canons of natural (or divine) justice are invoked to say that the strong should not oppress the weak, the victor should not kill the vanquished when the latter surrenders, even criminals should be treated in a human way inside the jails.

Criticism

(i) Like philosophical justice, the idea of natural or divine justice is a matter of myth.

(ii) It is abstract and metaphysical in nature.

3. The legal theory of justice: It identifies the idea of justice with the working of the courts. The Magistrate is the administrator of justice. He should interpret the meaning of law and then pronounce a verdict whether the accused is guilty of a certain crime or not and, if guilty, what punishment should be given to him. The advocates of imperative theory of jurisprudence like Hobbes, Bentham, Austin and Dicey fully endorse this view. The legislature has the authority to make a law. The courts have authority to administer justice according to the law of the land. Where law is silent, the courts may act according to the norms of natural justice from which arises a new kind of law based on the principles of equity. A dispute must be settled by a court of competent jurisdiction. The accused must be given opportunity to defend himself. The procedure of trial must be fair and open. The judges should act freely and honestly. The accused should be given punishment according to the nature and magnitude of the wrong.

Evaluation

Legal theory is the best of all theories on this subject. It constitutes the basis of Western jurisprudence. Proper implementation of this theory leads to the creation of an ideal situation what Dicey calls the 'rule of law'.

4. The Marxian theory of justice: In Marxian theory law and justice are identified with the fact of class domination. State is an instrument of exploitation and oppression by one class over another. Law and justice are nothing else than a part of the entire State structure, The legislature makes a law that is in the interest of the ruling class. The courts act in a way that strengthens and defends the position of the class in power. If the instruments of law and justice protect and promote the interests of the bourgeois class, they will serve the purpose of the proletariat after the successful socialist revolution. The judiciary should have a 'committed' character. It should not defend the system of exploitation in a bourgeois society. It should finish the class of exploiters in a socialist society.

Thus, while the liberal interpretation of justice is quite flexible that places judiciary in an impartial and independent position, the Marxist notion desires its committed form. The liberal theory is too flexible and amenable to diverse, even conflicting, interpretations in various important directions. The Marxist view is inherent with very rigid postures. Highlighting this essential point of distinction between liberal and totalitarian (including Fascist and Communist) varieties, W. Friedman says: "In modern democratic society the judge must steer his way between the Scylla of subservience to the government and the Charybdis of remoteness from constantly changing social pressures and economic needs...the administration of law under these systems becomes a predominantly political function and an instrument of the government policy."[11]

KINDS OF JUSTICE

1. Social justice: It relates to the balance between an individual's rights and social control. It ensures the fulfilment of the legitimate expectations of the individual under the existing laws. It assures him benefits thereunder and protection in case of any violation or encroachment on his rights. It is consistent with the unity of the nation and needs of the society.[12] Social justice requires the sacrifice of certain rights of an individual at the altar of general interest. However, viewed in a wider perspective the idea of social justice aims at the proper reconciliation of the interest of an individual with the overall interest of the community or prevalence of the latter over the former in the event of any conflict. It constitutes "an essential part of the great complex of social change, for which something may have to be sacrificed for a greater good."[13]

The concept of social justice is a very wide term covering within its fold everything pertaining to the norm of general interest ranging from the protection of the interests of the minorities to the eradication of poverty and illiteracy. It relates to the observance of the principle

11. W. Friedman, *Law in Changing Society*, pp. 65-66.
12. Bakhshish Singh, *op. cit.*, p. 73.
13. Boalding, "Social Justice in Social Dynamics" in R. Brandt (ed.), *Social Justice*, p. 92.

of equality before law and independence of judiciary. It also relates to the eradication of gigantic social evils like those of pauperism, disease, unemployment and starvation. All this also relates to the liquidation of vested interests that obstruct the achievement of common good. In the backward countries of the world, the idea of social justice enjoins upon the State to make concerted efforts for the improvement of the lot of the downtrodden and weaker sections of the community. Its area widens itself to cover the economic domain of a people's life because it demands non-exploitation of the working class.

Criticism

1. The ideal of social justice lacks a precise connotation on account of varying social and economic theories and in view of the conflicting interpretations of thinkers and jurists belonging to the liberal and the Marxist schools.
2. Allen observes: "We hear much today of 'social justice'. I am not sure that those men who use the term most glibly know very clearly what they mean by it. Some mean distribution or redistribution of wealth; some interpret it as 'equality of opportunity' — a misleading term, since opportunity can never be equal among human beings who have unequal capacities to grasp it. Many, I suspect, mean simply that it is unjust that anybody should be fortunate than themselves and the more intelligent mean that it is just — I would rather say benevolent — that every effort should be made at least to mitigate the asperities of natural human inequality and that no obstacle should be offered, but rather help offered, to practicable opportunities of self- improvement."[14]

2. Economic justice: Social and economic justice are closely related. Social justice demands eradication of gigantic social evils. Most of these such as exploitation of the workers by the capitalists or concentration of national wealth into fewer hands etc., find their place in the economic sphere. As M.C. Chagla said, "Freedom is meaningless if it prevents the achievement of economic justice. To a hungry man or to a man who is denied human dignity, political freedom is an empty word. The problem of today is how to bring about economic and social justice without sacrificing the individual to the ever-increasing power of the State."[15]

The idea of economic justice means non-discrimination between man and man on the basis of economic values. In positive terms, it

14. Allen, *op. cit.*, p. 3.
15. M.C. Chagla, *The Individual and the State*, p. 8.

implies adequate payments for work without any discrimination on some artificial ground. It enjoins freedom for all in the sphere of production and distribution of goods subject to the conditions of social welfare. It demands that the State of national economy be reshaped in a way that the benefits are made more and more available to the common man. Thus, the idea of economic justice comes to imply a socialist pattern of the society.

Like social justice, the economic justice is also a matter of acute controversy between the liberal and Marxist thinkers. It is a matter of acute controversy among the proponents of liberalism. The Communists desire to abolish the institution of private property for the sake of bringing about an era of economic justice. The liberals invoke varying standards ranging from the maintenance of private property system to the imposition of reasonable restrictions on its use and enjoyment by the people. Both notions suffer from inherent fallacies. While one may say that the Marxist formula 'from each according to his ability, to each according to his work' in the era of socialism and 'from each according to his ability, to each according to his need'. In the final stage of socialism (communism) it would be contrary to the just principle of distribution as well as to the humanistic norm of helping the weak and the disabled even when they do not work. The norm of regulatory legislation or reasonable restriction as laid down by the courts of free and democratic countries, would make the whole idea of economic justice fluid, perhaps touching the verge of meaninglessness. Justice and ideas about it are, therefore, to seek a new balance and a new harmony in the present conflicts between large national economic and social interests, on the one hand, and the individual or group rights and interests on the other.[16]

3. Political justice: Political justice stands for a free and fair participation of the people in the political sphere. It involves the guarantee of universal adult franchise without distinction on some artificial grounds in matters of recruitment to public services. What the policy of the state should be, and how the society should be organised in political and economic directions are matters which should be decided by the people themselves according to prevailing needs and circumstances. The idea of the preservation of political rights of the individual dominates the scene. The very notion of justice assumes an individualistic tenor in view of the fact that despite being a social creature, some of his deeper pursuits in the field of knowledge, mind and spirit are individual affairs. As a matter of fact, they "are the springs from which civilisation grows."[17]

16. P.B. Mukherji, *The Elemental Principles of Indian Constitution*, pp. 12-13.
17. *Ibid.*, p. 20.

The notion of political justice requires that the State must protect and preserve certain valuable rights of the individual so that he may develop his personality as a citizen and thereby contribute his share to the welfare of the political community. It desires a liberal-democratic order in which rights of the individuals, including those of the minorities, are well-protected. It covers much of what falls under the category of social and economic justice. It makes itself coterminous with the case of a full-fledged democratic order. It involves recognition and protection of rights relating to the maintenance of a political creed. It also enjoins the prevalence of right to dissent and duty to tolerate.

4. Distributive justice: The earliest notion of distributive justice was given by Aristotle, who said that equals should be treated equally and unequal's unequally. Injustice arises when the reverse comes to take place. It establishes an organic relationship between the norms of justice and the principle of equality. The modern interpretation of this term, however, establishes an organic relationship of a juristic norm with a particular system of economy. In this sense, distributive justice desires equal distribution of income among the equals only. It is traceable in the writings of J.W. Chapman and John Rawls.

(i) *View of Chapman*: Chapman seeks to integrate the idea of justice with his principles of 'economic rationality of man' and 'consumer's sovereignty' coupled with individual's claim of 'moral freedom.' To him; the first principle of justice is the distribution of benefits which maximise benefits in accordance with the principle of consumer's sovereignty. The second principle is that a system is unjust if the material well-being of the few is purchased at the expense of the many. In simple terms, it implies that no one shall gain at the expense of another.[18]

(ii) *View of Rawls*: Rawls sets out two basic moral principles of justice which constitutional democracy should satisfy. Firstly, each person engaged in institution affected by it has an equal right to the most extensive liberty compatible with a like liberty for all. Secondly, inequalities as defined by the institutional structure or fostered by it are arbitrary, unless it is reasonable to expect that they will work out to everyone's advantage and provided that the positions and offices to which they attach or from which they may be gained are open to all.[19] Such a

18. J.W. Chapman, "Justice and Fairness" in Friedrich and Chapman (eds.), *Justice in Nomos*, VI, pp. 30-34.
19. Rawls, "Distributive Justice" in Peter Laslett and W.G. Runciman (eds.), *Philosophy, Politics and Society*, III Series, p. 61.

view of distributive justice has been offered by the thinkers of the liberal school. They have made serious efforts to reconcile their notion of an affluent society with a challenge posed by the socialist order. In their' affirmations, democracy "is reduced from a humanistic aspiration to a market equilibrium system."[20]

5. Corrective justice: It is contained in the verdict of the judicial bodies that is delivered after hearing the statement of parties in a dispute. It aims to correct the erratic behaviour of the party in dispute. It emanates from the decisions of the courts in which we find an interpretation of the law of the land, a wise distinction between 'just' and 'unjust' situations, award of punishment to the wrong-doer, strictures passed against the delinquent authority and the like. In certain cases the courts may significantly reduce the scope of inequality created by the statutory provisions of the land. In brief corrective or 'positive' justice is what is done by the courts to correct the erratic behaviour of a person by following the law of the land.

Thus justice is essentially a normative concept having its place in various spheres like religion, philosophy, ethics and jurisprudence, though its ramifications also cover social, political and economic spheres. Justice is necessarily related with the function of judicial organisations. It is the bond that connects important political values like those of rights, liberty, equality and fraternity. There can be no liberty if there is no equality. There can be no equality if there is no justice. Again, there can be no liberty if there are no rights. There can be no protection of rights if there is no well-organised system of law so as to ensure proper administration of justice. Thus, justice is the synthesiser and reconciler of great political values. In the words of Daniel Webster "justice is the chiefest interest of man."

QUESTIONS FOR EXERCISE

1. What is meant by justice? Describe legal, political, social and economic dimensions of justice.
2. Write short note on social and economic justice.
3. Define justice and discuss its political, social and economic dimensions.
4. Write short comments on justice and its kinds.

20. C.B. Macpherson, *Democratic Theory*, pp. 78-79.

18

Political Obligation

MEANING OF POLITICAL OBLIGATION

Connotations of Obligation

The term 'obligation' originates from a Latin word 'obligate' implying something that binds men to an engagement or performing what is enjoined. The term obligation has its various connotations in different realms:

1. In the realm of ethics: In ethics obligation informs a man to fulfil or discharge a duty enjoined on him and acceptable to him by his rational understanding.

2. In the field of jurisprudence: Here, obligation requires a man to obey law by which he is tied to some 'performance.' Law regulates the social life of men. Hence, the principle of legal obligation takes the form of a bond between private persons tied to one another for the performance of some act as desired by the enforcement of law.

3. In the world of politics: In politics, obligation takes the form of a bond between man as a citizen and the authority under which he lives "to perform. an act, or a number of acts, for the governing authority."[1] In the words of Benn and Peters, it implies that as man is a political animal, he is bound to live under some authority and, as such, it becomes his obligation to obey its commands. Hence, when the authorising rule is law, and the association a state, we call it "political obligation."[2]

Thus, political obligation is acceptance of the 'commands' of men-in-authority roles. The idea is integrally connected with the pattern of man's life in an organised whole. There can be no life if there is no order. And since order implies obedience, there can be no order if there

1. Barker, *Principles of Social and Political Theory*, p. 184.
2. Benn and Peters, *Social Principles and the Democratic State*, p. 298.

is no acceptance of it. A people cannot live well without accepting the commands of the persons in charge of maintaining peace and order in the society. Thus, the principle of political obligation is based on the maxim of common prudence. As Benn and Peters observe: "Of course, there are plenty of good reasons for accepting authority in general (though they may not always apply in particular). We are often in a situation where it is more important to accept an umpire's judgement than to insist on our own... An army will usually do better even with bad generals than with no generals at all. We accept authority, because most social enterprises would be hopelessly without it."[3]

Political obligation rests upon issues relating to the nature of authority that involves within its fold the whole world of existing rights, laws and political organisation generally. It covers the opposite situation in which people have a legitimate claim for the disobedience of authority. As Laski points out it "is the enterprise that counts; the authority is conditional on the way it promotes or preserves it."[4] The people not only obey the laws of the State or the 'commands of the sovereign', they also scrutinise those orders in terms of the satisfaction they seek from life. Therefore, from time to time, they reject them on the ground that they are a denial of those satisfactions. To quote Laski, "Obedience, that is to say, is the normal habit of mankind; but marginal eases continually recur in which the decisions to disobey is painfully taken and passionately defended."[5]

ESSENTIAL CHARACTERISTICS OF POLITICAL OBLIGATION

1. Honest public service: As government is a difficult art it is the duty of every conscientious person to be seriously interested in the management of public affairs. Those placed in high offices should direct their thought and action to the general good. Not merely of an intellectual character; political obligations involve obligations of an honest public service.

2. Political legitimacy and effectiveness: Political effectiveness implies actual performance in the light of the extent which the political system provides for the performance of the basic functions of the government as the people and powerful groups in society perceive them. Political legitimacy refers to the capacity of the system to engender and maintain the belief that the existing social, economic and political institutions are most appropriate for the society.

3. *Ibid.*, p. 329.
4. Laski, *The State in Theory and Practice*, p. 17,
5. *Ibid.*

3. Critical attitude: The idea of political obligation not only informs people to obey the authority of those in power, it also desires them to be critical about the way authority is exercised. The people should scrutinise the actions of their rulers. They should resent any invasion on their liberties. Thus, political obligation involves resistance to authority.

Summing up the whole idea of political obligation Bern and Peters write: "There are good grounds for accepting authority in general, but there may be good grounds for rejecting it in particular cases; if authority derives from a constitution, there would generally be good grounds for rejecting any exercise of it which is unconstitutional. Again, if its legitimacy depends on the way it is used, an invasion of a sphere where political authority is inappropriate might be a ground for disobedience or, in extreme cases, for resistance."[6]

THEORIES OF POLITICAL OBLIGATION

1. The divine theory: It finds its place in religious doctrines. In it the source of obedience to the commands of men-in-authority roles is traced in matters of faith. The necessity of the Divine Will stands above and apart from the citizens and the governing authority. The ordinance is "I am obliged to obey the governing authority, because I am obliged to obey God and because any governing authority is essentially an emanation and delegation of divine authority."[7] Thus, the authority of the ruler "stems not only from inheritance according to custom, or from popular acclamation, these are regarded as the consequences rather than the grounds of authority. The true source is divine and his authority is, therefore, independent both of human choice and custom."[8]

The divine theory sacrifices the nature of authority. It commands persons to obey authority as if it is an emanation of God. It led to the emergence of the dogma of divine rights of kings found various religions like Hinduism and Christianity. It leaves no room for right to resist political authority. As it is the "march of God on earth" the State can do no wrong.

Criticism

With the growth of new knowledge of secularism in modern times this theory has lost its significance. The new realisation is that "if men are disposed to doubt, they want reasons related to their situation, rather than dogmatic assertions that everything is as it ought to be. Any approach to political obligation that left no room for discussion in the light of the

6. Benn and Peters, *op. cit.*, p. 329.
7. Barker, *op. cit.*, p. 184.
8. Benn and Peters, *op. cit.*, p. 301.

particular situation, might confirm the faith of the faithful; it could not convince the doubter."[9]

2. The prescriptive theory: According to this theory political authority and reverence to it are based on the principle of established 'customary rights' ripens into an association wherein lies the source of its legitimacy. As Jean Bodin says as the authority of the patriarch (head of the family) is based on the fact of historical prescription, so the authority of the king (head of the State) finds its source in the fact of long possession. An established practice has a significance of its own because it embodies the 'wisdom of the ages'. The people obey their rulers, because obedience is a well-established convention. According to Edmund Burke all settled political institutions have a prescriptive character. He condemned the logic of the French revolutionaries that political institutions could be demolished and built anew as desired by the people. He argued that people revere their traditions in which the wisdom of the past is hidden. Such traditions have a very long record of evolution. They can be changed gradually over a very long of time. Thus, political obligation is a result of very long traditions which the people observe as if having a 'divine' character. Thus, according to this theory, "all authority is legitimate, if it is sanctioned by custom; no further question need be asked."[10]

Limitations

(i) The source of political obligation lies not only in paying reverence to the well-established practices of the realm but also in doing away with them. People desire change and if there is frustration of their hopes, they take to the path of revolution. The advocates of this theory stick to the fact of reverence to the past and feel allergic to the idea of a revolution.

(ii) People observe their traditions so long as they have their utility. They resort to break them down when their usefulness is no longer existent. Therefore political prescriptions may change with time.

3. The idealistic theory: It finds the source of political obligation in the 'moral nature' of man. It does not sanctions the right to resistance. The State is a natural association. It is a moral organism. It alone can give 'good life' to its members. It is like 'a partnership in virtue'. It is a *koinonia* having its highest aim in ennobling human personality. Therefore, man should obey, rather worship, its authority. As the State represents the

9. *Ibid.*, p. 303.
10. *Ibid.*, p. 307.

real will of its members there can be no conflict between the will of the individual and the will of the State. Rousseau says that it is impossible for a sovereign to maim or harm its people. Justifying the case of a God-state Hegel says: "Nothing short of the State is the actualisation of freedom." Treitschke says, that "man should fall down and worship the State." Joad concludes: "It, therefore, follows that the actions of the State in so far as they proceed from General Will, must always be irreproachably right in the sense that they represent what is best in individual wills......The state can never act unrepresentatively."[11]

Difficulties

(i) This theory is too abstract. It places very ordinary things in a highly philosophical, even metaphysical, form that cannot be understood by a man of average comprehension.

(ii) To teach the people to adulate political authority like deaf and dumb creatures is to open the way for totalitarianism. All great idealists except Green subscribe to blind obedience to thc authority of the State. Referring to the ideas of Hegel, in this connection L.T. Hobhouse says: "When we are taught to think of the world which we know as a good world, to think of its injustices, wrongs, and miseries as necessary elements in a perfect ideal, then, if we accept these arguments, our power of revolt is atrophied, our reason is hypnotised, our effects to improve life and remedy wrong fade away into a passive acquiescence in things as they are; or, still worse, into a slavish adulation of the Absolute in whose hands we are mere pawns."[12]

4. Social contract theory: It is the theory of *consent of the individuals.* It dwells on the factor of consent of the people as revealed in a hypothetical social contract on which the entire structure of political obligation rests. As the people are the makers of the State, they are also its mutators. God has no place in the making of the State. In the 17th century England, Hobbes and Locke stressed that political authority is derived from a social contract. The people are collectively bound to obey it so long as the government works for the general good and keeps itself within limits laid down by the compact. As Locke says: "No one can be subjected to the political power of another, without his own consent."[13]

11. C.E.M. Joad, *Modern Political Theory*, p. 13.
12. L.T. Hobhouse, *Metaphysical Theory of State*, p. 19.
13. Locke, *Second Treatise of Civil Government*, Sec. 95.

Value of Contract Theory

The system of a democratic government stands on the premise of the contract theory. This theory alone attaches importance to the 'will of the people'. The people institute a sovereign authority for the sake of their own preservation. If the sovereign puts their life in danger, they may revolt to make another contract. Locke sanctions people's right to revolt in case the government abuses the trust of the people. Thus, this theory has its distinctive merit.

Demerits of Social Contract Theory

(i) It makes State a conventional association.

(ii) It informs people to rise in revolt whenever they feel dissatisfied with the functioning of their government.

(iii) It creates fertile grounds for the occurrence of revolts. C.E. Vaughan remarks that Locke formulated not a theory of the government but a theory of rebellion.[14]

5. The Marxian theory: It denounces State as an instrument of exploitation and oppression by one class over another. People are not obligated to obey a State that is a discredited organisation. They should destroy it by revolutionary means and create a 'new state' in the form of the 'dictatorship of the proletariat' or a State of the workers and peasants. Such a State alone must be obeyed. Its aim is first to establish a classless society. It will wither away to pave way for the emergence of a stateless condition of life or a golden era in which all public affairs would be managed by the free and voluntary associations of the people and 'glorious human values' prevail. In Marxism, the theme of political obligation is converted into the theme of social obligation. Marx "envisaged the fully socialised man as one who would see no distinction between private and public interest and whose activity would be attuned to the latter."[15]

Limitations

(i) This theory on the subject of political obligation has three aspects — no obligation to a 'bourgeois state', all obligation to a 'socialist state', and eventual conversion of political obligation into social obligation in the final stage of socialism (communism). A bourgeois state is not a thoroughly discredited institution. It cannot be identified with an instrument of exploitation and oppression by one class over another. A

14. C.E. Vaughan, *Studies in the History of Political Philosophy*, Vol. II.
15. Michael Evans, *Karl Marx*, p. 162.

socialist state, as conceived by the Marxists, may not be the genuine state in which people must render full obedience to its authority.

(ii) Revolution is a sacred affair in a capitalist state, but it becomes profaned when a socialist order is established.

(iii) In this theory the very theme of political obligation disappears in the final stage of social development. The ambivalent attitude of the Marxists "reduces the question of political obligation to a question of political expediency, and ignores the independent individual whose experience alone counts in the determination of his obedience to the laws of the State."[16]

6. Theory of Harold Laski: Discussing various theories of political obligation one may appreciate one that stands the test of experience. One should look into the case of political obligation from a pragmatic point of view that desires "to contend for truth as tested by reality and its fruits."[17] Such a view is the approach of Laski who says that men "obey the state not merely for the sake of order, but also on account of what they deem that order to make possible. They are, in fact, judging the State from the angle of satisfactions, they think it should provide. Their judgements, no doubt, vary with time and place, expectations of what is legitimate are always born of experiences; and the demands of one society at one period will differ from those of another society at another period. But the implication is the clear one that the exercise of political authority in a society is never unconstitutional."[18]

THEORIES OF GROUNDS OF RESISTANCE

1. *Thomas Hobbes*: He tells us that though the State is based on a social contract whereby people surrender their all rights in favour of a Leviathan without taking any commitment from him. They are bound to obey every law of the State to keep the horrible 'State of nature' away. They have a right to break the contract if the sovereign commands the people "to kill or wound themselves, or not to resist those who assault them or to abstain from the use of food, air, medicine, or any other thing, without which they cannot live."[19]

2. *John Locke*: The State is a creation of social contract. Society, state and the government are distinguishable. The society has a pre-political character. The State is a creation of the first or open contract. It continues

16. Ray and Bhattacharya, *Political Theory*, p. 150.
17. C.E. Merriam, *History of Political Theories*, p. 15.
18. Laski, *op. cit.*, p. 17.
19. Hobbes, *Leviathan*, Ch. 14.

to exist even when the government is dissolved or changed. But the government is a creation of the second or tacit contract. It implies that the king or the government is bound by the terms of the 'contract'. The people may revolt or 'make an appeal to the heavens' if they find their king acting against the terms of the contract. They may resist the abuse of political power. They may change their ruler acting like a despot. They may have a new one of their trust in his place.[20] Explaining the meaning of the situation identifiable with the abuse of the trust of the people by the king, Laski says, "The substitution of arbitrary will for law, the corruption of Parliament by packing it with the prince's instruments betrayed to a foreign prince, prevention of the due assemblage of Parliament all these are perversions of the trust imposed and operate to effect the dissolution of the contract. The State of nature supervenes and a new contract may be made with one more fitted to observe it."

3. *T.H. Green*: He was an idealist like Rousseau and Hegel, but he was a liberal too. He followed the English liberal tradition. He recognised people's right to resist political authority in the event of 'cruel necessity'. He justified revolt against the abuse of political authority if it is sanctioned by the force of public conscience as being in the interest of the people as a whole.[21]

4. *Harold Laski*: He connects the subject of political obligation with the factor of 'moral adequacy'. According to him, people must obey the authority of the State, if it meets their satisfaction. They may disobey it, if they find that the commands of the State lack the force of utility and moral adequacy. Thus, right to resistance should be substituted by the 'duty to disobey'. It is a claim to a right which a citizen cannot surrender without denying himself the full meaning of his citizenship. It is an obligation arising out of the acceptance of and loyalty to the idea of the common good. There are circumstances in which resistance to the state becomes an obligation if claims to rights are to be given validity. However no general rule of either time or situation can be laid down as a guide to such an action.[22]

5. *M.K. Gandhi*: His view is based on the premise of practical idealism. Authority is legitimate when it is based on truth and non-violence. If it is violent or untrue, the people have a right to resist it by means of *ahimsa* and *satyagraha*. The purity of means is essential for the achievement of a legitimate end.

---

20. Laski, *Political Thought in England (Locke to Bentham)*, p. 37.
21. T.H. Green, *Lectures on the Principles of Political Obligation*, p. 115.
22. Laski, *A Grammar of Politics*, p. 96.

As different answers may be furnished by different persons faced with such a situation or a series of such situations, Margaret MacDonald feels that "necessary and sufficient grounds for political obligation are not to be found."[23]

QUESTIONS FOR EXERCISE

1. What is political obligation? Explain its essential characteristics.
2. Critically discuss various theories of political obligation. Which is the best and why?
3. Describe various views about grounds of resistance of political authority.

23. Cited in Benn and Peters, *op. cit.*, p. 331.